T0245623

All
Hands on
Tech

All
Hands on
Tech

The AI-Powered Citizen
Revolution

Thomas H. Davenport and
Ian Barkin
with Chase Davenport

WILEY

Contents at a Glance

Preface   xv

Introduction   xxvii

PART 1   Background, History, and Context   **1**

Chapter 1   Why Citizen Development Is Inevitable   3

Chapter 2   A History of Citizen-Led Innovation   21

Chapter 3   The Citizen Journey   33

PART 2   Calling All Hands   **49**

Chapter 4   Citizen Development Using Low-Code/ No-Code Tools   51

Chapter 5   Citizen Automation   63

Chapter 6   Citizen Data Science   81

Chapter 7   The Skills and Personality of Citizens   101

Chapter 8   The Citizen Champion: With and Without Air Cover   123

PART 3   Getting to Work   **133**

Chapter 9   The Citizen Tech Landscape   135

Chapter 10 Benefits of Citizen Development   151

Chapter 11 The Organizational Response to Citizen Technology   161

PART 4 Setting Sail   **175**

Chapter 12 Preparing to Set Sail   177

Chapter 13 Genesis   187

Chapter 14 Governance   201

Chapter 15 Guidance   215

Chapter 16 Guardrails   227

Chapter 17 The Future of Citizen Development   235

Appendix A Citizen-Ready Checklist   245

Appendix B Citizen Development Challenges
                Organizations Are Likely to Face   253

Appendix C Additional Resources   255

Acknowledgments   *257*

About the Authors   *259*

Index   *261*

Contents

Preface   xv

Introduction   xxvii

PART 1 **Background, History, and Context**   **1**

Chapter 1 Why Citizen Development Is Inevitable   3
           What Are Citizens?   4
           Why Is Citizen Development Growing?   6
           The Front Lines of Digitalization   9
           Monarchy, Federalism, or Anarchy?   12
           Like Seemingly Everything Else, Citizen
                 Development Is Social   14
           Making Citizen Development Safe and Effective   16
           Generative AI and the Future of Citizen Development   18

Chapter 2 A History of Citizen-Led Innovation   21
           Outsiders and Insiders in Business Improvement   21
           The Open Innovation/Crowdsourcing Movement   23
           Open Source in Software   25
           The Maker Movement   26
           The Growth of Citizen Science—Starting with
                 Ornithology   28
           A Slow but Pronounced Shift   30

Chapter 3   The Citizen Journey   33
                 Diverse Journeys   33
                 Initial Capabilities   34
                 Automation Comes Next   36
                 The Journey to More Sophisticated Analytics   36
                 The Citizen's Career in a Large
                     Organization—for a While   37
                 Citizen Data Science in an Organization That
                     Welcomes Them   40
                 A More Dramatic Career Transformation   41
                     The Citizen as Rogue Agent   43
                     The Citizen as Entrepreneur   44
                     A Citizen Data Science Startup   46

PART 2   **Calling All Hands**   **49**

Chapter 4   Citizen Development Using Low-Code/
                 No-Code Tools   51
                 How Did We Get Here?   53
                 It's Not Just Citizens   53
                 What Can an Organization Do with Low-Code/
                     No-Code?   54
                 Citizen/Professional Collaboration and Fusion Teams   56
                 Generative AI as a No-Code Solution   58
                 How to Succeed with Low-Code/No-Code   59
                 Management Challenges with Low-Code/No-Code   60

Chapter 5   Citizen Automation   63
                 Citizen Automator   64
                 Types of Work Well-Suited to Automation   64
                     Integrating Between Systems as Human APIs   65
                     Performing a Series of Tasks: Workflow   67
                     Making Decisions Based on Defined Rules   68
                 The Offices Where Automation Plays   69
                     Back Office   69
                     Front Office   69
                     Middle Office   70

The Origin Story of Broad Automation Adoption 70
Who Is a Citizen Automator? 72
Where Does Citizen Automation Belong? 73
What Is the Upside of Citizen Automation? 74
  Idea/Execution Overlap 74
  Prototyping the Future State 75
  Increased Speed 76
  Employee Experience and Loyalty 77
  Fostering Cross-Departmental Innovation 77
What Can Go Wrong? 78
  Overhyped and Under-Delivered 78
  Paving Cow Paths 78
  Technical Debt 79
The Future of Citizen Automation 80

Chapter 6 Citizen Data Science 81
Citizen Data Analysis 82
True Citizen Data Science 85
What Is the Upside of True Citizen Data Science? 87
What Kinds of People Become Citizen Data Scientists? 88
  What Can Go Wrong? 90
What Kinds of Problems Should Citizen Data
  Scientists Take On? 92
  Citizen Data Science for Generative AI 93
Citizen Data Science and Data Flow Automation 95
How Can Citizen Data Scientists Work in Data
  Science Teams? 96
How Will the Citizen Data Scientist Role
  Evolve Over Time? 98

Chapter 7 The Skills and Personality of Citizens 101
Workers of the Future, in the Future of Work 101
Personality Traits of a Citizen Developer 103
  Passion 103
  Curiosity and Willingness to Learn 104
  Perseverance and Grit 105
  Creativity and Innovation 106

Mindset   107
    Entrepreneurial Mindset   107
    Computational Mindset   108
    Hybrid Mindset   109
Skills of the Future   109
Skills of Citizen Developers   110
    Domain-Specific Skills   111
    Literacies   112
        Data Literacy   112
        Analytics Literacy   113
        Digital Literacy   115
    Technical Skills   116
    Human Relationship Skills   119
        Communication and Collaboration Skills   120
        Political Skills   121
The Final Tally   121

Chapter 8   The Citizen Champion: With and Without Air Cover   123
Shell: High Air Cover   124
Dentsu and Tinuiti: Air Cover, but Citizen Focus
    When Ready   125
Arcadis: Growing Air Cover Over Time   126
Quiet Growth in Citizen Development at Amtrak   128
Lessons from Citizen Development Champions   130
The Long-Term Fate of Citizen Development
    Champions   132

PART 3   **Getting to Work**   **133**

Chapter 9   The Citizen Tech Landscape   135
Information Technology Is Important—Duh!   136
What Makes a Tool Citizen-Ready?   136
The Evolution of Programming Languages   137
Current Citizen Tools and Platform Landscape   138
    Low-Code/No-Code Application
        Platforms for Citizen Development   138
    Citizen Automation Technologies   139
        Robotic Process Automation for Execution   141

IDP: Helping RPA See   142
Other Tools in the Automation Stack   143
Citizen Data Science Technologies   143
New Developments for Citizens in Business
   Intelligence   145
The Generative AI Era of Citizen Development   147

Chapter 10 Benefits of Citizen Development   151
Targeting and Scaling Improvement Benefits   152
Innovation and Experimentation Benefits   155

Chapter 11 The Organizational Response to Citizen Technology   161
The Two Stereotypical Positions   161
Beyond the IT Resistance Stereotype   163
An Emerging Third Party   165
"Governance" of Citizen Technologies   167
Citizen Technology in Highly Regulated Businesses   170
Putting It All Together: Balancing Risk and Reward   172

PART 4   Setting Sail   **175**

Chapter 12 Preparing to Set Sail   177
Maturity Models   178
   Citizen Development Maturity Model   178
      Stage 0: Random Acts of Citizenry   179
      Stage 1: Awareness   179
      Stage 2: Acceptance and Focused
         Exploration   180
      Stage 3: Formal Adoption   180
      Stage 4: Industrialization   181
      Stage 5: Absorption   181
Cast of Characters   182
   Leading Roles   182
      Citizen Developers   183
      Citizen Automators   183
      Citizen Data Scientists   184
      A Citizen by Any Other Name   184
   Supporting Roles   184

	Citizen Champion	184
	Citizen Coach	184
	Citizen Librarian	184
	Stakeholders	185
	The 4G Approach to Citizen-Readiness	186
Chapter 13	Genesis	187
	Genesis Fork 1: Submit or Just Commit	187
	Submit, Then Commit	188
	Commit	189
	Fork 2: Create or Orchestrate	190
	Create Your Citizenry	191
	Orchestrate Your Citizenry	192
	Fork 3: Revolution or Evolution	193
	Revolution	193
	Evolution	194
	Starting Strong with the Fundamentals	195
	Benefits	195
	Talent	197
	Key Performance Indicators	197
Chapter 14	Governance	201
	Fork 4: Tolerate Risk or Avoid Risk	202
	Risk Tolerance	202
	Risk Avoidance	203
	Fork 5: Bottom Up vs. Top Down	204
	Top-Down Governance	204
	Bottom-Up Governance	205
	Fork 6: Centralize or Federate	206
	Centralized Governance	207
	Federated Governance	207
	Enabling a Successful Voyage	209
	Risks	209
	Organizational Structure	211
	Governance Models	212
Chapter 15	Guidance	215
	Fork 7: Solo or in Teams	215
	Go Alone	215
	Go Together	216

	Fork 8: Direct or Explore	217
	Direct Instruction	218
	Project-Based Learning	219
	Nurturing the Crew	220
	Training	220
	Levels of Citizen Certification	221
	Citizen Lite	224
	Community Building	224
	Ideation and Creativity	224
Chapter 16	Guardrails	227
	Fork 9: Stewards or Shields	228
	Stewards	228
	Shields	229
	Facilitating Best Behaviors	230
	Human Guardrails	230
	Automated Guardrails	231
	Financial Guardrails	231
Chapter 17	The Future of Citizen Development	235
	Citizen Development: Too Pervasive to Have a Name?	236
	The Future of the IT Function and IT People	237
	Coaching and Assessing, Not Developing	238
	Ultimate Fusion	239
	Broader Tech and Data Leadership	240
	The Role of AI	241
Appendix A	Citizen-Ready Checklist	245
	Preparing to Set Sail	245
	Genesis	246
	Governance	247
	Guidance	248
	Guardrails	250
Appendix B	Citizen Development Challenges Organizations Are Likely to Face	253
Appendix C	Additional Resources	255
Acknowledgments		*257*
About the Authors		*259*
Index		*261*

Preface

Jay Crotts: Bringing "Shadow IT" Into the Light

It's fitting to begin this book with the story of an unlikely hero of citizen development. Jay Crotts is a semi-retired former chief information officer of Shell PLC, the energy giant. Jay Crotts was executive vice president and group CIO of Shell from 2015 to 2023, and about halfway through his tenure he had a bit of a revelation. Shell was in a race to digitalize its business, and Crotts just didn't feel like it was happening fast enough. His global IT function had a multibillion-dollar annual budget and more than 8,000 staff and contractors, but they still couldn't satisfy the demand for applications, automations, and analytical models around the company.

Crotts kept telling his people that they needed to get closer to the business in order to create value, but he realized that there were plenty of people in the business who could create value with IT as well. People were getting citizen-oriented tools in their hands, but he was a bit worried about what they were doing with them.

Crotts was based in the Netherlands, and the European Union had passed the General Data Protection Regulation (GDPR) in 2016. He was afraid that citizen development would get out of control and that employees would violate the law by inadvertently making available critical personal data—the medical records of sailors on Shell tankers, for example. He felt that there were lots of smart engineers and other employees at Shell doing innovative things, but there was no safe place to access and store the data they needed to use. Crotts knew those people were thinking, "I want to be productive, but there is no place to do it. Crotts' group says no, because there is a risk of GDPR violations or cybersecurity issues." He looked around the energy industry and elsewhere to see if anyone else had solved the problem, and they hadn't. Many CIOs were still viewing citizen development as undesirable "shadow IT," but Crotts saw it as a way to bring it out of the shadows and into the light.

So Crotts put Nils Kappeyne, one of his trusted business unit CIOs, in charge of the do-it-yourself (DIY) initiative. They didn't want to call it citizen development because they were afraid engineers might think they were being taught how to vote. Crotts thought the initiative would work out well, but he wasn't sure. The critical thing, he believed, was finding a safe place to access and store data for citizen use. He told Kappeyne to find a place to put the data, and then data owners—which already existed—throughout the business would determine access to it. He said to Kappeyne at the time, "What will bring people to your platform is where the data is."

As the DIY program was rolling out, Shell was deepening its partnership with Microsoft, and that vendor was making big bets on both cloud and citizen development. The data at Shell for citizen use ended up being stored in Microsoft's Azure cloud. And the vendor had also just introduced its Power Platform—a collection of citizen-oriented tools for application development, business intelligence, web portal development, and later workflow automation. Crotts and Kappeyne placed their DIY bets on these Microsoft tools and a few others from vendors like `Salesforce.com`.

Kappeyne thought that he could keep his day job as a business unit CIO while getting DIY going, but Crotts felt otherwise. "It needs to be big," he said. Kappeyne, already a Shell VP, suggested that the program wasn't worthy of a VP title, and he could take a demotion. "It needs to be big," Crotts said, "and you should keep your VP title." Kappeyne also thought that he could establish the DIY program within a couple of months. Crotts doubted it but didn't say so. Kappeyne stayed in the job for a couple of years and then reluctantly handed it off to somebody else.

Crotts also supported a collaboration with Shell's research function on citizen data science. Dan Jeavons, the head of that initiative, reported into the research organization but was formally included in the IT leadership. Shell collaborated with Microsoft Azure to be able to run models at scale in the cloud. As with the application development DIY program, data was provided to the data scientists, "and they could go to town," Crotts remarked. The DIY approach, accompanied by effective cloud security, enabled data science to thrive. It was a good fit for a culture where, as Crotts put it, "engineers—many of them come out of school knowing Python these days—question a model if someone else develops it."

Some IT people worried about losing their jobs, but Crotts thought that they—or some, at least—would move from being developers to coaches and enablers. And that is what has happened. Shell still has plenty of professional developers, and in many cases the DIY program has brought the business and the IT people into closer collaboration.

One influential aspect of the Shell DIY approach to citizen development is the "zone" program, in which different zones (green, amber, red) get treated differently in terms of governance. We'll describe the approach later in the book, but suffice it to say here that it has been adopted by a variety of organizations. Microsoft has endorsed it for Power Platform customers, for example, and the Project Management Institute has adopted it for its teachings on citizen development. Several companies we spoke to said they had adopted the Shell zone approach.

But perhaps even more influential for the worldwide spread of citizen development has been the idea that a corporate IT organization can get behind citizen technology activity and give it the support it needs to thrive. Crotts is pretty modest about this achievement:

> People really liked it, and it's one of the fastest things going. A significant number of engineers adopted DIY, and we've given them credit for the work. The tools are easy to use, and the data is there. Once other CIOs understood it they thought it made sense.

Crotts mentioned several DIY projects that have enabled energy transition activities or substantially reduced fuel consumption in Shell operations. He doesn't say that citizen development has transformed the huge company, but as he put it, "We've hit singles all across the globe."

Benjamin Berkowitz: A Finance Professional Turned Citizen Automator

One shining example of citizen automation turning a domain expert into a digital transformation leader is Benjamin Berkowitz. A self-professed "finance guy," he was motivated to solve operational and budgetary challenges in the hospitals where he worked. He studied history and psychology in college and earned an MBA. He's now pursuing a PhD in management and organizational behavior. He wanted to know what made enterprises tick.

Berkowitz began his career in the healthcare field, working first as a financial analyst at Boston Children's Hospital before moving to Mass General Brigham (MGB). Based in Boston, MGB is the largest hospital-based research enterprise in the United States, with revenues of nearly $19 billion and more than $2 billion in annual research funding. It is, in short, a hospital with a lot of work for its finance department. Berkowitz's 11-year career at MGB afforded him the chance to experience and impact almost every part of it. Starting as a team lead for payer strategy and contracting, he then moved to lead revenue calculation and revenue finance systems, finally becoming director of financial analysis and strategy, and chief of staff of revenue cycle operations—the lifeblood of any healthcare business, since it's how the organization gets paid for its work. But on this journey he found himself doing more than simply overseeing financial functions.

Berkowitz had always been interested in making work processes more efficient and effective. Early in his career that meant using Microsoft Access to automate reporting. He then graduated to using SQL to process large data sets in order to process revenue models. This trend then accelerated in his revenue cycle job at MGB. In his own words, Berkowitz was "bouncing around from department to department, automating as he was going." He didn't know he was a citizen automator; he hadn't even heard the term. He was just applying his penchant to problem-solve to challenges as they presented themselves and using the automation tools at his disposal.

Berkowitz's pivot to becoming a full-time champion of automation began while looking at budgets, as finance people are wont to do. The growth of MGB's operations over the previous decade had been strong. Staff levels grew accordingly. But Berkowitz was now facing a challenge. He had 800 people in the RevCycle and Shared Services Center and no end in sight to growth in hiring. The challenge was compounded by talent shortages and rapid wage inflation. Clearly the status quo wasn't sustainable. As part of a budget planning conversation, he said to his VP, "There must be a better way for us to manage all of this work."

His next steps (highlighted in an article[1] Berkowitz coauthored) addressed the growing scale of work to track and catalog an increasing number of healthcare providers. The current system was slow and inefficient. It took three different hospital administrators to collect, aggregate, and export data, all of which was performed manually.

In response, Berkowitz and his colleagues recruited external developers and partnered them with a process specialist from the finance department to redesign workflows to better facilitate automating the tasks sequence involved. They developed automations to collect provider data, format it, and present it to members of the finance team. Their solution also highlighted the next actions, so as to assist the team in efficiently moving each process forward. The results were frontline finance employees being free to focus on higher-value work and the ability to handle provider growth without having to hire more staff.

Berkowitz was hooked. But his organization needed more convincing before jumping headlong into automation. Berkowitz then pursued lots of research, conferences, discussions with experts, and proofs of concepts to help settle on robotic process automation (RPA) as the tool of choice. His tenacity paid off, and he was able to convince his leadership to set up a new department. In 2019, with strong support from his CFO, he established the intelligent automation department with himself as director, reporting to the VP of finance and administration. Always budget conscious, Benjamin then faced the choice of how to staff the initiative. He decided rather than bringing on a large team of developers, he would recruit internally for citizens like himself. What's more, he would focus his efforts on the five to six departments where operational improvements from automation would have the biggest impact. He didn't want to leave out other, smaller departments like legal and contracts, so he set up a small central team of developers to support their needs.

He opened up internal recruiting to anyone who wanted to be an "embedded developer"—a name chosen to emphasize that the team was made up of subject-matter experts (SMEs) working closely with and serving their colleagues. These citizen automators could have the business-level

---

[1] Ben Armstrong and Benjamin Berkowitz, "Scaling Automation: Two Proven Paths to Success," *MIT Sloan Management Review*, February 28, 2024, `https://sloanreview.mit.edu/article/scaling-automation-two-proven-paths-to-success`.

discussions that IT would struggle to have, and they knew who to go to for answers to their questions.

Next, he needed to generate buzz, recruit talent, and put in place a series of best practices. In addition, since he was reporting up to finance leadership, he was conscious that he needed to nurture a strong working relationship with IT if this was to be a success, The embedded citizen developers and centralized developers would all report to him, and they would surely encounter issues involving integration with multiple systems.

To attract talent, he provided a clear and rewarding career path, with a new job code, a different pay scale, and three levels of qualification—junior, normal, and senior automation developer. He also created an intake lead role in which a person could play part champion, part ambassador, working with departments to look for opportunities to leverage the tools and capabilities of the team. Berkowitz described this role as similar to a primary-care physician: helping a department diagnose a workflow situation and working with the right specialists to develop automation solutions that fit their needs.

The success of Berkowitz's department was no secret; one day in the spring of 2021, he got a call asking if he wanted to come to work at the pharmaceutical company Vertex, a pioneer in the development of treatments for serious diseases like cystic fibrosis and sickle cell. Ready to try out a different industry and a different set of potential challenges, he said, "Let's give it a go."

Berkowitz now serves as the director of digital automation at Vertex. Unlike at MGB, he works for IT and has a centralized team. As stated on his LinkedIn profile, he is "creating pathways for citizen developers throughout the organization, further democratizing automation tools and accelerating the return on investment of the program." Vertex is rolling out a different tool set than he used at MGB, which is more focused on cloud-based citizen development.

Of note, Vertex's leaders have set a bold top-down mandate of discovering five new drugs in five years.[2] Berkowitz hopes that leveraging his team's automation capabilities will contribute to making this bold goal a reality.

As for the MGB program, its success gained the attention of the IT organization. Upon his departure, the IT department laid claim to the team.

---

[2] https://www.bizjournals.com/boston/news/2024/02/05/vertex-2023-earnings.html.

"Mr. Citizen"—The Citizen Development Pioneer with the Arrows to Show for It

Although in our research we found many examples of organizations embracing citizen development, that doesn't always happen. One prominent proponent of the idea—we'll call him "Mr. Citizen" because he works for a consumer products company, which didn't want us to identify the company or him—advocates strongly for the idea internally and externally in social media (from which we take this description), but hasn't always received support from his organization.

Mr. Citizen wasn't always a citizen developer. For many years he spent most of his workday entering data into Excel. The area in which he works is a data-rich activity, but the data typically comes from all over the place: ERP systems, supply chain management systems, marketing projections, sales databases, and lots of spreadsheets. He became very good at moving data in and out of Excel spreadsheets, but he knew that he—like every other human—occasionally made mistakes in this process. He crammed so much data into Excel that the program often broke. And it wasn't much fun. It also didn't allow much time for thinking about big-picture improvements in his business process.

Despite the tedium of the Excel work, Mr. Citizen did it for years because he knew of no alternative. He wanted to spend less time on data entry and manual reporting, and more on statistical analysis of the data. He and his colleagues had asked his company's IT department for systems that would make this process much easier, but they never got much encouragement—the IT backlog was too long, and they wouldn't take on any project that wasn't an enterprise process.

So Mr. Citizen began looking for alternatives to Excel. He tried a popular business intelligence tool, but it didn't really help much. So then he explored a tool known for its analytics and "data pipeline automation" capabilities called Alteryx, and a system called Tableau for the visual analytics of the data and statistical analyses. Later he experimented with a tool for automation of data integrations and APIs called Parabola. These tools saved him lots of time, and he became an advocate for their use both inside and outside his organization. These tools weren't supported by the IT department, but Mr. Citizen found them easy to download and use. He wasn't banned from using them, but IT told him that he didn't need Alteryx because all it did was write SQL queries. Why didn't he just write them himself, they asked. Of course, it was because he is not a SQL programmer. Still, he struggled to get his IT organization to put Alteryx and the other tools on the list of approved software. He continued to build tools to save himself and his colleagues time and drudgery, reducing the need for IT professional help, but getting no respect for it.

Mr. Citizen could probably spend all of his time as a citizen developer, but he believes that a key aspect of his value—and that of any citizen developer—is his combination of citizen technology skills and business function expertise. Because he possesses both types of skills, he can now not only build many technology solutions for his part of the business, but also communicate effectively with IT professionals about requirements for enterprise-level systems they might build. He commented on social media that he believes entry-level workers should spend their time learning some aspect of the business (supply chain management, for example) and not learning professional IT skills.

On social media, Mr. Citizen wrote a sort of "open letter to IT teams" blog post (it's long, so we won't reproduce it all here) that expresses his relationship to them, as well as listing some of the accomplishments he and his team made with citizen technologies:

> . . .And if I'm being honest, you weren't always the best to work with. You had a real command-and-control approach to technology: We'd ask you for something and you'd gather a bunch of requirements just to disappear for 6 months and come back with something that usually missed the mark.
>
> Remember that huge business intelligence initiative we did? We were going to modernize our whole reporting infrastructure into a one-stop shop for all our supply chain analytical needs. You came to me with big promises.
>
> But when it came time to gather requirements, I was vague. I had no idea how to tell you what I needed, and you didn't know the business well enough to understand me. In the end (18 months late and way over budget), you left me with the same stuff I had before, in a slightly prettier package.

This doesn't have to happen anymore. Your approach is changing, it's less about command-and-control and more about enablement—empowering operators with a flexible stack and all the tools we need to solve our problems on our own.

I'm changing, too. I'm using low-code/no-code tools—as a citizen developer—with loads of benefits:

- **I've saved a ton of time and money** (without having to bug you much). Literally thousands of hours, millions of dollars.
- **I'm more data literate.** I've been building my own data pipelines, working with relational databases and creating my own data models.
- Because I'm more data literate, **my communication with you is becoming more effective.** I don't give you vague requirements anymore—I talk in terms of selection criteria, filter criteria and modeling steps.
- **And that huge backlog of yours – I can help *alleviate* it.** There aren't enough of you to go around, so you rightfully prioritize the big stuff – and there are lots of smaller things that I know you'll never get to. We can take care of that stuff ourselves now.

Here are some examples of what my team and I have been able to do with little to no help from you:

- **We automated our product allocation process,** a highly manual process that in my 11+ years here you never wanted to touch. We were able to save over 40 hours *per week* (not to mention the huge morale boost for our allocation team).
- **We built out a data model and a suite of analytics to support our promotional planning process.** It routinely identifies millions of dollars worth of planning errors. But the need for this was specific to our market, so it was never going to make it to the top of your backlog.
- **We built functional prototypes of data models** that supported our demand planning and claims teams. In fact, they're serving as inspiration for your product teams to build global solutions.

> You might be skeptical. You're worried about governance and best practices. I get it. But that's no reason to tell us not to use low-code/no-code tools – it's a reason for you to help us learn these practices. You've developed them over decades – we won't get it overnight, but with your support, we'll get there.[3]

Mr. Citizen, as his remarks suggest, is conscious of governance in citizen development himself, and writes social media posts to people in other companies counseling them to follow responsible citizen practices like building only small solutions, producing documentation, and testing for data quality. The IT group in his company, as he also acknowledges, has finally admitted that citizen development might be useful in some circumstances, but the group still appears to be more interested in controlling it than encouraging it.

Like some other citizen developers we've observed whose work is not appreciated by IT or their broader organization, we'd guess that Mr. Citizen is likely to eventually leave the company. However, we have no doubt that he'll find another company or entrepreneurial venture in which he can create value from the combination of skills he now possesses. We also suspect that his employer—even its IT teams—will miss him.

The Future of Work

Stories like Jay Crotts's, Benjamin Berkowitz's, and "Mr. Citizen's" are becoming more common in enterprises across the globe. This sort of change is taking place at companies of every size, in every industry, across every function, department, and team.

Challenged by staffing shortages and inflation, facing heightened competition, and coming to grips with the reality that every element of a business is now inextricably attached to data and software, leaders and individual contributors in companies of all sizes are stepping up and stepping in to drive the changes they know are needed. They are beginning to succeed, empowered by an enormous shift in the power dynamics that have long defined enterprise operations.

---

[3]"IT Teams—Can We Talk?" Parabola.io blog post, Feb. 2024, https://parabola.io/blog/it-teams-can-we-talk.

Technology is no longer owned by any one department or function. Data and its analysis are no longer the property of only the PhDs and the hard-core number crunchers. And these genies cannot be put back in their bottles. From now on, all employees have the ability to be system designers, data analysts, coders, and creators. Every one of them is empowered to act on their unique set of experiences and their specific levels of expertise with process, product, customer, partner, or whatever other component of the elephant they touch every day. No one knows it better. And, until now, no one was able to contribute such well-informed insight toward making things better. The value of this grassroots, bottom-up, SME-first approach to transformation cannot be overstated. Creation of technology at the front lines will fundamentally change the way change happens. And there is no going back.

However, there is certainly more to be done to ensure that we can all move forward successfully. Because, while employees are more empowered than ever before, the question is, are they ready? Are their enterprises ready? Are the policies, procedures, and controls ready to safely enable this new reality?

We think the answer is no—or at least not yet in most organizations. But there are significant efforts being made to prepare. Some of these efforts will prove successful; others will not. Our discussions with leading global organizations, midsize national organizations, and small local firms has revealed a wide range of awareness, preparedness, and maturity of mechanisms in place to make the most of what can only be described as a revolutionary new way of imagining, enacting, and driving change. This book is our attempt to distill what we've seen and what we believe enterprises need to consider in order to jump onboard a train that has already left the station. Failing to do so will likely result in entire enterprises finding themselves in the way of that very train.

Introduction

When we began discussing the idea for this book, the COVID pandemic was just receding, leaving behind it a tumultuous set of realities about how work was to be conducted going forward. Bosses and their employees were trying to determine where work should occur (return to offices or continue to work virtually) and who would be doing the work (talent shortages were only just starting to become the new reality of enterprise growth and resource management).

We knew that automation and intelligent machines were already a significant force in enterprise operations. Tom had recently published his 22nd, 23rd, and 24th books—all about artificial intelligence (AI) and the role that it was playing in transforming business operations, analytics, and skills needed for the future. Ian had just co-authored his first book on intelligent automation. He had recently sold his robotic process automation (RPA) consulting firm, which had helped large enterprises grasp, adopt, and manage process automation in their front- and back-office operations. There was no doubt in our minds that AI-powered automation was a hot topic. But, the question remained, who was going to be doing the automating? Similarly, there was also no doubt that data was taking a center-stage role in almost every transformation discussion. But who was going to be doing the collecting, cleaning, and analyzing of it?

The labor shortage left companies with big plans and small teams to achieve those plans. The one bright light in that reality was that technology was clearly getting "easier." Amateurs were building applications that could previously only be created by professional technologists. Data science teams were able to do more with the teams they had—harnessing capabilities like automated machine learning (autoML) that allowed data scientists to leverage more sophisticated models in less time, sometimes taking advantage of people with quantitative—but not PhD level—skills. IT teams were able to develop testing scripts more quickly and integrate systems with easier tools than application programming interfaces (APIs), once the only digital glue that could hold a company's plethora of systems together. A little later, generative AI came along and transformed everyone's notions of how best to communicate with smart machines for citizen development and many other purposes.

Amid the reality of talent shortages and technology advancements there would emerge two major forces that we believe will forever alter the landscape of work—and we're confident that's not hyperbole. Those developments are the converging trends of technology becoming more human and humans becoming more technical. This book is our exploration of that reality, in which everyone (if they so choose) can play a significant role in shaping the type of work they do and how they do it.

We see this as a good-news story. It's an aspirational tale of the unleashing of human ingenuity at scales never before seen or, until now, possible. This is a reality in which anyone with the gumption and a get-up-and-go spirit can design, build, and use complex information creations of their own imagination.

That said, this is also an environment in which much could go wrong if those same creators are not guided, supported, and overseen by those with greater knowledge of data security, compliance, and general best practices. The last section of the book is devoted to these risk-reduction approaches.

Our Experience

This book is the culmination of many years of discussion and sharing of our respective points of view on the trends and changes occurring in the world of work.

Tom's points of view came from his extensive research, consulting, and writings on AI, data science, and the application of analytics in enterprises. His publications in both journals and in book form have covered a wide range of topics including automation (*Only Humans Need Apply*), analytics (*Competing on Analytics, Analytics at Work*), and AI (*The AI Advantage, Working with AI, All In on AI*), and low-code/no-code development ("When Low-Code/

No-Code Development Works—and When It Doesn't" in *Harvard Business Review*). Ian's experience was a bit more hands-on, having come from the outsourcing industry and cofounding an automation consulting firm that was an early pioneer in applying RPA and other intelligent automation tools to digitize routine work tasks and processes. He also developed a series of courses hosted on LinkedIn Learning that helped enterprises upskill their teams on topics such as RPA, intelligent automation, process mining, process discovery, and conversational AI—the tools that were helping to empower employees.

We met a few years ago and continued to talk over time about automation, AI, and digital transformation. We shared our disappointment about the slow pace of digitalization in organizations and the excessive marketing claims of some AI and automation vendors. While conversing about these topics, we realized we also shared an interest in citizen development. We started by researching and coauthoring a couple of articles ("We're All Programmers Now" in *Harvard Business Review*, and "Harnessing Grassroots Automation" in *MIT Sloan Management Review*) and then decided we'd keep things moving with a book. Since then we've interviewed more than 50 executives and companies involved in citizen development and had many, many Zoom conversations, a few podcasts and webinars, and a couple of face-to-face meetings to digest all the learnings from early adopters.

We're convinced that citizen enablement with technology is here to stay and will have major implications. So in this book we will examine the elements and frameworks that we believe will shape the next decade or more of enterprise operations. We will examine the technologies that are in play today and appear inevitable on the near horizon. We will discuss the skills that are needed, and are in high demand, in enterprises of every size across the globe. We'll describe the individual roles necessary to make citizen initiatives effective, including the frontline worker, the IT manager, the executive leader, and the customer. Each of these roles is being altered, empowered, and compelled to adapt in order to survive and thrive in an environment where technology is as pervasive as process.

For Whom Is This Book Intended?

We're confident that reading this book and moving into citizen development is of benefit to a variety of audiences. For different types of readers, however, the ideas and lessons we hope to transmit are somewhat different. If you're an enterprise leader, we hope to persuade you that citizen development is both inevitable and beneficial. Your actions and support can accelerate the movement and make it more successful, however. One option is to simply get out of the way, but we believe that a better one is to get on board, encourage the productivity and innovation it can engender, and try to align it with your organization's strategies and objectives. In addition, there are likely to be some cultural changes necessary for citizen development to thrive. One key example is to adequately motivate and reward citizen development and the benefits accruing from it so that productive citizens stay in your employ. Those types of changes can happen only with senior management support.

We're also targeting this book at the millions of technically savvy people in organizations who are or can be citizen developers. Throughout it we try to describe both organizations and specific individuals (as in the preface) who are enabling this revolution. If you're in the individual contributor category, read on to find out the benefits to you and your career of jumping on this bandwagon. You'll also learn about what technologies you could be using; what types of applications, automations, and models you might develop; and how you can get support from the rest of your organization. Overall we believe that your jobs will be more fulfilling and productive if you use these powerful tools to improve work.

There may also be some generational differences in how individuals approach citizen development. If you're in Gen X or Y or are a Boomer who's still in the workforce (as Tom is), you've accumulated a lot of domain expertise about the businesses in which you've worked. Unless you have made an effort to master each new technology that comes along, you may feel that you are a bit less tech-savvy than those digital natives who live on their smartphones. We will argue that citizen development will change your job too, however, and you will want to embrace the change. Your domain expertise makes you incredibly valuable as a citizen developer, and we hope you'll either become one or work closely with some you encounter at work.

If you're in Gen Z or Alpha (more power to you for an early start!), you are less likely to have a lot of business experience, but you are probably quite comfortable with the personal use of various technologies. If you adopt citizen tools as you learn about business, you'll probably be much more productive and effective than most of your peers.

This book is also for information technology professionals (or professional automation or data analysis/science folks). You may not be terribly positive about citizen development, but we hope to persuade you otherwise. More and more IT organizations are embracing this trend, and we hope you will too. Citizens could certainly use your help, and their business expertise combined with your technical chops could make for some great outcomes.

Overall, the citizen revolution is a good news story for all the groups listed. But, it's also a wake-up call and a call to action. Unlike any previous wave of technology, this generation of citizen-oriented tools is more accessible, enterprise environments are more porous and easily disrupted with citizen-class technologies, and the citizens are clamoring for the opportunity to apply their expertise and make things happen. We have structured the book to share what we've learned in our research, outline frameworks and approaches we believe will set you up for success, and leave you with a bit of inspiration that the future of work has a place for us all and that all hands will (in some way or another) be on tech.

Why Is Citizen Development a Good Thing?

There will be many places throughout the book where we explore the benefits of harnessing the ingenuity of domain experts, augmenting them with technical superpowers never before available. We dedicate Chapter 10, "Benefits of Citizen Development," to exploring the benefits in depth and showcasing the numerous ways in which this wave of grassroots innovation will serve to transform both the future of work and the workers involved. But we felt it important to draw your attention to some highlights right up front.

In our research, we were able to speak to dozens of global organizations, most very large, several in the medium to small category. We surveyed several hundred firms thanks to LinkedIn polls and webinar surveys we were able to deploy during discussions of the two journal articles we mentioned earlier that served as the catalyst for this book. What we found was strong evidence that citizen development is both real and really valuable.

Enterprises that are able to launch and support citizen programs report higher degrees of process innovation, more rapid and agile experimentation and solution deployment, operational efficiencies, cost savings, and perhaps most encouraging, higher levels of employee satisfaction and retention. If done on a large scale, with senior executive support and substantial resources and with substantial attention to change in jobs, business process, and organizational culture, citizen development can be a transformative force—a game-winning home run—for organizations. Even at a minimum it's a great way to score runs with walks, singles, and an occasional extra-base hit.

Empowering domain experts with the ability and the freedom to turn their ideas into applications, automations, and higher-order analysis, is good for all stakeholders involved. Furthermore, the citizen development movement is a blueprint for how the work of the future can incorporate breakthroughs in generative AI and other forms of AI, while ensuring that the focus is on a humans + AI equation for optimal outcomes.

What You'll Learn In This Book

Here's a breakdown of each chapter in the book.

Chapter 1: Why Citizen Development Is Inevitable

Citizen development refers to the process of employing easy-to-use tools to create and deploy custom applications, automations, or data analyses by nontechnical users. This approach empowers business users, citizen developers, or power users to create software solutions without having to rely on IT departments or professional developers, analysts, or data scientists. Citizen development has emerged as a solution to the growing demand for digital transformation and the need for speed, efficiency, and agility in software development. We assert that this trend is both impactful and unstoppable.

Chapter 2: A History of Citizen-Led Innovation

Harnessing the creativity of employees is not new. Throughout the history of enterprises, approaches have been used and improved in order to tap into the ingenuity, creativity, and subject-matter expertise of those closest to the tasks and processes that make up a modern operation. This chapter explores the history of citizen-led innovation, creation, and solutioning.

Chapter 3: The Citizen Journey

Citizen developers can play a number of different roles in organizations, have a variety of paths toward becoming citizens, and have a range of career progressions as a result of their technology orientations. In this chapter, we explore these variations in depth, along with some of the factors that drive different outcomes for citizen roles and careers.

Chapter 4: Citizen Development Using Low-Code/No-Code Tools

Low-code/no-code (LC/NC) application development tools are the original citizen development technologies. Leading software vendors have embraced the idea, and many companies are now encouraging citizens to develop applications for individual or departmental use. This chapter covers the types of applications to which LC/NC tools are put, the role of IT in collaborating with citizens, and the likely future of citizen development using generative AI for coding and broader application development.

Chapter 5: Citizen Automation

Citizen automation complements app development, introducing software as a means of handling the routine and transactional work common in every enterprise. Citizen automators use the intelligent automation tech stack, including RPA, intelligent document processing (IDP), and other cognitive tools to integrate between systems, digitize workflows, and automate rule-based decision-making. In this chapter, we explore the roles played by work optimization, outsourcing, and automation, and we speculate on the advancement of the citizen automation toolkit in light of generative AI and large action models.

Chapter 6: Citizen Data Science

Citizen data science—and its less demanding cousin, citizen data analysis—involves developing not applications or automations but data outputs such as dashboards, displays, predictive models, and AI-based recommendations. Data analysis is well-accepted for citizens in most organizations, but "true" data science is more problematic. In this chapter, we discuss the state of citizen data science and analysis, provide some leading examples, and speculate on what tools like generative AI will do to change the situation.

Chapter 7: Skills and Personality of a Citizen

There is no one personality profile or skill set that makes for an ideal citizen. However, there are characteristics and traits that help to identify those likely to embrace the opportunity to apply domain expertise to the pursuit of technology-enabled problem-solving and solution development. In addition, just as people have traits, so too do companies and departments. In this chapter, we explore the telltale signs of productive and creative citizens and citizen-ready organizations. We'll also break down some of the specific skills necessary for citizen application development, citizen automation, and citizen data analysis/science.

Chapter 8: The Citizen Champion: With and Without Air Cover

A critical aspect of making any citizen initiative successful is a savvy and energetic champion within organizations. This chapter describes some of the activities they perform and the value they provide. A key distinction among champions is how much "air cover" or executive support they have. We show how their strategies for making citizen development thrive differ with different levels of support and resources.

Chapter 9: The Citizen Tech Landscape

What are the popular citizen tools, applications, and platforms? Citizen development platforms typically offer drag-and-drop interfaces, visual builders, and prebuilt components that simplify and accelerate the development process. Some of the popular low-code or no-code platforms used by citizen developers include Appian, Microsoft Power Apps, Salesforce Lightning, OutSystems, and Mendix. These platforms offer a range of features and functionalities, such as data integration, workflow automation, and mobile app development. We also discuss citizen automation and data science/analysis tools and the directions they are all likely to take in the future.

Chapter 10: Benefits of Citizen Development

Citizen development offers several benefits to organizations, such as increased agility, faster time to market, reduced IT backlog, and cost savings. By enabling users to create applications, businesses can streamline processes, automate workflows, and improve decision-making. Citizen development also has strategic implications when done at scale. It also promotes strategic benefits like innovation and creativity by giving users the freedom to experiment and try new ideas without the need for technical expertise.

Chapter 11: The Organizational Response to Citizen Technology

Historically, there have been two key parties involved in battles over citizen development: citizens, who support it, and IT organizations, which oppose it. We describe these two camps and their positions in some detail. We also describe how third-party groups can help citizen development thrive. We provide several detailed examples of how organizations have responded to citizen development.

Chapter 12: Preparing to Set Sail

While citizen development offers many benefits, it also comes with some challenges and risks. To ensure successful citizen development, organizations should establish governance policies, provide training and support, prioritize security and compliance, and foster collaboration between citizen developers and IT professionals. Other best practices include identifying business needs and goals, selecting the right platform, and measuring the impact of such initiatives.

Chapter 13: Genesis

It is likely that your organization has citizen development activities underway and in every department, region, and function. That said, a formal program depends on a solid beginning. Even if the train has left the station, the importance of starting strong cannot be underestimated. This chapter outlines the features of a strong start and proposes best practices for setting the tone, clarifying the mission, and launching a sponsored and enterprise-grade citizen development program.

Chapter 14: Guidance

Once an initiative is announced and the mission is declared, the next steps are to select a leader, identify citizen candidates, and provide the necessary training and tools to get to work. This chapter showcases the elements that leading citizen development initiatives use to create strong behaviors, habits, and capabilities across the team. In addition, the chapter highlights levels of training and methods with which to incentivize performance.

Chapter 15: Governance

The success of a citizen development initiative is measured both in the outcomes created and in the safety and rigor with which the outcomes are delivered. Recognizing that citizen developers are not formally trained in security, compliance, or risk management, this chapter explores ways in which to adapt traditional governance measures to balance control with a level of freedom. This is done to encourage citizen-led creativity and development, while also safeguarding an enterprise's systems and data.

Chapter 16: Guardrails

A close relative to an overall governance strategy, this chapter explores various guardrails that high-functioning citizen initiatives have put in place to ensure compliant development and automation development. This chapter also explores other forms of guardrails that include financial controls and security protocols—all catering to the level of awareness and authority that a citizen is granted within their enterprise's development environment.

Chapter 17: The Future of Citizen Development

In this chapter, we try our hand at being futurists, forecasting the direction of travel for enterprise tech, organizational change, and the fate of domain experts. We explore the impact of natural language coding, which will truly allow all hands to be on tech. We also consider the role of IT in this new world of fusion teams, broadly embedded technical skills, and an empowered ecosystem of internal stakeholders. Finally, we leave you with our hopes for the future of work, the worker of the future, and the leadership in that future. We wish them all smooth sailing.

Appendix A: Citizen-Ready Checklist

This appendix provides a "citizen-ready" checklist to determine your organization's readiness for extensive citizen development.

Appendix B: Citizen Development Challenges Organizations Are Likely to Face

This appendix lists a set of citizen development challenges that organizations are likely to face.

Appendix C: Additional Resources

This appendix provides additional resources for readers wanting to learn more about citizen development.

Background, History, and Context

1

Why Citizen Development Is Inevitable

This is an unprecedented time in the 70-year history of business information technology. Amateurs, or *citizens*, are riding a new digital horse, and enterprise IT organizations can no longer fully control the reins. The repercussions will be profound.

Throughout the history of modern enterprise, IT organizations, automation groups, analytics and data science functions, or other professionals have been the sole or primary developers of enterprise capabilities in data and technology. This has led to great frustration in organizations due to greater demand than supply because IT professionals couldn't meet demand in a timely fashion. It has also led to frequent communication breakdowns between technical experts and business leaders and users.

Today, however, new technologies as well as more digitally oriented employees are making possible the development of technology solutions by amateurs outside of IT or other specialized groups—known as *citizen developers*, *citizen data scientists*, or *citizen automators*, depending upon what types of technology they are trying to create. Given the rapid developments in AI that cross these boundaries—generative AI systems can already create application programs, automation workflows, or data science analyses—the best future term might be *technology-enabled citizens* or something similar. These citizens no longer need professional intermediaries to obtain the information and digital capabilities required to do their jobs. This development constitutes a revolution in how humans and machines combine to meet organizational objectives.

Once derided as "shadow" or "rogue" IT, applications, automations, and AI models developed by amateurs are already powering substantial components of organizations. IT organizations that were once unalterably opposed to citizen development have begun to encourage it. As companies seek to digitize much of their operations, they increasingly realize that the large population of enabled IT amateurs is essential to their success. Some companies still resist significant citizen development, but it seems inevitable in the long run.

What Are Citizens?

A *citizen* in this context is someone who develops applications of information technology outside of a formal information technology group within organizations. It is rarely a formal title but rather an informal description or persona. There are various versions of citizens, including *citizen developers* (typically using low-code/no-code application development tools), *citizen automators* (using robotic process automation tools or other automation systems), *citizen data scientists* (who develop sophisticated analytical or machine learning models), and even *citizen data engineers* (who use data management tools to manipulate data). As other professional roles using technology emerge, it is likely that there will eventually be citizen versions of them.

Our definition of *citizen* with regard to information technology is similar in some ways to Brook Manville's and Josiah Ober's notion of citizens in Athenian democracy. They wrote:

> Underpinning all the achievements [of that society] was a system of governance based on personal freedom, collective action, and an open, democratic culture. Athens was at heart a community of citizens—a "politeia," to use the Greek word—and each of those citizens had both

the right and the obligation to play an active role in the society's governance.[1]

Just like Athenian citizens, technology-focused citizens need community, freedom, and responsibilities. Citizen developer communities are critical to individuals' ability to learn about new technologies and build on the work others have already accomplished. Freedom comes into play because being a citizen with information technology is a voluntary activity; it doesn't work well to force people to undertake it—they may lack either the skills or motivation, or both. And there are multiple different citizen activities from which to choose. Responsibility and obligation in the citizen technology user context involves adhering to guidelines and guardrails for effective technology use and being transparent about the technology capabilities a citizen has developed and how it was done. Developing technologies and systems may not be the citizen's only or even primary job, but it's a role that needs to be taken seriously.

As we've suggested, citizens generally hold jobs outside of IT organizations. They occupy an almost infinite variety of primary roles—doctors, marketers, supply chain analysts, financial analysts, entrepreneurs, human resource specialists, researchers, product developers, etc. But all of these jobs today involve information generation, manipulation, and consumption. Technology helps collect, store, process, and analyze that information. In many cases, citizens do more than create technology and manage information for their own jobs; they take on that responsibility for their department or business unit. Citizen-developed technologies, then, can be intended for use by one person (in which case they may not need a lot of governance or controls) or multiple people (when they probably require a bit more oversight). Some citizens have developed tools that are used by the entire enterprise, although this is somewhat rare.

Citizens are defined as people outside of IT, but they may move in and out of IT-related organizations over time. IT groups may realize that they would benefit from a citizen perspective in the creation of IT systems.

---

[1] Manville, Brook and Ober, Josiah, "Beyond Empowerment: Building a Company of Citizens," *Harvard Business Review*, January 2003, https://hbr.org/2003/01/beyond-empowerment-building-a-company-of-citizens.

Earlier, these business-focused IT employees were referred to as *business systems analysts*. Today they take on other roles. For example, in data science groups (which may be in IT or may be in other parts of a company), professional data scientists were at one time the only real job role. Now, however, there are intermediary or hybrid roles that are increasingly found within data science projects and products. They may include data product managers, translators, or citizen data scientists. These people can develop or help to create data science models with citizen-level skills and can also oversee some of the operational and people-related changes that are required to make data science successful.

Somewhat confusingly, *citizen development* is used throughout organizations and the literature as both a broad term for citizen technology activity and a term for citizen application development using low-code/no-code technology. But we're also discussing citizen automators, citizen data analysts, citizen data scientists, citizen web developers, etc. So in many cases we'll use the term *citizen technology enablement* to describe all of the types of information technology activity that may be performed by citizens.

Why Is Citizen Development Growing?

As we've suggested, citizen development is growing because technology is becoming more human, and humans are becoming more technical. The first trend is a generally slow but continuous evolution toward technologies that are easier for nonprofessionals to use. Vendors began to produce tools for end users to create or customize solutions as early as the 1980s. The particular technology domains in which we have seen great progress include low-code and no-code program development, easy-to-use visual analytics tools, automated machine learning, web page development systems, mobile app development platforms, and automation programs. Even programming technology has become easier to use over time, and many professional programmers already draw from code repositories for much of their projects. Most automation tools were always point-and-click, drag-and-drop activities, but vendors have added even more easily mastered versions of their tools for citizens. Automated machine learning systems have made it possible for amateurs to generate complex machine learning models. Automation programs, such as robotic process automation tools or Service-Now, have special versions intended for use by citizens.

The trend toward increased usage of these technologies became apparent to Gartner systems engineering researcher and analyst Eric Knipp in 2009, when he published a research report that first named citizen developers.[2] Gartner predicted at the time that within five years a quarter of all applications developed in organizations would come from citizens, although no one seems to have assessed whether that specific prediction came true.

Citizen-oriented tools became more common and more powerful between 2015 and 2022, slowly shifting the balance of power away from IT departments and toward the hands of citizens. However, the explosion of generative AI onto the scene in late 2022 has accelerated the democratization of powerful technologies in ways that almost no one was prepared for, least of which are IT departments and business leaders within enterprises. It has turned an evolution into a revolution. In many domains technology has become more citizen-oriented.

At the same time, most humans have become more technology-oriented. Virtually every participant in advanced economies today uses powerful technology on a daily basis—at the very least, downloading and using apps of multiple types on a mobile phone. Everyone has more computing power on their desktops and in their pockets than was contained in data centers a couple of decades ago. Online and inexpensive courses in multiple aspects of technology abound. While there remain some forms of detailed knowledge about IT development that are not possessed by amateurs, the gap between them and professionals is shrinking.

In addition to the increased supply of tech-oriented citizens and citizen-oriented technologies, the demand arising from traditional IT/business conflicts is also still at play. Business discontent with IT backlogs and the pace of IT development is a perennial issue, as is the communication gap between business stakeholders and IT professionals. It's been a long-standing truism that businesspeople understand their business, IT people understand their technology, and seldom shall the twain meet. While these factors haven't necessarily worsened, the broad digitization initiatives within companies may have decreased the willingness of citizens and their managers to tolerate them.

---

[2] The Gartner research report is proprietary, but the research is described in Darryl K. Taft, "Gartner: 'Citizen Developers' to Deliver 25% of Apps by 2024," *EWeek*, October 23, 2009, https://www.eweek.com/development/gartner-citizen-developers-to-deliver-25-of-apps-by-2014.

To quantify the level of discontent, a 2021 survey of about 1,000 "business decision makers" (sponsored by a citizen-oriented technology vendor) found that:

- 3–12 months is the average backlog for planned IT projects, and the situation is worsening as business project demand outstrips IT budget growth.
- 55% of respondents say business units already do more than IT to procure or develop new applications.
- 53% of business decision-makers believe the volume of applications built or sourced by non-IT business units will increase over the next 12 months.[3]

IT professionals became an important role when businesses had limited direct access to information technology; mainframes and minicomputers resided in temperature-controlled data centers and serviced entire corporations. But today, technology is everywhere. Data and information are everywhere too. Large language models provide access to massive troves of intelligence, at a price that is virtually free. And, thanks to ChatGPT (and equivalents), coding is soon to be everywhere, since it is no longer a skill out of reach for most "nontechnical" people. At home and at work, we've all become constant users of computers, software, local networks, and the Internet. If it's "shadow IT," we're all in the shadows now. More likely, however, shadow IT is being brought into the light.

Thanks to the mass simplification of technology development, we are all now the potential builders of the next generation of these tools. It's only natural that the creation of business systems would shift from professionals to these pervasive and increasingly knowledgeable IT amateurs. One chief information officer told us that in meetings between IT professionals and knowledgeable business users, it is increasingly difficult to tell who belongs to which group—they all can discuss business issues (even if citizens understand them a bit better) and IT solutions to them (even if IT professionals understand them a bit better). There is no easy way to help IT understand

---

[3] "IT's Changing Mandate in an Age of Disruption," Economist Intelligence Unit report sponsored by Appian, `https://appian.com/learn/resources/resource-center/whitepapers/economist-survey-its-changing-mandate.html`, 2021.

the business better (other than having them work more closely on projects with citizens), but there are plenty of technologies available to help businesspeople develop better IT solutions.

The Front Lines of Digitalization

Copious data suggests that enterprises struggle with a chasm of digital capabilities. A quick Internet search for "why digital transformations fail" yields a plethora of blog posts, articles, and books on the subject. Digital transformation is taking too long, in part because millions of application development, coding, data science, and tech-associated jobs are going unfilled. To compete in the future, companies know they need more IT capabilities, and the current supply chain has failed to provide the necessary resources. The only way for companies to fill the void is through greater emphasis on skill development of their existing staff—their citizens.

Imagine two different organizations. Both have explicit initiatives underway to digitally transform their businesses. In one, the IT organization tries to carry the load by itself. There, the mandate to digitize has only created more demand for new applications, automations, and data analyses—but no new supply. Department leaders and digitally oriented professionals initially submitted request after request, but as the backlog grew, they became discouraged and stopped bothering to ask when their solutions would be forthcoming. After a couple of years, no one even mentioned digital transformation anymore.

In the other organization, digital transformation was a broad organizational mandate. IT was certainly a part of it and had to update a variety of enterprise transaction systems as well as moving most systems to the cloud. They had their hands full with this aspect of the transformation.

Fortunately, in this hypothetical company many citizens were engaged in the transformation process as well. They built individual and departmental applications and even an occasional mobile app for customers—mostly with a quick review from a helpful IT professional. They automated their own processes after improving them. They built dashboards, scorecards, and even some straightforward machine learning models for marketing, supply chain management, and human resources. Digitizing the company was regarded as everyone's job, and thousands of initiatives took place all around the company. Not surprisingly, the company began to outdo its competitors—not only on digital capabilities but on market share and profitable growth as well.

These two organizations are fictional, but they are reflective of a variety of companies we've seen and researched for this book. Almost every company, nonprofit, and governmental organization wants to be more digital these days, and for good reason. It leads to less friction in dealing with customers and suppliers, product and service offerings that are better attuned to customer needs, more satisfied employees, a better fit between production and consumption, and so forth. It's a worthy objective, so why not try to achieve it with all the resources available to an organization? Noel Carroll, a business school academic at the University of Galway, researches citizen development and has concluded that organizations employing it broadly have considerably more "digital agility" than those that do not. We wholeheartedly agree.

Citizens as we've defined them are the front lines of digitalization. Just as we rely upon frontline workers to figure out better ways to do their work, to satisfy customers, and to make good use of their work hours, we can now rely upon them to use information technology to make themselves and their departments or functions more effective and productive. Where we once depended upon frontline employees to practice Lean Six Sigma or other approaches to quality improvement, we can now also allow them to create applications, mobile apps, automated workflows, and data analyses. Not everyone wants to be a citizen developer of technology, but increasing numbers are willing to volunteer—particularly if the communications, tools, and incentives are right.

When frontline employees develop their own technologies, there is often a very different attitude about them than with centrally developed systems that are imposed by IT. We've all experienced systems that we have to use by central mandate, and we often don't like them much. We focus on their shortcomings more than their advantages, and we resent having to learn the new tools or to change our work processes to incorporate them. But when we develop the technologies ourselves, we're much more tolerant of any problems, and we're more likely to be positive about workflow adjustments that we've imposed upon ourselves.

It's also possible—though just speculation at this point—that citizen enablement could play something of a leveling-up role in financial inequality. Satya Nadella, the CEO of Microsoft, has argued that citizens on "the front line" in many industries could learn new skills, accomplish new tasks, and be paid more as a result. The phrase he used in a speech was that "IT level wages can go to the front line." If this seems self-serving for the CEO of a company offering citizen development tools, then David Autor, a respected labor economist at MIT, has made a similar point. But Jeremy Kahn, a *Fortune* magazine editor, argues that this leveling function is far from certain—in that, for example, citizen enablement could end up reducing the compensation of IT people—so it is far too soon to count on any reduction in inequality. He compared writing software by citizens to a time-consuming and unrewarded task like making travel reservations; he wrote:

> The same may not happen with the task of building software or compiling and analyzing data—workers will now be expected to do it themselves, without any increase in pay or compensating reduction in primary responsibilities. So our jobs might just get a little more stressful and more miserable.[4]

Kahn's perspective suggests that to make citizens happy in their jobs, we'll have to figure out ways to motivate and incentivize citizen development. And our research suggests that many organizations haven't figured out how to do that well yet.

Not every citizen-developed technology will function well or advance the broader digital cause, but many will—and far more than just professional IT developers can create. Of course, there are risks to citizen tools and activities, and we detail them in this book. But after talking with more than 100 people involved in citizen development—citizens themselves, sponsors, IT leaders, vendors—we have yet to hear any disaster stories.

---

[4] Jeremy Kahn, "Microsoft CEO Satya Nadella Is an AI Winner. He Doesn't Like to Talk About the Potential Losers," Fortune *Eye on AI* Newsletter, Jan. 16, 2024, https://links.newsletter.fortune.com/e/evib?_t=5c2d888702774d17aa3d0350287b6d73&_m=311acf79dbf244828a364b900a35975c&_e=4G0Hw7D4GkaYxYrnqlsLzhT5cLZVa0RdeAEkXuXNwMUNggQeXqz6jGNH7247xFq6.

With proper guidance and governance, development of technology by people at the front lines of organizations can be empowering, productive, and safe.

Monarchy, Federalism, or Anarchy?

More than 30 years ago Tom coauthored an article called "Information Politics" in which he and his coauthors compared data management approaches to political power structures.[5] The primary alternatives were monarchy (or more broadly, autocracy), federalism (a common form of partial democracy), and anarchy (we won't discuss here two others: technocratic utopianism, or assuming that technology solves all problems, and feudalism, in which there are multiple monarchs). Citizen development approaches can be similarly classified.

In some organizations, IT is the king or queen, and citizen enablement, if allowed at all, is viewed as a lowly activity practiced by commoners. Such a monarchy, of course, is not the best environment for citizen activities to flourish. Under federalism—which Tom and his coauthors deemed the most desirable model for information management—there are some domains reserved to central IT groups, such as transactional systems of record and key data definitions. The remaining types of development are allowed and encouraged to be done by citizens. We think that federalism is generally the right model for facilitating citizen development. As in federalist democracies, however, effective federal models for citizen development do require some strategizing (and perhaps even arguing) about what activities are allowed by what parties.

The third model, anarchy, is what could happen in organizations if citizens had no oversight or governance. There might be, for example, as many systems and information results as there are employees—"infinite versions of the truth." The organization might become dependent upon citizen-developed systems that no one even knows about or for which the developer has long departed the company. IT budgets could become both bigger and more difficult to control, as many individual users contract separately with (the same in some cases) vendors of software and data. And poorly developed systems by citizens could be hacked into by cyber-crooks.

---

[5]Thomas H. Davenport, Lawrence Prusak, and Robert Eccles, "Information Politics," *MIT Sloan Management Review*, Fall 1992, https://sloanreview.mit.edu/article/information-politics.

Many organizations are moving rapidly toward an information politics model that is closer to federalism than monarchy. And as we've stated, some monarchs (IT leaders) welcome the change. Just as in nation-level democracies, there are plenty of reasons to urge more citizen involvement. On the positive side, widespread citizen enablement could usher in a much broader and faster approach to technology-based innovation in organizations, including digitization, automation, and data analysis. With no need for an intermediary to misunderstand requirements, more systems that are developed will fit the business need and will actually be used. IT professionals wouldn't become obsolete, but they could focus on monitoring citizen-developed tools and building complex systems and technologies that truly require their expertise.

Of course, the citizen revolution raises questions about what is the ultimate fate of IT organizations within companies and how they can facilitate and safeguard citizen development without placing too many obstacles before it. Passing on the benefits of citizen development is economically infeasible, and not to manage it effectively is equally untenable. We'll address this tension at several points throughout the book.

Another potential benefit of citizen development, if it is executed in an aggressive fashion, could also change the relationship of employees to organizations. Information technology has historically involved *creators* (IT professionals) and *users* (some might prefer the term *victims*, but we think that's a bit exaggerated) who are relatively powerless users of the technology developed by others. But just as legions of Six Sigma colored belt–wearers transformed process improvement around the turn of the 21st century, citizen development could spark a new era of digitally enabled business improvement. Citizens could not only improve or streamline their own business processes and tasks but could automate and analyze them as well. In Chapter 15, "Guidance," we even propose a citizen development belt hierarchy, although it doesn't approach the complexity of the five- or six-level (depending on your source) Six Sigma belt assortment.

Such widespread citizen activity could have two different and opposing impacts. It could spark increased engagement with work and would likely improve employee satisfaction and retention. Or it could lead—as social media conversations suggest it already has—to employees automating key tasks in their own jobs and using the freed-up time to find second or third jobs or to surf popular Internet sites. While we believe the first outcome is more desirable for the organizations that sponsor and cultivate citizen capabilities, they have to work out appropriate motivations and rewards for citizens to avoid the latter outcome. Either way, we suppose, citizens will be happier in their job (or jobs).

Like Seemingly Everything Else, Citizen Development Is Social

Another reason why citizen development is a growing and successful movement is the social nature of the activity. If you're a citizen in a large company, chances are good that there are regular meetups, hackathons, etc., to discuss different aspects of citizen development. Creating such a community is usually a fundamental responsibility of the citizen development champion, as we discuss in Chapter 8, "The Citizen Champion, With and Without Air Cover."

But even if you're a citizen developer who labors from a basement couch, there are plenty of online social sites in which citizen technology efforts can be discussed. There is the "overemployed" branch of citizenry, which regularly discusses on social sites their ability to use citizen-developed solutions to hold down multiple remote jobs. Another prominent site that we'll describe in Chapter 2, "A History of Citizen-Led Innovation," in the context of citizen data science is Kaggle, which is primarily viewed as an online data science competition venue (with more than 16 million members, now owned by Google). In addition, however, it offers learning tools, previously developed machine learning models and notebooks, and a discussion board for every competition. Some of the Kaggle participants are professional data scientists looking to make a few extra bucks in a competition, but many of them are amateurs.

There are also a variety of "community" sites run by citizen-oriented vendors. Alteryx, for example, has an Alteryx Community site with an academy for learning the tools, a discussion board, and a "gallery" of previously developed workflows and other Alteryx assets to share. The discussion board often reveals its citizen focus; the first post we looked at starts with this:

Hi community,
 Maybe this is a dumb question so apologies in advance.

Microsoft also supports a large online community site for Power Platform users (when we first accessed the site, it boasted 882,000 members).

It also includes forum discussions, events, user groups, and tutorials. Its citizen orientation was also revealed by the first post we read, which included this:

> Hoping someone can guide me with some steps since this is the first time I have worked with Copilot Studio.

Even general-purpose discussion boards sometimes address citizen development topics. For example, Tom's former coauthor Julia Kirby referred him to a posting on Reddit by a user ("Chonny") who used machine learning language analysis models to analyze the New Testament chapters attributed to the apostle Paul. He wanted to determine how likely they were to be written by Paul (many were not, he concluded). Although the work seems to us a pretty sophisticated analysis, he made it clear that it was an amateur effort.

> I have a bit of time and access to good NLP [natural language processing] models at work. . . This isn't intended to be serious research, but could be considered a starting point or template for those curious to pursue this further. Note that the Epistles were originally written in Greek, while the classifier is trained in English. Better results would likely be obtained using a model trained in ancient Greek.

After posting his results, he received some constructive criticism from other Reddit users, suggesting, for example, that he did really need to analyze the original Greek texts. But some were quite encouraging, such as this post:

> Seems like a fun "napkin-math" experiment and while some might be confused by the indeterminate results, having a bit of background in the tech I think the fact your model had such a significant result for Titus was a surprising success.

However, Tom's friend, Julia, suggested that the religious establishment might not be happy about this sort of work.

This is a fun example to me because of course what he's proposing would be a big deal to the Catholic Church, which has of course immense resources it could use to equip people in its hierarchy with AI tools but presumably is not doing so . . . and probably isn't crazy about the idea of some amateur sleuths making findings with the potential to undermine doctrine. (They're still getting over that Luther guy.)

In other words, corporate IT organizations are not the only potential objectors to citizen development.

But the larger issue is that the social nature of citizen development makes it generally more successful. For vendors, online social activity takes away some of the support requirements that would otherwise be necessary. For citizens themselves, not only do they get suggestions about how to do their IT work better, they also feel like they are part of a larger group that is doing this work and is passionate about it. Any opposition they face from inside their organizations might be countered by support (or at least interest) from the online community.

Support from social sources, however, doesn't mean that citizen development is safe. As we've noted, without proper controls and guardrails, widespread citizen development could usher in chaos. We'll describe some approaches to preventing such chaos throughout this book and preview some of them here.

Making Citizen Development Safe and Effective

Because citizen development can—even if rarely—cause problems and create risks for organizations, it's important for IT organizations—or whichever group is primarily overseeing citizen activity—to institute approaches and policies to make citizen-developed IT systems effective and safe. It's common to refer to such approaches as *governance*, but that term is only a part of what organizations need. *Enablement* is perhaps more appropriate because it encompasses all activities designed to make citizen-developed tools work well. Enablement consists of four components: genesis, governance, guardrails, and guidance. Each is described briefly here.

- **Genesis:** A journey of 1,000 innovations begins with a single step. In the case of citizen development, it is important to understand and support who takes those first steps, and how. Most citizen initiatives are often grassroots and happen rather organically, based on the creativity and inspiration of individuals in various operating departments and teams across an organization. As such, the tools they use, the solutions they develop, and the approaches they take are almost entirely ad hoc. We showcase such grassroots efforts by a finance professional at Mass General Brigham Hospital, a supply chain expert at a large consumer products company, and countless others. Some other organizations have a much faster launch, creating a support organization and orchestrating citizen learning and technology adoption. This approach, exemplified by Shell, is generally more desirable but less common. In studying the citizen trend, it's particularly important to understand how these initiatives take root, and provide the most supportive and clear environment and set of systems to ensure high rates of early (and compliant) success.

- **Governance:** This is the typical term used to describe how organizations ensure safe systems and data. It has not been a popular term with many businesspeople; who wants their work to be governed? But it is sometimes necessary, particularly when citizen systems or models have a negative impact on transactional systems of record or when they use key data elements and modify them in ways that create "multiple versions of the truth." Companies in highly regulated environments will also be concerned about analytical or AI systems that use personally identifiable data in ways that may not be private or secure. Approaches to governance may involve mandatory reviews by the IT organization, or, at the least, appointment of some manager within the citizen's organization to perform data stewardship activities. Another approach to governance, in a healthcare provider, automatically identified any data that might be of interest to external regulators.

- **Guardrails:** Companies may also try to build in automated or semi-automated guardrails that make it easy to do the right thing with citizen technologies and difficult to do the wrong thing. One insurance company, for example, used a citizen automation tool that automatically alerted the IT organization when it was created. Other examples of guardrails might include data catalogs or libraries in which clean and official versions of data are stored and made accessible; application program interfaces (APIs) to transactional systems that are read–only; and repositories of code, automation programs, or machine learning features that have been tested and can be easily reused. AT&T, for example, has an extensive program of citizen automation and data science with an extensive automation code library and a voluminous feature store for machine learning models.[6]

- **Guidance:** Citizens also need guidance on whether the applications they have developed are safe and effective and how to master new technologies. Some companies offer individual guidance to citizens; for example, Mayo Clinic's AI Enablement organization encourages employees with ideas for AI applications to talk with a professional about the idea and how it might best be developed. If there are regulatory or technology infrastructure issues with the proposed application, the citizen is informed about how best to proceed. Other organizations offer regular community meetings of citizens to discuss new technologies and how best to use them. Wolters Kluwer, for example, has an "Addicted to Learning" series that teaches citizen developers, automators, and data scientists about new technologies that are relevant to their jobs and the company.

With this multifaceted approach to enablement, organizations can build citizen capabilities while ensuring a low level of problems with the tools they develop. Further, the concept of "enablement" is much more appealing to citizens who just want to get their work done and do not view a heavy governance hand as positive. Enablement activities signal respect for citizens rather than control. In Chapters 13 through 16 we'll describe each of these "4Gs" in greater detail and discuss organizations that have successfully embraced all three aspects of enablement.

Generative AI and the Future of Citizen Development

Although generative AI only became known to most audiences in late 2022 with the release of ChatGPT, it already seems apparent that it will revolutionize citizen development. It's clear that it is or will be a very com-

---

[6] Thomas H. Davenport, "Citizen Data Science and Automation at AT&T," *Forbes*, Jan 30, 2023, https://www.forbes.com/sites/tomdavenport/2023/01/30/citizen-data-science-and-automation-at-att/?sh=72a820f21b32.

mon interface to software for code generation, low-code/no-code development, automation offerings, and analytics and machine learning. It may even replace the need for some of these programs; the Advanced Data Analysis feature in ChatGPT Enterprise, for example, can create machine learning models (by generating Python code) that rival those from specialized machine learning software. The only barrier to supporting many different business tasks with sophisticated technology will be the ability to express what one wants to accomplish in simple language. Even that barrier may be eased as generative AI systems develop conversational approaches to prompting.

Citizen development already seemed inevitable, but generative AI will only make it more so. Companies should begin now to prepare for this situation by educating citizens about the possibilities that generative AI offers them. Generative AI and the systems it controls or interfaces with will need clear access to high-quality data—both structured and unstructured—to perform data analysis and create applications and models, so data preparation and ongoing curation are other important preparatory activities. And since generative AI is likely to lead to a substantially larger number of citizens in most organizations, organizations should prepare for a greater degree of enablement activities to ensure the quality and ease of citizen development.

It may be that generative AI is the final straw that breaks the model of most IT development coming from professionals. There is little doubt that advanced levels of IT expertise will continue to be necessary, but the bulk of it may be devoted to guidance and oversight of citizen development. Active involvement by IT leaders in building citizen capabilities will undoubtedly make the movement more successful in organizations. Some IT professionals may find this a distasteful future for their profession, but others are likely to welcome and thrive in it.

2 | A History of Citizen-Led Innovation

There are many antecedents and inspirations of the citizen development idea over the last century or so. We won't go into detail about any of them, but we want you to know that the idea stands on the shoulders of previous ideas and movements. Citizen development is one of many approaches to improving business performance that have come before it, although we don't think there is anything exactly like it. Culturally, however, it has much in common with a long-term trend toward empowerment and encouragement of innovation by amateurs, either alone or in collaboration with professionals.

Outsiders and Insiders in Business Improvement

The desire to improve how work is done may go back multiple centuries, but one of the first systematic approaches to this objective was created by Frederick Taylor around the turn of the 20th century. His work is relevant to citizen development primarily because he pioneered the study of work-flows, which are critical to the effective use of citizen (and professional, for that matter) automation. Were Taylor alive today, he would no doubt advocate the idea of not automating a bad process. As we discuss in Chapter 5 on citizen automation, we agree with Taylor. The combination of process improvement and workflow automation is a powerful one to which Taylor didn't have access.

But Taylor, like many types of business improvers, was not a citizen. Rather, he was a manager (at Midvale Iron Works, Bethlehem Steel, and other companies) and eventually a consultant. As an outsider to front-line work he wasn't intimately familiar with the work processes he attempted to improve; instead, he carefully observed them and made recommendations for or instituted changes. That's one way to learn how to improve the business, but if the people who actually do the work are available, why not rely on them for improvement suggestions?

Since Taylor, most of the business improvers used by organizations have been people outside the business who make themselves available for hire. They may be consultants, coaches, market researchers, or advisors. Don't get us wrong—we believe that such individuals can be helpful, and we've both had jobs in those roles. They often have expertise in business improvement methods and tools that internal employees don't have. Of course, the internal employees have more expertise in how the business works, and they have to somehow communicate it to the external advisors.

And even when outsiders' specialized expertise is necessary, we believe the best ones are those who teach insiders how to improve. For example, in the heyday of Six Sigma and Lean, consultants were certainly involved, but the goal was typically not to do all the process analysis and improvement themselves but rather for them to teach employees how to do process improvement as a component of their own work.

Consultants are also often hired for system development and technology architecture work, particularly when the technologies involved are new or complex. Over time, as technology gets easier and employees become more experienced in its use, it makes sense to shift the work inside. As one head of automation in a big company (who didn't want to be named) put it,

> When we started with automation and RPA we used some consultants. Even though it wasn't very difficult work they charged us full rates. Now we view automation work—at least the type involving rules-based decisions—as pretty commoditized. Our own employees can do it unless there is some complex AI for document analysis or something like that. Most large consulting firms have realized that the work can be

done by client employees and have moved on to new technologies like generative AI.

We've also seen the same type of diminished consulting opportunities in data reporting and visualization. Before the advent of easy-to-use data visualization tools such as Qlik and Tableau, creating visual dashboards was a perfectly respectable task for consultants, or for that matter business intelligence specialists within a company. Today the great bulk of that work is done by citizens.

However, bottom-up improvement isn't practiced only by people who are trying to improve processes or provide better information. There are a range of activities that were previously restricted to professionals that have been opened up to "regular people." Some of these, such as suggestion boxes in corporate cafeterias, have not been terribly successful. But some have been of substantial value to organizations. Tom and some colleagues wrote in 2003, for example, about "idea practitioners" who bring in ideas to organizations about how to improve business and work.[1] They had observed it in the case of several improvement domains they had worked in: business process reengineering, knowledge management, and (after the article) analytics and big data. These were not generally senior managers but rather curious, well-informed middle managers or individual contributors who could see a match between new management approaches and a set of problems needing solutions.

Several other bottom-up improvement activities, which we describe in this chapter, have taken off at least to some degree. Some involve information technology as a core activity, and some have it on the fringes of that particular movement. All of them, however, have individual creation by amateurs as the core of that particular movement. Culturally, they all have a lot in common with citizen development.

The Open Innovation/Crowdsourcing Movement

One of the earliest cultural antecedents to citizen development is the idea of citizen innovation in products and services. Eric von Hippel, a long-time MIT

---

[1] Thomas H. Davenport. Laurence Prusak, and H. James Wilson, "Who's Bringing You Hot Ideas, and How Are You Responding?" *Harvard Business Review*, Feb. 2003, https://hbr.org/2003/02/whos-bringing-you-hot-ideas-and-how-are-you-responding.

professor, has been one of the earliest and most persistent advocates of citizen development, although he did not use that term. His overall focus was on innovation in various domains, and his lifelong passion has been on innovation by "users"—what he calls *distributed innovation*—rather than professionals.

Over about 50 years of research he's been interested in many versions of users—lead users who are some of the earliest adopters of a product or service, customers in general, consumers, clinicians, open-source software developers, and the like. For most of his research the focus was on new products and new uses of existing products, but his attention to open-source software suggests that software and information systems are the primary domains for innovation today. The innovation may be substantial and product-oriented—as with generative AI, for example—or may just be a new solution to a small problem inside an organization.

Von Hippel described "lead users" in one of his early papers.

> Lead users are users whose present strong needs will become general in a marketplace months or years in the future. Since lead users are familiar with conditions which lie in the future for most others, they can serve as a need-forecasting laboratory for marketing research. Moreover, since lead users often attempt to fill the need they experience, they can provide new product concept and design data as well.[2]

We can easily transfer the lead user idea to that of citizens. Citizens—particularly those good at "scouting" or understanding the need for a new system—are "familiar with conditions which lie in the future for most others." Their awareness and their development efforts can serve as a "need-forecasting laboratory" for IT organizations or business leaders who need to redesign their workflows, their transactional systems, or their data analyses.

Von Hippel's research preceded a variety of innovation approaches that are philosophically compatible with citizen development. The open-source software and crowdsourcing movements are forms of innovation that he and his students helped to nourish over the past few decades. And, like citizen development, both startups and some large companies have embraced them.

---

[2] Eric von Hippel, "Lead Users: A Source of Novel Product Concepts," *Management Science* 32, no. 7 (July 1986):791–805.

We won't go into the historical detail of von Hippel's research, but we want nervous readers to be aware that "all hands on tech" is not a new idea, and it is one that has been quite successful in the domain of product innovation. There is much to be said for professionals in any innovation domain but also much to be said for amateurs. Were it not for Eric von Hippel, amateurs would have been overlooked by many organizations.

Open Source in Software

Most people are familiar with the idea of "open-source" software, which is when software is released to the world without anyone having to pay for it. This was quite common in the early days of software development, when universities and corporate researchers collaborated on software programs. It largely disappeared when companies found they could make considerable profits from software sales but has come back over the last decade or two. Now in generative AI, many companies (including Meta, Google, etc.) have released open-source versions of their models. In short, open-source software is a success. But how does it relate to citizen development?

There are some common attributes. Developers of open-source software and citizen developers don't expect to be paid for their technology products, although both would like some recognition. Both work on a voluntary basis, and their outputs can be shared by numerous users.

But that's about the extent of the similarity. These are the big differences:

- Open-source software developers are usually professionals, not amateurs. It's just the opposite for citizens.
- Open-source code goes out into the larger world. Citizens develop technology offerings only for use within their own organization.
- Since open-source code will generally be used a long way away from its creator, the code must be well-documented if it's to be successful. On the other hand, much citizen-developed technology is intended for usage by local colleagues, and it may be poorly documented and still be useful.

Although these are important differences, it's still likely that the rise of open source has made some IT people more comfortable with citizen development. After all, if an organization is using open-source software created by people from outside the organization's walls who could only be contacted with difficulty, isn't it somewhat less risky to use technology developed by your own employees, even if they aren't official IT people? We think so.

The Maker Movement

The "maker" movement is another antecedent/fellow traveler of citizen development. It's an amateur-led approach to building physical things, sometimes accompanied with software. It originated around the turn of the 21st century. Shortly after the idea of makers was propagated by futurists such as Neil Gershenfeld of MIT's Center for Bits and Atoms, 3D printers approached being a mainstream technology as it became cheaper and more reliable. Armed with a printer, a set of software parameters, and plastic or resin, makers could make almost any small physical item. Makers congregated in "makerspaces," physical facilities that provided not only the equipment to make things but also the social relationships to make making fun.

As in citizen development, makers are generally amateurs, and the activities are voluntary. Also like citizen information technology, it's often considered empowering to its participants, and both types of activity can be innovative. The maker movement is close enough to citizen development in its culture that it might be referred to as *citizen making*. As one article about the lessons from the maker movement, which advocated its creator orientation within companies, put it,

> The maker movement is a cultural phenomenon that celebrates shared experimentation, iterative learning, and discovery through connected communities that build together, while always emphasizing creativity over criticism.[3]

All of the same points might be made about citizen development, although the "creativity over criticism" element has yet to be explored by the organizations we have researched.

Again, however, there are some key differences. Makers generally make physical products (although some makers do "hack" computing capabilities, often using the inexpensive Arduino circuit board), while citizens develop

---

[3] Simmi Singh, "Lessons from the Maker Movement," *MIT Sloan Management Review*, Summer 2018, https://sloanreview.mit.edu/article/lessons-from-the-maker-movement.

business-focused software or data analyses. Making is typically more a fun hobby than something done at work for business purposes, as with citizen development. There may be some citizens who make software at home for fun—in fact, we're sure there are some, and no doubt it helps make them better citizen developers—but that's not the primary purpose of citizen activity.

Although citizens don't need a physical facility in which to create software, the "makerspace" idea could be an appealing add-on to citizen development initiatives. A "citizenspace" could be a locus for help and advice from development coaches, a place for citizens and IT professionals to meet and collaborate, a place to try new software for which the organization hasn't yet purchased an enterprise license, and, of course, a place to get good coffee.

For example, at Tom's employer Babson College—a business school with a strong focus on entrepreneurship—the Weissman Foundry was established as a makerspace in 2018. Upon completion, Babson's website described the facility and its role at the school and its near-neighbor colleges.

> The purpose of the building is to serve the needs of students pursuing entrepreneurial ventures where physical prototyping is central, promoting greater collaboration with the Olin College of Engineering, and Wellesley College; and complementing existing "innovation spaces" on campus. . . particularly by providing a dedicated "messy" project workspace where students can work on projects at all hours.[4]

In 2023, however, Erik Noyes, an entrepreneurship professor who oversees the Foundry, led the formation of The Generator, an organization to facilitate generative and traditional AI understanding and use on campus. The Foundry became the home of The Generator as well, and has hosted a number of student and faculty events. It also has student coaches who understand generative AI and can help student and faculty "citizens" learn about the technology.

---

[4] Complete: Weissman Foundry, Babson College Facilities Management Department, `https://www.babson.edu/facilities-management/capital-projects/weissman-foundry`, accessed March 16, 2020.

The Growth of Citizen Science—Starting with Ornithology

It's not surprising that the citizen movement has taken root in information technology systems; after all, they're cropping up everywhere. The "citizen science" concept, for example, involves the pursuit of scientific activities by amateurs who have an interest in advancing science. As with information technology development, there was historically a fairly strict separation between scientists and the rest of society. Now, however, there is some consensus that amateur scientists can at least be of value in helping to collect data, and perhaps to analyze it as well.

Citizen science is related to the ideas of "open innovation" and "crowd-sourcing," approaches that are practiced in a variety of domains. Eli Lilly pioneered the concept of open innovation in the pharmaceutical industry by creating two companies—Innocentive and YourEncore (a partnership with Procter & Gamble focused on retired scientists)—to enlist outside "solvers" to help find solutions to medical, biology, and chemistry problems. These organizations were created more than 20 years ago, and the concept has become somewhat mainstream by now. Kaggle, an open innovation program in data science formed in 2010, is now owned by Google and has more than 15 million registered users. Although some users are professional data scientists, Jeremy Howard, former president and chief scientist of Kaggle, once tweeted that "almost every Kaggle contest was won by someone outside the field of the contest."

There are many different versions and examples of citizen science. One of the earliest involved ornithology, in which citizens participate in the collection of bird populations and migration.[5] The Audubon Society's Christmas Bird Count is a prominent example; it began on Christmas Day in 1900 and is still practiced today by citizen ornithologists. According to the Audubon Society,

The data collected by observers over the past century allow Audubon researchers, conservation biologists, wildlife agencies and other

---

[5]Vanessa Lavesque and students, Sustainability Methods and Perspectives, "Introduction," Pressbooks Open Educational Resources, 2019, https://pressbooks.pub/sustainabilitymethods/front-matter/titleandpreface.

interested individuals to study the long-term health and status of bird populations across North America.[6]

There are many other domains in which citizens are encouraged to help scientists and researchers by gathering data. In fact, the US government maintains a website—CitizenScience.gov—that lists, when we last checked, 503 projects that allow citizen participation in data gathering.[7] They range from beach sand grain size photo-taking (SandSnap) to annotating gene expression data in humans and mice (Omics Compendia Commons). The latter project also allows for citizen data analysis, as do several others in the list.

In some cases citizen science even extends into citizen medical research. The U.S. National Institutes for Health (NIH) has a program called Biomedical Citizen Science, and the Department of Health and Human Services has citizen science programs in a variety of other areas. The National Library of Medicine manages the All of Us program, which seeks to gather genome data from a million volunteers. Because many of these programs involve data gathering and data analysis, they increasingly overlap with citizen development of information technology.

Cancer treatment is of particular interest to some citizen scientists. Tom has a friend, Brad Power, who runs the Cancer Patient Lab.[8] It organizes hackathons and discussion groups to help cancer patients use their own genomic and other forms of data to make highly personalized decisions about cancer treatment. Power, a former management consultant and cancer patient who is neither a physician nor a biological scientist, argues that cancer treatment is changing rapidly and can be highly data-driven if activist patients and their doctors use all of the resources that are available. In his view, patients with complex cancer cases will have better outcomes if they become citizen scientists themselves. He does recognize the value of professionals; many of the discussions he organizes involve oncologists and cancer researchers.

---

[6]Audubon Society, "History of the Christmas Bird Count," https://www.audubon.org/conservation/science/christmas-bird-count/history-christmas-bird-count, accessed Jan. 6, 2024.
[7]https://www.citizenscience.gov/catalog/#, accessed Jan. 6, 2024.
[8]CancerHacker Lab website, https://cancerhackerlab.com, accessed Jan. 7, 2024.

Of course, as with citizen development, different citizen science programs have different levels of citizen involvement. In some cases citizens only provide or gather data for researchers to analyze, and the protocols of the scientific experiments are also created by professionals. Other programs are somewhat more collaborative in nature and allow citizen domain expertise to be employed. That may involve data analysis or specialized expertise. For example, a program organized by professional researchers of orca killer whale health took advantage of a citizen scientist named Maya Sears. She had cultivated the rare skill of identifying particular orcas in a large pod for observation and testing.[9] This type of amateur/professional collaboration is consistent with the collaboration among citizen developers and IT professionals, sometimes called *fusion teams*, in many organizations.

We aren't experts on citizen science, but we'd argue that the rise of this movement is highly related to the rise of citizen technology development. In both cases there is a recognition that there are too many problems to be solved by professionals alone, and people who understand the problem domain in detail have a lot to add to the process of developing solutions to it. Just as smart IT managers are opening the door to citizen development, smart researchers and scientists are trying to find ways to enlist citizen scientists in addressing hard scientific problems. Finally, of course, the effective use and analysis of data is key to both citizen science and citizen development—some citizen scientists are citizen developers, and vice versa.

A Slow but Pronounced Shift

We hope we've persuaded you that although the citizen development movement has several unique aspects, it has a lot in common with other movements that are intended to empower amateurs to do work that was once reserved only for credentialed professionals. This slow but definite trend is also in keeping with the idea that those traditional credentials may no longer be necessary for someone to be hired or promoted within organizations. Many companies have begun, for example, to consider hiring individuals who don't have college degrees but do have experience-based expertise or "micro-credentials" based on online learning programs.

---

[9] Emily Anthes, "These Vets Make House Calls for Killer Whales," The *New York Times*, Dec. 26, 2023, https://www.nytimes.com/2023/12/26/science/orcas-killer-whales-veterinarians.html.

At the heart of this movement is the idea that the line between amateur and professional is not a hard and fast one. It is instead a spectrum of expertise, or in many cases a set of spectra of different types of expertise. Amateurs may not have the highest level of technical expertise in science or product development or manufacturing, but they may have some useful knowledge. And they often have more expertise than professionals in aspects of the problem being addressed—they know the business, they know their cancer symptoms, they know the products they want to make, and they can certainly have high levels of creativity and motivation. This suggests not only that amateurs or citizens should be empowered in the search for good ideas and solutions but also that they should be engaged in collaboration with professionals as often as possible.

Of course, citizen development isn't happening in every work setting, and that's probably a good thing. We're not advocating, for example, citizen brain surgery or citizen nuclear power generation for obvious reasons. And even when some citizen-driven activities are technically feasible—as in citizen journalism, for example, since lots of people today can write and publish their perspectives on current events—it doesn't always work out well. Citizen journalism tends to lack the professionalism and objectivity of journalism practiced by professionals in established institutions, and it has been a substantial source of misinformation. But we haven't seen similar problems in the area of citizen technology development, and we view it as an effective domain for extensive—if well-managed—activity by amateurs.

We don't know how far this will go, but overall we think it's a helpful and hopeful trend. The problems faced by humans in this world are too difficult and numerous to be solved by professionals alone. Instead, we should enlist as many citizens (in the broader sense) as possible in addressing them.

3 | The Citizen Journey

Every citizen is unique in some respects, but there are patterns in how they develop their technical capabilities and apply them to their jobs and organizations. Even if the specific details vary a bit, it's useful to understand their journeys to facilitate more people becoming citizens. By "journey" we mean not only how they became citizen users of technology but also what it means for their long-term careers.

We'll first discuss the typical progression of citizen activity over time and then discuss the longer-term career implications of citizen activities. For the former discussion we are indebted to Alan Jacobson at Alteryx—until recently the chief data and analytic officer at that vendor and previously director of global analytics at Ford Motor, where he led a citizen development effort that eventually included more than 12,000 people.

Diverse Journeys

While we describe some typical paths that citizens take in becoming more technology-oriented, it's important to make clear that citizens come from diverse backgrounds and go into diverse citizen-oriented roles. They also inhabit diverse geographies. For example, the Microsoft Power Apps webpage has a section entitled "Six people who changed careers with low-code from Power Apps." Without endorsing that particular technology, we found the diversity of backgrounds and roles quite fascinating. They include the following:

- A senior audiologist in Australia who became a low-code developer analyst for her traveling hearing service
- A geospatial technician who built a variety of apps for an electrical utility in South Africa
- An IT support manager who became a low-code consultant developer for a UK consultancy
- An HR specialist overseeing CPR teams for the American Red Cross who became a Power Platform solution architect for an IT solutions developer
- An owner of a UK secretarial and typing services business who became an application developer for that business
- A bricklayer who became a "digital transformation specialist" at a manufacturing company in Pennsylvania

There are many other such stories, and we will add to them in this book. We'll describe lawyers who become AI application developers, English majors who become citizen data scientists (of sorts, anyway), and front-line operations people who become translators interfacing with professional data scientists. Each of the examples suggests that the combination of powerful, and accessible, technology with the growing awareness and skills of those in non-IT/non-data roles will serve to significantly enhance and advance the way businesses innovate and transform in the future.

Initial Capabilities

Most of the citizens we have observed or researched did not go from being technophobes to technophiles. They always had a familiarity and comfort with technology. As Kristen, an underwriter in a life insurance company who is working to improve AI applications in her company, put it,

> I never studied technology—it wasn't even on my radar in school. But now it's clear that it's the evolution of underwriting. I have always been willing to try new things, and learn new things. I am not a professional

developer but I work with them a lot to make our algorithms and processes better and faster. If you adopt a digital mindset you will be fine.

One of the first attributes of an effective citizen, then, is a positive orientation toward technology experimentation (or a "digital mindset") and a willingness to employ it in her or his work.

But a digital mindset is valuable only if there is a business context to which it can be applied. The initial capabilities of an effective citizen also need to include a business domain such as underwriting, marketing, sales, supply chain management, or customer service. With the combination of technology experimentation and domain knowledge, a citizen can figure out how to transform a work process by applying a new technology. As one company representative put it, "The combination of data science and subject-matter engineering is very powerful."

For example, we've already described "Mr. Citizen," the supply chain practitioner at a large consumer products company and a passionate convert to all forms of citizen enablement. He describes himself in his LinkedIn profile thusly:

I am a thoughtful and analytical person with a drive to improve the work-lives of my colleagues through process improvements and efficiencies. Thanks to my curious and innovative nature, I have "led from behind" a digital transformation in the supply chain organization. By adopting new analytical tools to automate and improve our processes, my colleagues and I are changing the way we work with data in our supply chain, improving insights and saving hundreds of man-hours in the process.

As we've discussed, this citizen decided he'd spent way too much of his life entering data into Excel spreadsheets, so he found some tools that could automate the process of data entry and then of displaying data analyses. His boss, who owned all of the supply chain operations, thought that other departments such as logistics and distribution could benefit from the same tools. So he and two other citizen types were pulled out of the business to automate information flows and improve reporting displays for all of supply chain operations. They became the supply chain operations technology and analytics group, but none of the group members have any IT background or affiliation.

The group is also getting into automation of other types of operational and administrative processes with the company's preferred robotic process automation tool. Even with this recognition from his group and department, however, this citizen still struggles with recognition and support of citizen-oriented activities and technologies by the company's IT department.

Automation Comes Next

"Mr. Citizen's" journey with citizen activity is typical in that he increasingly automated the data-driven process for which he was responsible. He started with Excel, business intelligence, and visualization tools but moved beyond them to automate the production of analytical investigations. It's painful to create new analyses every time there is some new data to analyze, so citizens like to automate the process of extracting data, getting it into an analysis tool, and doing the analysis—often including a visualization component.

Another path to automation is from process improvement. In the old days (late 20th and early 21st centuries), process improvement involved only manual process improvement. Typically people employed tools like Lean or Six Sigma to make incremental improvements in their individual or work group business processes. These approaches were fine for their time, but even after the process was improved, a human still needed to perform the tasks in it. Today it makes sense not just to improve a process but to improve it with robotic process automation or the various other tools that can automate information-intensive work. This is pretty easy for someone with any degree of technical competence to do, and the tools to automate are becoming simpler all the time. In a growing number of companies, process improvement groups are adding automation capabilities or merging with other groups that already possess them.

The Journey to More Sophisticated Analytics

Tom's passion over the last couple of decades has been to persuade people to adopt more sophisticated approaches to analytics instead of just being happy with descriptive statistics and bar charts of them. Predictive analytics that predict future outcomes based on past ones (the same thing as machine learning, at least the simpler forms of it) and prescriptive analytics (analytics that recommend a specific action or decision) are generally more valuable than simple descriptive tools. The technology enabling "citizen data scientists" is getting easier to use all the time, and much of the statistical heavy lifting is taken care of by programs like automated machine learning and generative AI.

However, it is important to point out two factors that limit the use of more sophisticated analytics, and we will cover them in detail in Chapter 6, "Citizen Data Science." One is that you need to have a pretty good understanding of math and/or statistics to make sense of even pretty automated data science programs. Let's face it—many people don't have that level of quantitative ability, and what's more they don't want to acquire it.

The other limiting factor is that even if a citizen understands the basics of math and statistics, some of these data science tools can get into rather esoteric territory. If you're informed by an automated machine learning tool, for example, that the model best fitting your data is a support vector machine, you may struggle to understand what that means. It's also possible that something about your data and analysis approach may violate some key assumptions of a particular algorithm type. Therefore, if you are doing any important analysis as a citizen, we encourage you to make friends with a qualified data scientist and run your analysis approach by your new friend to make sure it checks out. A hard-core professional data scientist may prefer to create their own machine learning models over reviewing yours, but they need to get used to the citizen revolution.

The Citizen's Career in a Large Organization—for a While

Because many organizations haven't yet fully embraced citizen technology activities to a substantial degree and because citizens are typically hybrids of technology and business orientations, the citizen career path inside large companies is usually poorly defined. There are exceptions, as we'll describe at Kroger and their 84.51° analytics and AI focused subsidiary.

Some citizens are perfectly comfortable with being outside of mainstream career paths within organizations. But in many cases we've observed, citizens' frustration with problematic career paths can lead them out of large companies and into consulting, vendors of citizen-oriented technology, the ranks of the remote-working "overemployed," or entrepreneurial opportunities. One citizen automator at an ad agency even decided to open an ice cream shop, although it seems unlikely that she is using a lot of automation capabilities in her new business.

Charles Coleman's experience as a citizen automator and data scientist is perhaps illustrative of this career path issue. Coleman was educated at Georgia Tech as a mechanical engineer, and he initially went into a geotechnical engineering role for a construction company. He performed tasks like soil testing, site planning, and foundation design until the bottom fell out of the residential construction market in 2009. He eventually went back to school and got an MBA, emerging with supply chain, marketing, and business technology and analytics skills.

When Coleman secured a job at Home Depot as a senior analyst in assortment planning, he felt like he'd found a great place to apply his skills. Home Depot, like many data-driven retailers, wanted to move in the direction of customized product assortments at each store based on what customers actually want to buy. He was hired to input store sales data into Excel and build visualizations in Tableau for assortment planners. At the time Home Depot had 750 different merchandise categories (like hammers, wires and cables, or Halloween products), and the goal was to review each category at each store every five years. If that sounds like a long wait between reviews, it's because each assortment planner could handle only six to twelve assortment reviews per year—each category required between six and eighteen weeks to enter data, do the needed analyses, and create reports for stores. The great majority of Coleman's time was spent entering data into Excel.

Needless to say, he did not find this a particularly fulfilling task, so he often looked for ways to shortcut it. One weekend he downloaded a free trial version of Alteryx, a software tool that provided automation for "data blending" tasks and for performing analytics on the resulting data (not surprisingly, we learned about both "Mr. Citizen" and Coleman from sources at Alteryx). It rapidly became clear to Coleman that this tool could free up enormous amounts of time for himself and the Assortment Planning teams; his data input time went from several hours to several minutes, and he eventually found that he could cut at least two weeks off the time necessary to optimize a particular category. Previously the assortment planners didn't have time to run through alternative assortment plans for the categories to determine the impact on store performance, but now they had much more time, and running through a particular assortment took half an hour instead of weeks.

With his own time freed up, Coleman began to work with assortment planners on different clustering schemes—alternative assortment plans—for Home Depot's 2.5 billion SKU/store combinations. The clustering models ran both in Python and in a vendor-sourced proprietary tool. Then the high-performing clusters would feed into automated Tableau visualizations and got sent to internal customers who could act on the recommended product movements within each store. The internal IT and analytics groups weren't thrilled that Coleman was doing this work—much of the analysis took place on an extra company laptop under Coleman's desk—but they eventually came around to grudging support given the results the company was getting.

The system worked as intended, and Home Depot made a lot of money as a result. When Coleman received the "Merchandising Employee of the Year" award, he was told that he'd personally contributed somewhere between $2 and $4 billion—note the *b* there—in additional Home Depot revenues. To recognize his contributions, Home Depot gave him a framed certificate, took his picture with the CEO, and handed over a gift card—Coleman thinks it was either for $25 or $1,000, but he's not sure which. In either case it's a tiny, tiny fraction of what he contributed to the company.

But Coleman liked working at Home Depot and wasn't primarily bothered by the low monetary rewards. What did bother him, however, was that his direct boss told him that he was irreplaceable in his current role and would not be allowed to take any other job at the company. He might be eligible for a one-level promotion, but that was the ceiling for him. Citizens like Coleman enjoy learning and growth in their jobs, and he was told that he wasn't going to get either of them.

Coleman had presented his work at Alteryx and Tableau conferences, and one person in the audience ran a small analytics and data-oriented consulting firm in Atlanta. He quickly realized that Coleman could make a big difference to his company and offered him a job. Coleman took it and kindly trained a replacement for himself at Home Depot.

Coleman has now been at the consulting firm for more than eight years and greatly enjoys working with companies to understand and improve how they analyze their data. He's still working with citizen tools and views himself as a citizen automator of data science tasks and processes—in other words, one of the many hybrid citizen types we have seen. He estimates that he's worked with more than 75 clients across a broad variety of industries on these issues. He even offers on his LinkedIn page to do this type of project for free for nonprofit organizations—that's how much he likes the work.

We've found many other citizens who have found themselves in similar career paths, although few have created as much value for their companies as Coleman. But his career journey is illustrative of the issues citizens face. They do great work at one company, but then the company wants them to continue doing that work (or even worse, wants them to stop it because it's not approved by the IT or analytics bureaucracy) and doesn't recognize their need for advancement and task diversity. The rewards they receive from the company are not at all proportional to the value they produce for it. They are not embraced by the company's technology or analytics groups, or any support is grudging. It's no wonder that many of them don't stay in big companies for long. There are certainly exceptions to that rule, but it requires organizations to recognize and reward the value that citizens are producing.

Citizen Data Science in an Organization That Welcomes Them

The "citizen data scientist" is among the rarer breeds of citizen developers. To be or emulate a data scientist, you have to like math and computing. The tools to make data science accessible to the less technically inclined user have been available now for a decade—they are generally referred to as *automated machine learning*—but they can still be a bit intimidating to the quantitatively averse. Even though that software—and even more recent generative AI programs—can do sophisticated data analysis and create excellent machine learning models with very little input from the user, there is still some interpretation needed of the output. Some companies we've worked with have found it difficult to recruit citizen data scientists because of the math intimidation factor.

So it's not surprising that our example of a citizen data scientist comes from 84.51°, the wholly owned data science subsidiary of the Kroger Co. that is named after the longitude of its headquarters city, Cincinnati. As might be expected from a company named after a number, many of the people at 84.51° are hard-core professional data scientists who spend their workdays trying to figure out how to create a better-fitting random forest model. But the leaders of 84.51° have figured out that data scientists alone can't do it all; to help Kroger and its consumer products partners make better data-driven decisions, they also need people who understand the business problem, empathize with those who need to solve it, and partner with them to deploy it in business processes.

That is basically the job of Amanda Woodly, whose job title is "Solution Design Director for Kroger Merchandising." She worked for 10 years in footwear and fashion retail and has been at 84.51° for four years. Her role involves translating between business stakeholders and 84.51°'s data scientists to understand the need, gather requirements, and deploy solutions.

Woodly could probably qualify as a data scientist in many less quantitative companies. She wasn't focused on engineering, programming, or analytics in college—she majored in business—but in her retail jobs she began to appreciate the need for quantitative and data-driven decision approaches. She doesn't program or tune machine learning models herself, but she understands how they work, and can explain them to Kroger Co. business leaders, who are responsible for implementing them. She has realized that she's good at math, but she is also a "synergistic, holistic brain person who needs to understand how systems, processes, people, and vendors all connect."

She has explored and can use automated machine learning tools, but she actually prefers the process of building machine learning solutions from the ground up—particularly, she says, if the resulting model is somewhat transparent and can be explained to businesspeople. "We make sure we are leveraging science that can be bought into by business users," she elaborated.

She believes that citizen roles like hers are successful at 84.51° and Kroger because many of them came out of business roles and have empathy and understanding for the problems business leaders face. "We use their language and make sure we understand their process and system," she said. There is plenty of training available at 84.51°, but she feels that hiring people with the right backgrounds is just as important. 84.51° has a values-based leadership model focused on "limitless minds, fearless hearts, and relentless delivery," and she tries to live up to those values every day.

A More Dramatic Career Transformation

Stevie Sims is a credentialed citizen developer at Shell, whose citizen program we will mention multiple times throughout this book. It's one of the most advanced initiatives for citizen-driven technology work we've seen, and Sims is one of its poster children. He works at the Shell Norco Manufacturing Complex along the Mississippi River in Louisiana, which has been refining oil for more than a century and now also produces a variety of petrochemicals. Sims, who received an associate's degree in process technology, started work at Norco in 2013 as a process operator. The tools of that trade were Nomex suits, two-way radios, and hardhats, and he spent much of his day monitoring gauges and turning valves.

But as the Norco plant became more digitally focused, so did Sims. He learned about automated control system operations and dabbled in digitizing data, saving files, and troubleshooting operational systems. In 2018 he applied for a role in a temporary assignment as a "turnaround planner"—a turnaround being a very large plant shutdown and maintenance event involving hundreds of pieces of equipment, with many different schedules, spreadsheets, and work packages. He got the job and decided he needed to learn more about spreadsheets, which he'd never used. He "dove in head-first" to learn about spreadsheets, charts and graphs, and dashboards. It's probably indicative of his passion that he remembers the day (July 5, 2019, if you must know) that he learned about the Excel VLOOKUP function for finding data in a large table.

When the COVID pandemic hit in 2020, he learned about effective use of virtual tools for communicating and document sharing. Then he remembers that on August 4, 2021, he was told by a colleague that he should abandon Excel for data analysis and move to Power BI. A couple of weeks later Hurricane Ida slammed into Louisiana and the Norco facility, which became a "forced turnaround" with no time to plan and few resources. Using YouTube and Google search, he learned what he needed about creating Power BI reports and dashboards to display all the Ida recovery information for Norco. After the Ida recovery was over, he learned about Power Apps and created an application to manage work requests.

At that point Sims had become known as a citizen developer *par excellence*. He was recognized as a "Shell.ai DIY Hero" in 2020, and his boss told him it didn't make sense for him to return to turning valves. He developed a number of citizen applications and then in 2022 became a member of the Shell IT organization that developed high-value citizen-oriented tools for his business units on the Gulf Coast on the Microsoft Power Platform. By the time we spoke with him he'd built dozens of applications, one of which—called Idea Funnel—keeps track of all the citizen-developed applications that have been built for the Gulf Coast area of Shell. Now he is no longer technically a citizen developer, since he's building applications for others. But he came from the operations side of the business and still has a lot of domain knowledge for applications of that type. Most of his development activity is in what Shell calls the "amber zone"—we'll describe that in greater detail later in the book—but it means that they're for more than 50 users but short of the entire enterprise.

Stevie Sims has been promoted twice within a few years, and he feels that his career progress from process operator to lead Power Platform developer has been amazing. He's grateful to Shell for allowing him to progress so quickly, and even though he is getting a four-year college degree, he has no interest in getting a different job or monetizing his skills further elsewhere. "It's a fun journey, and I get to make a lot of people's jobs easier," he said. He's also part of the Microsoft citizen development community and has spoken at its conferences. His mom refers to him as a unicorn, and he doesn't seem to disagree.

The Citizen as Rogue Agent

Things don't always work out as well for citizens as they have for Stevie Sims. As in Coleman's case, organizations may not sufficiently recognize or reward the increased productivity and value that citizens provide. That leads some citizen developers to seek other approaches to monetizing their activity—in particular, holding down multiple full-time remote jobs at once with overlapping work schedules using citizen development tools to automate their tasks. This activity may stretch the notion of citizen-oriented technologies a bit; "automated mouse movers" is one we didn't think about until we read about them on these sites.

Ian discovered in the course of research for this book that there are discussion boards about this—typically named "Overemployed"—on Reddit, Discord and several other websites. These individuals refer to their jobs as J1, J2, J3 (we've seen comments going up to J5) and collect salaries from each—thus providing a clear monetary incentive to use citizen tools. Of course, many (including us) would argue that it's unethical to do so without an employer knowing about it.

Of course, this can be a perilous job situation, and the discussion boards mention hazards like too many Zoom meetings in which you are expected to show your face, face-to-face meetings called too frequently, etc. Post-COVID pandemic, there are fewer totally remote jobs, so being overemployed isn't as easy as it used to be. The discussion boards suggest that it's not uncommon for such individuals to be discovered and to lose one or more jobs. There is plenty of advice given about how to make this situation work, as in this post about understanding the culture relative to automation:

> I think you have to know what culture you're in. At my J1 I automated
> some things and no one gave a s. . . about it. Even people that had
> manually been doing these tasks for years on the daily/weekly/monthly,
> I think I made them look bad. After learning my lesson I only automate
> 90% and then I can still get credit for pushing the button manually and
> processing requests. This way I also avoid making the established team
> members look like s. . .
>
> Edit: I should also add at my J2 everyone believes in and cares about
> automation so it's just expected that I automate everything possible that
> I touch. If I didn't, I'd get in trouble; I do, so people like my work.

We would argue that organizations should view the "overemployed" as
a warning sign that they need to get incentives and motivations aligned
among their citizen employees. If they can produce twice as much as non-
citizens because of their automation and development actions, they should
be rewarded accordingly.

The Citizen as Entrepreneur

Of course, there are alternatives to staying within a large organization as a
citizen or becoming a consultant. One is to start a company that is based on
citizen development of key information systems in a startup (typically using
LC/NC tools). One example of such an entrepreneur is Heidi Ojha, a
trained and certified physical therapist who believed that musculoskeletal
(muscle, nerve, or joint pain) injuries were being over-treated by many doctors with unnecessary imaging and surgeries. She was confident that she
could dramatically reduce costs for small to midsize companies' health insurance by treating many such problems with telehealth-based physical
therapy. Her confidence was based in part on a multiyear clinical study that
she conducted while a professor at Temple University.

But while Ojha was confident about her business idea, she wasn't confident about the ability to build information systems to support it. She had
neither startup experience nor programming experience, and while she
hoped to recruit a technically experienced cofounder, the lack of any revenue for her startup made that prospect difficult.

Then one day she came across a digital ad and a website for an eight-
week virtual program called "The No-Code Startup," offered by another

startup called WeAreNoCode. It offered the possibility of building apps and/or websites with a video curriculum, live group coaching sessions, and online support. She signed up and worked on two LC/NC tools—a website development tool called WebFlow and a mobile app development tool called Bubble. She was able to develop both without writing a line of code within the eight-week program and was able to start offering her services to a couple hundred employees of her business customers.

With some customers and more than $25,000 in monthly recurring revenue to show, Ojha was able to bring on a technically experienced cofounder to refine her systems. She was also able to enroll in the TechStars accelerator and to attract pre-seed funding of about $650,000. Now she has almost 7,000 paying customers and more than $10 million in booked sales.

Of course, this isn't just one citizen development entrepreneur story, but two. Christian Peverelli and Eddy Widerker founded WeAreNoCode to help people like Heidi Ojha realize their startup dreams. Peverelli, who is the public face of the company, told us that he is "scratching his own itch." He tried several times to be a successful entrepreneur, but he didn't have much luck at it (although he did sell one of his companies successfully). He ran a startup accelerator in Los Angeles and looked at thousands of startups. For those who didn't make it, he said,

> It's a slaughterhouse. These entrepreneurs have spent thousands of dollars and years of their lives while making little progress. They are trying to figure out the technology they need by puzzling together things on the Internet, or hiring people to code for them who do it poorly. We started WeAreNoCode to help people build the software component of businesses. We try to give them tangible methods to break down every step of the startup process and to leverage no-code to do it.

Peverelli is now a YouTube star, providing edutainment on different aspects of citizen development and reviewing the tools to make it possible. Aware Health is only one of the company's successful customers. Others include companies selling T-shirts, Scottish salmon, AI-based appointment scheduling, and job-finding aids. Peverelli said he is still waiting for the first unicorn ($1 billion in value) company to be created by no-code citizen development, but he's sure it will eventually happen.

A Citizen Data Science Startup

Another alternative is for an entrepreneur to create a data science–oriented startup with data analysis tools. This is relatively easy now with more public sources of data and a variety of automated machine learning systems. But in 2016, when Daniel Schauber started his Frankfurt-based company exechange, Excel was perhaps the only citizen data analysis tool in broad use. Schauber was a financial journalist at a German newspaper, with a focus on covering industrial production technology and mechanical engineering manufacturers.

In university and graduate school he had studied linguistics and literature. But as a teenager he had an early digital orientation.

> I played with the Commodore VIC-20 home computer and also wrote simple computer programs in the Basic programming language. I was therefore familiar early on with the amateurish and pragmatic solution of even complex problems using self-created computer programs based on the trial-and-error principle.

After graduating from college he worked for several years at BASF, the large German chemical company. There he cultivated important domain knowledge and some useful skills.

> At BASF's corporate headquarters, I came into intensive contact with the very formalistic language of internal and external corporate communications and the special codes it contained, which fascinated me. In BASF's finance department, I also got to know the Microsoft Excel spreadsheet and was impressed by how this tool could be used to record, analyze and statistically evaluate large amounts of data.

While he worked as a journalist, he had always had an interest in corporate news releases. In particular, he was curious whether CEOs who departed their companies left voluntarily or were pushed out. In my spare time he collected, analyzed, and categorized corporate news releases, especially CEO departure announcements, and began to capture and analyze the data electronically. He began to think that there might be a business in revealing why CEOs left companies and focused on coding and recording factors that might allow that determination.

He collected, analyzed, and categorized the data from the CEO departure announcements himself, recording the data in Excel. He experimented with various approaches to structuring and classifying the collected data. His work was informed by his experience as a financial journalist. However, he said that whenever possible he sought interaction with practitioners and academics to perfect the classification method, and he observed the statistical methods that were used in academic research for linguistics classification and prediction.

The result was a straightforward machine learning model using a 10-point system for classifying CEO departures. He called the model the "Push-out Score" and published it on the exechange.com website for the first time in 2016.

Since that time, Schauber has gradually automated the steps in the coding and evaluation of data that he considers both feasible and worthy of automation. For example, the counting of words, the recognition and classification of common linguistic formulations from corporate CEO departure announcements, the analysis of share price performance, and the determination of the exact term of office of the departing CEO measured in days are data points for which he has automated the collection—all using Excel.

Schauber's company exechange sells both access to its database on more than 1,300 CEO departures since 2016 and reports describing the circumstances and score for individual CEO departures. The primary clients for these offerings are financial firms such as investment managers and private equity funds. Schauber also continues to write articles as a journalist on a freelance basis.

Schauber, like other effective citizen data scientists, is interested in getting to the truth about CEO departures, but not in esoteric algorithms and models. His company's website is quite clear about the combination of "pull out" and "push out" forces that the Push-out Score combines. The company's website provides 10 anonymized examples of how the score is computed. He also makes a simplified version of the Push-out Score algorithm available to academic researchers for free.

These diverse citizen journeys make clear that there is no one path for citizens within either large organizations or startups. And becoming a productive and effective citizen developer doesn't necessarily mean a fast route to career success. However, we suspect that organizations will increasingly recognize the potential value of citizen activity and recognize and reward it accordingly. In addition, becoming a citizen developer does seem to make employees more satisfied in their jobs—it's undoubtedly better than manually moving data from one spreadsheet to another. Over the next few years, we hope to see more rewarding career paths and journeys for individuals who adopt the citizen approach to their work.

Calling All Hands

4

Citizen Development Using Low-Code/ No-Code Tools[1]

The use of low-code/no-code technologies to create IT applications is at the heart of the citizen development movement. There are numerous prognosticators who have argued that the world will need far more application programs than IT professionals can produce; the IT research house IDC speculated that 750 million such programs will be needed by 2025.[2] Low-code/no-code (LC/NC) applications are expected to fill the void. Another prognosticator, Gartner, has speculated that 80% of technology products and services will be built by professionals outside of IT organizations by 2024—the year this book is being published—and LC/NC technologies

---

[1]This chapter draws in part on Chris Johannessen and Tom Davenport, "When Low-Code/ No-Code Development Works—and When It Doesn't," *Harvard Business Review*, June 22, 2021, `https://hbr.org/2021/06/when-low-code-no-code-development-works-and-when-it-doesnt`.

[2]The research is proprietary but is described briefly in this press release: "IDC Updates Its Future of Digital Innovation Framework," Oct. 12, 2022, `https://www.idc.com/getdoc.jsp?containerId=prUS49760222`.

will enable this production.[3] Of course, we'll never know exactly how many or what percentage of applications will be developed by citizens using LC/NC tools, but it's a safe bet that the number and percentage will be high.

So what do we mean by LC/NC technologies? Simply put, they involve using simple interfaces instead of traditional programming to create new programs or modify existing ones. There are many versions of this phenomenon, ranging from point-and-click and pull-down menus all the way to generative AI. The latter can easily generate code and, if prepared and prompted correctly, can also generate entire applications, web pages, mobile apps, and online games. LC/NC tools—and no doubt eventually generative AI—are even being used to create manufacturing applications.

Some argue that "low-code" tools are best suited for professional developers and that citizens should focus only on "no-code" options.[4] But there is no formal definition of what constitutes "low" and "no," and in many cases (including generative AI), no-code tools generate code that can be modified by the user. We believe, then, that while no-code technology may be better for nontechnical users as a class, there are certainly a number of exceptions in which low-code tools would be appropriate.

We've already mentioned this approach in passing throughout the book and described several examples of their use. These tools in the hands of citizens were at the heart of the Shell DIY movement, for example. One application developed within that program involved optimizing furnace burners (20 furnaces, each with 64 burners) at a Dutch refinery. The burners consumed 85% of the plant's total energy. The optimization process had previously been manual and was both time-consuming and inaccurate. A DIY application was developed by the furnace operators to recommend the optimum trim settings for each burner. Use of that application reduced energy consumption by 25–30% and saved $3 million per year. Shell's citizens—more than 6,500 have been trained—have developed thousands of such applications in just a few years.[5]

---

[3] Gartner Inc. press release, June 14, 2021, https://www.gartner.com/en/newsroom/press-releases/2021-06-10-gartner-says-the-majority-of-technology-products-and-services-will-be-built-by-professionals-outside-of-it-by-2024.
[4] Adrian Bridgwater, "The Low-No-Code Series – Exposition: What We Need to Know," *Computer Weekly*, March 2, 2022, https://www.computerweekly.com/blog/CW-Developer-Network/The-low-no-code-series-Exposition-What-we-need-to-know.
[5] More examples and details of the Shell DIY program are described in Noel Carroll and Mary Maher, "How Shell Fueled Digital Transformation by Establishing DIY Software Development," *MIS Quarterly Executive*, January 2023.

How Did We Get Here?

For the past several decades, organizations have had only two alternatives when they needed new IT applications. They could build a new system using their own system developers, or they could buy a system from an external vendor. The "build" approach, like a custom suit or dress, offered a close fit to business requirements. But as with custom tailoring of clothing, it typically meant higher costs and a long wait. Systems bought from vendors, like off-the-rack clothing, don't fit as well but are typically much cheaper and can be installed faster. Some such systems allowed companies to configure the systems they bought, but many firms found it easier to change their business to suit the system than vice versa. Both of these approaches were employed largely by IT departments.

But as you might expect to find in a book on citizen development, there is a third alternative that is becoming increasingly popular. LC/NC applications can provide a close fit to business requirements, can be implemented quickly, and typically cost much less than systems developed in-house. The way it accomplishes these benefits is not magic but by turning over development to citizens instead of professional system developers. With point-and-click or pull-down menu interfaces, a moderately capable citizen can usually design and implement their individual or departmental systems in a few hours. The software may also have a conversational or search interface. No programming skills are required. However, these are not typically intended for use in creating mission-critical or enterprise-wide systems.

LC/NC software development may still require some level of programming skills, and in addition to citizen usage, it is also sometimes employed by professional software developers or hybrid business/IT employees to improve their productivity. Use by citizens, of course, greatly expands the population of people who can build software applications within a business. However, the amount of coding and technical expertise needed to build an LC/NC system isn't binary, but on a continuum.

It's Not Just Citizens

As with other domains of citizen technology use, IT professionals recognize the need for citizens to make use of LC/NC tools. Siemens, which has adopted LC/NC tools widely internally and also bought Mendix, a leading low-code vendor, is one of the more prominent companies that advocates for the

technology—both internally and for customers. Siemens/Mendix did a global
survey in 2021 of more than 2,000 IT professionals.[6] Fifty-seven percent of
those surveyed said that the number of staff needed for software
development is increasing, and 76% say that demand for developers has reached
high levels. In addition, 61% say the cost of software development is rising.
Two-thirds of major software projects are currently being delivered behind
schedule, and for 62% of IT professionals, that backlog is only increasing. As a
result of these trends, 64% of the surveyed respondents said their organizations
have relied on nontechnical staff to relieve pressure on the IT department during COVID-19. It seems unlikely to us that the situation will go back.

Microsoft, with its Power Platform suite of LC/NC tools, is another
major vendor in this space and is perhaps growing faster than any other alternative. That company also commissioned a survey in 2021 suggesting that IT
managers and professionals are embracing LC/NC capabilities. Eighty-seven
percent of CIOs and IT professionals believed that low-code is very useful in
helping their organizations modernize legacy applications, and 45% said they
initially adopted low-code platforms to make up for staff shortages. Clearly
these easier-to-use technologies are helping citizens and professionals alike.

What Can an Organization Do with Low-Code/No-Code?

LC/NC software development approaches support a variety of application
types. Small business transactional systems are perhaps the most common.
These are applications that process business transactions; large firms might
have expensive packages or custom-developed programs to perform them,
but small businesses can generate their own easily. Types of applications successfully developed with LC/NC tools include human resource management
(e.g., performance appraisal), reservation management for restaurants or other
experiences, order quote creation, field service management, and so forth.

LC/NC programs can also be used to develop web and mobile sites.
More sophisticated versions of these programs can even process customer
transactions. Companies providing website design tools also often provide
hosting services and can also make available value-added LC/NC features
that aid search engine optimization and social media marketing and enable
the setup and management of digital analytics. Some LC/NC tools now

---

[6] "Mendix 2021 State of Low Code Whitepaper," no date, https://www.mendix
.com/wp-content/uploads/Mendix_2021_State_of_LowCode_
Whitepaper.pdf.

make it easier for citizen marketers to automate marketing activities such as website personalization, email marketing, and digital ad trafficking.

Technology product developers can facilitate configuration and device setup with LC/NC applications. They may have programming skills but want to preserve them for the product itself. Simple programs for configuration and setup by users can be created by citizens.

Departmental/facility level applications like the Shell one we described are typically small-scale applications serving a piece of a larger company or organization. They provide some benefit to a workgroup or unit but don't serve a mission-critical or enterprise-wide purpose. The most common types of applications would involve recording and monitoring small-scale transactions, displaying information, making moderately complex calculations, automating a series of manual steps, or enabling access to information for a small group of employees, customers, or suppliers. Any enterprise-wide applications would probably be developed by IT organizations, although LC/NC tools could be part of their toolkit as well. In many cases, companies have created citizen application review processes that consider whether the application has broader enterprise applications. If it does, an IT or professional development group typically refines, deploys, and maintains it.

For example, the professional services firm PwC created a "Digital Accelerator" program for employees who were interested in doing citizen development. They received training in one of several different technology domains, including LC/NC tools. They were encouraged to develop tools that might be broadly useful to the entire firm. Then they could be reviewed in an evaluation process. According to an article describing the process,

> A curation team needs to evaluate each contribution submitted to the laboratory platform and make sure it works, isn't a duplicate of another tool, has properly documented logic and application, and can be found using commonplace search terms. People will tend to download the apps and bots that are highly rated. As with any social media platform, people can see how many downloads that particular artifact has had and can read others' comments about it.[7]

---

[7] Darren Lee, Mike Pino, and Ann Johnston, "Six Keys to Unlocking Upskilling at Scale," *Strategy + Business*, March 12, 2020, https://www.strategy-business.com/article/Six-keys-to-unlocking-upskilling-at-scale.

The Digital Accelerator program has led to more than 6,000 applications being added to a repository for enterprise use. We'll also describe it in Chapter 5, "Citizen Automation." LC/NC tools can also be employed (and have been extensively at PwC) by citizens to create small-scale automations and workflows. They can also be used to compute and display analytics, particularly visual analytics, but we cover that technology in Chapter 6, "Citizen Data Science." In a sense, all citizen tools are low-code or no-code, even if the terminology is primarily oriented to application development.

Citizen/Professional Collaboration and Fusion Teams

One of the clear findings from our research on the LC/NC phenomenon is that it is not restricted to citizens at all. As the Microsoft and Siemens/Mendix surveys suggest, IT professionals are making use of these tools as well, particularly the low-code versions. Some LC/NC vendors, such as Unqork, clearly focus on IT developers. Others, including Mendix, have both low-code and no-code (visual interface) offerings.

The IT professionals in the Mendix survey, for example, are using LC/NC tools in their own work. Sixty-four percent of IT professionals agreed that they use low-code as a development solution. Thirty-three percent have used it to build mission-critical applications, and they estimated that more than half of their everyday development work (51%) could be done on a low-code platform.

One major benefit of LC/NC technology is that since both citizens and IT professionals use LC/NC tools, they can collaborate in their use. The professionals in the Mendix survey said that 59% of projects using low-code are collaborations between IT and business groups. This may involve sequential responsibility for a system. For example, a citizen could develop a prototype of a system based on deep understanding of the business problem or issue. An IT professional could refine the system using the LC/NC tool. It could go into the organization's portfolio of enterprise applications and be maintained by IT over time.

A 2023 survey by Mendix of its user base found that 85% work in IT department teams, but 47% work at least sometimes in "fusion teams" that combine IT professionals and businesspeople or citizens. This term, developed by Gartner, is described as "a multidisciplinary team that blends technology or analytics and business domain expertise and shares accountability for business and technology outcomes."[8] Fusion teams imply ongoing collaboration throughout a system's lifecycle, rather than sequential responsibility.

This approach is one of the primary ones taken by Siemens, the owner of Mendix, in its own IT development projects. The chief information officer of Siemens, Hanna Hennig, has argued in video presentations that while low-code technology still requires some facility with technology, the ability to expand the user base with LC/NC tools and create more effective collaborations between employees with business and IT backgrounds is one of the primary benefits of the technology.[9] An IT partner, Philipp Lutz, who focuses on low-code partnerships with business-side employees at Siemens, commented (in a marketing document for Mendix).

> You can get started with development much quicker, and you can have your developers talk to the business stakeholders right away because you're all speaking the same language. You can even model the data together. The gap between business and IT is much smaller now.[10]

There is clear evidence of expansion of the user base at Siemens and many steps taken to facilitate that objective. Every Siemens employee was able to get a Mendix license and was given access to training, community meetups, and certification as a Mendix developer. More than 15,000 people have registered as citizen developers. They can download existing programs, components, and connectors from a marketplace as a basis for modification and extension. Guidelines and guardrails for documentation and governance were established. Siemens has more than 300,000 employees, and more than 240,000 of them used Mendix in some way, with more than 2000 certified developers, most in IT. There are more than 500 applications developed using the low-code technology that are in production.

---

[8]"Fusion team" definition in Gartner Glossary, `https://www.gartner.com/en/information-technology/glossary/fusion-team`, accessed Dec. 27, 2023.
[9]Hanna Hennig, CIO of Siemens, in WebSummit video. `https://www.youtube.com/watch?v=n7Jm5bnQfJO`.
[10]Mendix customer stories, "Siemens Enables Rapid Digitization in a 175-Year-Old Enterprise," `https://www.mendix.com/customer-stories/siemens-enables-rapid-digitization-in-a-175-year-old-enterprise` (accessed Dec. 28 2023).

There are many examples of serious application development at Siemens using mixed IT/business teams and low-code technology. One system developed with this technology, for example, is a system for the Siemens Mobility business unit that keeps track of the standards and regulations for thousands of railway-related components and products. This is clearly an enterprise application, containing more than 50,0000 regulations and standards in a database, with 6,200 active users. It was developed by a team of IT and business developers, and an agile Scrum Master, in six months.[11]

Generative AI as a No-Code Solution

The rapid rise of generative AI over the past several years has—as a "fringe benefit," because it wasn't originally envisioned by the technology's creators—enabled a form of no-code development of application programs simply from natural language prompts. In other words, the user describes the application, specifying what language it should be programmed in, and out pops an application. Theoretically, this development could turn anyone who understands and can express what they want from a program into a programmer. Indeed, we co-authored a *Harvard Business Review* article on citizen development, and we (more accurately, our editor) entitled it "We're All Programmers Now."[12]

However, this may be somewhat of an exaggeration, at least at the time we published the article in September 2023. Today generative AI can certainly generate code, but it is best suited to improve the productivity of professional programmers. Well-trained programmers are best equipped to create high-quality prompts that yield high-quality code, to identify errors in code that are made by generative AI, and to execute the generated code in a particular hardware and software environment. Many observers (including Satya Nadella, the CEO of Microsoft) have argued that generative AI should be "paired" with a professional programmer in a new version of what previously involved two skilled programmers working together in a "pair programming" situation. That environment is often more productive than a single programmer working alone, and professional programmers often report up to 50/60% improvement in their productivity.

---

[11] Ibid.

[12] Thomas H. Davenport, Ian Barkin, and Kerem Tomak, "We're All Programmers Now," *Harvard Business Review*, Sept.-Oct. 2023, https://hbr.org/2023/09/were-all-programmers-now.

There is a broader context involved in effective programming that generative AI-based code development has not yet been able to master. As one programming expert put it,

> "Every software system has additional considerations—like logical and physical system architecture, data modeling, build and deployment engineering, and maintenance and management activity—that still appear to be well beyond current generative AI capabilities."[13]

So is there any help for citizen developers from generative AI? There is already some, and it will no doubt increase over time. Generative AI code development systems such as ChatGPT, GitHub CoPilot, and Google Codey are all good at generating small code snippets that a citizen could combine into longer programs. They are also good at correcting mistakes in programs that a human has written, as well as documenting existing code. In short, they could be used as a coach to anyone who is trying to learn how to program better. After a citizen has developed a modicum of coding capability, the role of generative AI can shift from coach to pair programmer.

In addition, generative AI could turn low-code programs into no-code programs.[14] It could make every citizen-oriented tool easier to use and less likely to require programming expertise. Over time, we expect that generative AI tools could engage in a dialogue with the citizen user and through detailed questioning help transform a high-level intent into a functioning computer program—even a complex one.

How to Succeed with Low-Code/No-Code

Ruben Mancha (Tom's colleague at Babson) and his co-author wrote an article about two companies that had successfully employed LC/NC tools to "fuel digital transformation" at a faster pace with broader involvement.[15]

---

[13] Quote from James Fairweather in Joe McKendrick, "Generative AI Could Help Low Code Evolve Into No Code—but with a Twist," *ZDNet Innovation*, Oct. 13, 2023, https://www.zdnet.com/article/generative-ai-could-help-low-code-evolve-into-no-code-but-with-a-twist.
[14] Ibid.
[15] Einara Novales and Ruben Mancha, "Fueling Digital Transformation with Citizen Developers and Low-Code Development," *MIS Quarterly Executive* 22:3, Sept. 2023, DOI: 10.17705/2msqe.00083.

In the article, the authors state that there are five activities that must be completed successfully if an organization is to succeed with this approach.

- Set a clear strategy for selecting low-code development use cases.
- Identify and assign low-code users and provide training to upskill/reskill tech-savvy employees.
- Establish a low-code team that provides organization-wide support.
- Ensure that the low-code architecture is up-to-date.
- Evaluate the technical requirements of the solutions to assess which low-code platform is the best fit.

We agree that all these steps are important. However, we'd add a few to, or at least elaborate somewhat on, these five. Senior executives—the CEO, the CFO, and the CIO at a minimum but ideally the broad senior management team—must buy into the idea of citizen development using LC/NC tools and know what to expect from it in terms of cost and value.

We also feel that it's important for the "organization-wide support" in their third point to include community development for the sharing of expertise and solutions. Community development is a broad category of activities that may include regular face-to-face meetings of citizen developers, hackathons and contests, reward and recognition for outstanding projects, and internal marketing of the community. An additional way to facilitate learning and sharing is to establish a hub or marketplace for citizen-developed applications and components that can be shared across the organization. Finally, we think it's important to establish a process that allows IT professionals to review citizen-developed applications if they are relevant to the broader enterprise, create any new data, or are connected to the Internet and the outside world. These are the types of criteria that Shell, for example, used in its "red/amber/green" classification system for citizen-developed applications.

Management Challenges with Low-Code/No-Code

There are great benefits from LC/NC software development but management challenges as well. Broad use of these tools institutionalizes the "shadow IT" phenomenon, which has bedeviled IT organizations for decades—but this could make it much worse. Citizen developers tend to create applications that don't work or scale well, and then they try to turn them over to IT. Or the citizen may leave the company, and no one knows how to change or support the system he or she developed.

LC/NC oversight can control this issue, however, and make common the handoff of applications from citizen developers to professional ones when appropriate. IT organizations need to maintain some control over system development, including the selection of which LC/NC tools the organization will support. If designed and executed well, these approaches can "bring shadow IT into the light," as several IT leaders expressed it.

The best situation may often be a hybrid citizen/professional development model. As we've discussed, in some cases the partnership will be sequential, where the user develops 80% of the model and hands it off to the developer for polishing. Or the user may develop the initial application using a graphic interface tool and then give it to a developer (or a generative AI system) to program it in Python or some other more scalable language. Perhaps the ideal situation, as adopted by Siemens and other organizations, is for citizens and professional developers to work simultaneously in teams, with citizens providing more of the domain expertise and perhaps initial software solutions and professional developers translating their expertise into finished code. In any of these cases, the developer can record that the system exists, ensure that it works correctly, connect it to any needed data or transactional system, and ensure that it meets cybersecurity criteria. We've already seen organizations where one professional developer supports ten or more citizen developers. Although some professionals object to this type of role, others seem to enjoy it.

The bulk of the responsibility for managing LC/NC development, however, will fall on department managers, since most of the resulting systems are at that level. Department managers should be encouraged to facilitate LC/NC development, and be educated about how the technology works, what tools the organization supports, and the desired relationship between citizen developers and the IT organization. They should also educate their department members on the opportunities and responsibilities of LC/NC development.

Department leaders and the executive champions, too, may need to become more educated about the best practices for scaling LC/NC tools, especially across large geographical footprints. New organizational models such as a federated Center of Excellence (CoE) may need to be created, supported by internal digital portals (or "storefronts") where citizen developers, system developers, and leaders can collaborate, learn, and quickly get help when encountering roadblocks. As LC/NC systems scale and create their own data sets around business processes, further investments in supporting monitoring and analytics capabilities and infrastructure might be needed to aid governance.

Almost every organization today needs more system development talent. LC/NC development by citizens isn't a panacea, but it can address some of these resource shortages. And over time, it's likely that systems will become even easier to build for common processes and use cases. As Chris Wanstrath, the former CEO of code-sharing repository GitHub, put it, "The future of coding is no coding at all"—by either professionals or citizens.

5

Citizen Automation

The heart of citizen automation is the digitization of the (often manual) processing of tasks and workflows that make up the majority of transactional work done today. What's more, *citizen automation* is a term that captures a long and distinguished history of process innovators, tinkerers, and inspired change agents across every part of an organization. While this activity is also generally called *citizen development*, there are distinct differences that merit a stand-alone category. While citizen development often refers to the building of applications to address discrete use cases and function-specific needs, citizen automation typically focuses on automating information-intensive process workflows. These are typically individual- or department-level workflows and are supported by a set of tools known as robotic process automation (RPA) or sometimes intelligent process automation (IPA). These tools aren't blindingly intelligent or fast, but they can perform structured digital tasks, move information from one system to another, make basic decisions, and generally act as if they are humans—except they work faster, more reliably, and over longer hours than humans.

Automating workflows isn't new. But it is a domain that benefits from an ever-evolving and increasingly intelligent set of tools and capabilities. These tools in turn have enabled bigger and bolder visions of what can be fixed, made more efficient, or perhaps removed altogether thanks to a number of categories of software. At all times, these citizens have been steered by a burning desire to do things better—most often driven by a frustration that IT was not there to lend a hand. Or that IT simply dismissed automation ideas from the business as "'not their lane'." In some cases, IT played an even more active role by fully preventing any business-led automation work, due to the perceived risk it posed. Today, however, most IT organizations are comfortable with automation technologies, use them within their own function, and support their use throughout companies.

Citizen Automator

For as long as there has been work, there have been people who know that work is not being done efficiently or not being transacted in a reasonable, effective manner. These agitators, innovators, and well-intended trouble-makers are keenly aware that things can be improved. As recognized by productive agitator Benjamin Berkowitz at Mass General Brigham (now Vertex Pharmaceuticals), "There must be a better way for us to manage all of this work."

At all times, inspiration has been informed by the tools available. Tools—once mechanical, now digital—automate manual work. But no matter the type of tool, the purpose remains the same: conquer the mundane. This mundane and manual work exists in every function and every branch of every organization across the globe.

Enterprises have made significant investments over the last several decades to digitize operations and automate manual work. They did so with large-scale technology investments, including enterprise resource planning (ERP), customer resource management (CRM), and other such systems. As these transactional systems are adopted, less of this work remains manual, but manual work persists. Automation technologies are intended to address much of the remaining work that exists in the interstices of large enterprise systems.

Types of Work Well-Suited to Automation

There are three broad types of work that humans have traditionally done that could be performed by automation technologies. As most people go about their work days, they are often integrating between systems, performing a series of tasks, or making decisions based on defined rules. No day, nor job, is typically just one of these components. Instead, we divide our time across an array of activities that may include absorbing information, executing tasks, making decisions, or interacting with colleagues, clients, vendors, and more. While we would assert that most jobs are safe from automation, it's also clear that many individual tasks done in most jobs—especially in white-collar jobs—are candidates for automation. Many estimates peg the percentage at somewhere between 35–50%, though they have increased with the advent of generative AI.

To truly understand a "'job'" is to break it down to an atomic level, mapping and defining the tasks performed. Then each atomic task must be combined with others to form larger collections of work, ultimately rolling up to full end-to-end processes or workflows that achieve outcomes for internal or external customers. Put simply, tasks combine to create sequences, sequences create processes, and a collection of processes approximately explains how an organization operates.

So, let's take a closer look at the three types of automatable work: integrating between systems, performing a series of tasks, and making decisions based on defined rules. These are the realms in which citizen automation is most often found adding value and transforming the mundane and manual.

Integrating Between Systems as Human APIs

The work that we refer to as "routine," "repetitive," "manual," and "boring" is often the work of filling information gaps between systems. No function, industry, or department is free of these gaps. Your HR and personnel files, for instance, are likely spread across numerous systems—making your onboarding an act of duplicative data entry. HR-related activities often take place over multiple systems. Whether you look up your vacation days allotment, request vacation days, change healthcare beneficiaries, take sick leave, have a baby, get paid during maternity or paternity leave, get promoted, receive a pay raise, request to leave your job, get paid for unused vacation days, or perform a myriad other actions—all will likely require a member of your HR team to navigate and integrate across the systems involved in tracking and enabling these activities. Each will likely incorporate a number of systems for any specific process or transaction. And that number is growing.

The natural lifecycle of any enterprise, if it is successful, involves growth, expansions of operations, and often acquisition of other entities. Each of these elements comes with greater levels of complexity on all levels, including people, process, and technology. Teams grow, processes extend to capture the work being performed, and systems proliferate. What results is best illustrated in what's called a spaghetti diagram of interconnected systems and solutions to power the business. This complexity consumes resources to maintain and operate. And yet, this growing catalog of systems almost certainly doesn't get all of the work done, because there are always gaps. There are gaps between the legacy mainframe systems and the more modern systems on top. Gaps between the financial systems-of-record, and the applications used to coordinate supply chain logistics, e-commerce, customer relationships, and more. Gaps everywhere.

One way to solve this problem—to fill the gaps—is to introduce new applications that perform the activities currently not digitized or that sit somewhere in one of the gaps mentioned. That is in part what low-code/no-code (LC/NC) citizen developers do. Another way to address this is to implement more comprehensive software solutions—solutions like ERP and CRM systems—that connect with all existing systems, with the promise of enabling a more complete end-to-end transactional environment in which to run the business. But these are expensive, and they never seem to close all the information gaps. The third alternative is to plug the gaps. If the applications each have the right connectors and if IT has the budget and the bandwidth, this plug is called an application programming interface (API).[1]

Until recently, people were the APIs. Today we can use RPA and related tools to close the information gaps among systems.

A survey by Sapient Insight Group in 2021 found that the average organization deployed 16.24 HR applications.[2] The average number in 2020 was 10.23 and 8.85 the year before, for a cumulative average growth rate (CAGR) of 35%. That's an enviable growth rate for revenue, profit, or customers, but not enviable when it's the growth in systems an enterprise needs to pay for, implement, learn, and maintain. In addition, the more systems, the more gaps between systems. It is not uncommon for large

---

[1] An application programming interface (API) is a set of rules and protocols that allows different software applications to communicate and interact with each other. It defines how software components should interact and specifies how requests should be made and responses handled.

[2] https://hrexecutive.com/hr-tech-number-of-the-week-hr-systems-overload.

enterprises to have hundreds of systems. And the app sprawl is only accelerating with the software-as-a-service (SaaS) trend that Gartner believes to be a $195 billion market.[3] Large organizations with more than 10,000 employees use about 447 SaaS applications on average, and that number is rapidly climbing.[4] Smaller organizations use fewer, but the number is also growing while the size of the IT team may not be.

This same scenario plays out in finance and accounting systems, supply chain systems, procurement systems. . .you get the point. Lots of systems, lots of gaps. All being filled by people. That's all to say this is an excellent reason to implement systems that automatically take data out of one system and put it into another, perhaps with a decision or data manipulation in between. That's a big part of what RPA does.

Performing a Series of Tasks: Workflow

That's not the only reason for using automation tools, however. They can also perform tasks that come together in logical order to achieve outcomes. The tasks may be as simple as creating a file folder to store an applicant's submitted documentation. It may be as complicated as bringing together parts from multiple manufacturers, to ultimately construct a product for delivery. These activities may span systems; they may also span people, departments, and even companies. If they're done by citizens, they're generally less complex than full end-to-end process automations.

Ian has seen a lot of these citizen-developed workflows, since he was an RPA guy from its beginning. But Tom encountered his first citizen automator at Dentsu International, a very large advertising agency that decided to create a substantial group of citizens to automate small workflows. The first person he interviewed was Jessica Berresse, who worked in an operations team for Carat, a media buying agency within Dentsu. She told Tom about her favorite automation project, which involved one of her own job tasks. When she started in the operations role, one of her assigned tasks was "timesheet police officer." The finance team owned time reporting, but they were complaining that too many people weren't filling out their

---

[3]https://www.gartner.com/en/newsroom/press-releases/2022-10-31-gartner-forecasts-worldwide-public-cloud-end-user-spending-to-reach-nearly-600-billion-in-2023.
[4]https://pages.bettercloud.com/rs/719-KZY-706/images/2021-stateofsaasopsreport.pdf.

timesheets on a timely basis. They asked the operations team to address the issue, and Berresse found herself reviewing the reports of late timesheets and sending the same emails each month to habitual timesheet offenders found in the report. She was able to quickly build an RPA bot to go through the report, find the offenders, and fill in the details of email templates. She was very happy never to have to be timesheet policewoman again. This is typical of a citizen workflow—small, tedious, information-based, and not difficult for a human to give away to a bot.

Making Decisions Based on Defined Rules

One last element to discuss is the act of making decisions during the course of any of the workflows mentioned earlier. It is all but certain that there are various transactional avenues and options to choose between. For instance, what amount of tax should be added to a particular invoice? How many dependents should be added to a tax extension filing? What charge should be assigned for shipping of a particular product from the warehouse to a customer in Kalamazoo? There are also calculations to select and execute in order to reach necessary conclusions. These steps depend on decisions being made, and the decisions are based on a clear set of rules. Things like, "If the package is going to ZIP code 49003 and it weighs less than 5 pounds, then charge $28.50 for shipping."

Making decisions based on defined rules is a cornerstone of automation tools—RPA in particular. The rules should be nicely structured, definable, easily understood, and auditable. In fact, rules-based decisioning is a cornerstone to a large majority of work tasks and, therefore, a cornerstone of the automation of this work. Using more complex data-based tools and algorithms is, no doubt, more precise than a rule, and such machine learning models can be interfaced with RPA. But that's getting into the realm of data science. Most workflows will do just fine with less "smart" forms of automation technology, which are perfectly suited for citizen automators. Many decisions can be accomplished with one or more if/then statements that securely allow an enterprise to transact, act, and perform in ways that are both useful and compliant with policies—be they internally or externally legislated. As Ian noted in his LinkedIn Learning course "Introduction to Robotic Process Automation": "These robots are not dumb; they are just well behaved."

The Offices Where Automation Plays

The manual work in question exists in numerous places across an enterprise value chain, most easily broken into front-office, middle-office, and back-office functions. We don't intend to define and model all elements of this value chain, but for the sake of broad generality, we define *back* and *front*— and a bit of *middle* — to serve our purposes for this chapter.

Back Office

Back-office work encompasses the internal operations, financial, and administrative functions. It does not involve direct interaction with customers. It includes tasks such as accounting, data entry, payroll, financial management, human resources, compliance, IT services, and logistics. Back-office employees are crucial for processing transactions, managing inventory, onboarding new employees, and providing the data and support necessary for strategic decision-making and efficient business operations. Although back-office work is less visible to customers, it is essential for maintaining the operational backbone of a company, ensuring that customer-facing operations can be performed efficiently and effectively. It is here that a recent automation technology, robotic process automation, really blossomed. Back-office work is repetitive, based on straightforward rules, and involves inputting, processing, and outputting information—all tasks at which RPA excels. Back-office functions in telecom and banking have served as the introduction of RPA to many future adopters and service providers.

Front Office

Front-office work refers to the part of a company that directly interacts with customers. This includes departments such as marketing, sales, and service. The primary function of the front office is to establish and maintain contact with customers, often being the first point of contact for a customer when they interact with a company. Front-office staff are responsible for a variety of tasks, including but not limited to, communicating with customers, sorting emails, assisting with printing and typing tasks, and operating office equipment like printers and phones. These tasks can increasingly be automated, although they have less structure and repetition than some other types of work. However, communicating with customers and understanding their communications typically requires AI in addition to automation tools, and that typically would require more expertise than citizens possess.

Middle Office

Some companies and industries also have a middle office. While back- and front-office functions are somewhat universal, middle offices tend to be a specific set of tasks that connect the front and back office. For instance, the middle office in financial services institutions, such as investment banks or hedge funds, serves as a critical bridge between the front office (customer-facing roles like sales and trading) and the back office (administrative and support functions). It is primarily responsible for managing risk, calculating profits and losses, and overseeing information technology (IT) systems. The middle office ensures that transactions initiated by the front office are accurately booked, processed, and reconciled by the back office. A firm's IT function plays a key role in risk management by tracking and processing all deals made by the front office, supporting both the front and back offices with IT services, and ensuring compliance with legal and regulatory requirements. This department emerged due to the increasing complexity of financial transactions and the need for specialized skills in risk management and technology. Middle-office personnel typically possess college degrees and are essential for the firm's infrastructure, although they do not directly generate revenue. Similar middle-office functions are performed in other industries with a need for quality and compliance review, such as insurance and healthcare. The middle office is often a relevant and attractive place in which to explore automation programs. However, as in the front office, decisions may need to be more data-driven and analytical than is often possible with RPA, so citizens may need help from data science professionals.

The Origin Story of Broad Automation Adoption

Automation arose from a trend to centralizing and outsourcing work. Later came the effort to digitize that work that had been centralized and outsourced. The second wave was the fertile soil in which early process automation software emerged. It wasn't always usable by citizens in the early days, but it became easier to use over time.

To further aid in the efficiency of outsourced work, delivery centers introduced a few physical mechanisms to expedite and support the effort of doing more work quickly. Those mechanisms were the additional computer monitor and—believe it or not—the swivel chair. Other physical mechanisms such as delivery floor layout designs, visual measures, and general ergonomics were also important, but less so for our point about automation.

Almost all this work was repetitive and required a person to navigate across the vast number of systems we mentioned earlier. Opening and closing a client's applications repeatedly in the process of accessing, copying, pasting, and transacting constituted much of the tasks. The purpose was plugging gaps, executing workflows, and making decisions based on policies and procedures. Multiple computer monitors on every agent's desk were a way to quickly navigate between applications as efficiently as possible.

The other mechanism, the swivel chair, serves as a metaphor for the very act of navigating the systems and scanning an array of monitors. The rotation of a simple desk chair, apparently a mechanism invented by Thomas Jefferson in 1775, enabled the rapid rotation of one's head, without rotating one's neck. This type of furniture is so embedded in operational lore that work in offshore delivery centers has come to be described as "swivel chair integration." Integration of disparate systems is "automated" by a screen and a swivel chair. Something had to change.

But the idea that automation at scale could supplement, and even replace, such delivery centers didn't fully take off until 2012. The release of the white paper "Greetings from Robotistan, Outsourcing's Cheapest New Destination" by HFS Research, written in collaboration with Blue Prism (one of the earliest RPA vendors), helped to reframe the idea of automation. The paper stated, "Outsourcing has always been about people, process and technology. Scratch that. It's about process and technology, with people an optional extra."

It was about this time that *digital labor* entered the work lexicon, and enterprises were told that their success in the future would hinge on their ability to employ digital labor in all departments and functions across the business. While a compelling concept (at least to the finance teams looking to save money), this concept mostly just created anxiety in human labor, while overstating the degree to which any particular job was fully automatable.

Who Is a Citizen Automator?

Domain experts, creators, empowered subject-matter experts (SMEs), makers, super SMEs…in our discussions we heard all of these terms, and more, used to describe citizen automators. Citizen automators are not professional IT people. They are not computer science graduates. Nor do they typically have backgrounds or formal training in workflow or application design. They are, instead, members of business teams who spend their days working with the systems and the processes across their organizations. They interact closely with customers, suppliers, vendors, and partners. In short, they are uniquely qualified to weigh in on what is working and what could be working better. And now, thanks to the democratization of automation technologies, these businesspeople are able to turn ideas into action.

These ideas don't need to be specifically constrained to the scopes of work that they themselves are responsible for, although this is the most common scenario we see. These also don't necessarily need to address only internal processes and can cross organizational boundaries to include channel partners, vendors, or customers—although internal processes are the most common scenarios we see.

These automators are most often self-identified tinkerers and problem solvers. Stevie Simms of Shell is a citizen automator driven by questions like, "How can I save files in certain locations, digitize some things, and help out my local teams?" Renee Liu of Jabil is also a citizen automator, having learned about RPA from a colleague in the shared services entity. She wondered, "How can I apply this in my situation?" The countless professionals who say, "This can be better," and then make it so are all citizen automators. The key is that they use one or more tools in the automation tech stack available to them.

These automators often don't think of themselves with that description. Like Benjamin Berkowitz in our preface, they automate out of necessity but don't necessarily consider themselves automators. As expressed in a LinkedIn post to Ian by someone who took his introductory RPA course, "I've been trying to do RPA at my organization without knowing what RPA is!" Ultimately, the labels are less important than the objective and the result. These automators often begin simply with simple tools and scale from there as they become more aware of the options available to them.

In our discussions with citizen automators, the tool of choice to begin with is usually Microsoft Excel macros. From there they expand, leveraging web-based tools, more advanced tools in the Microsoft suite, and ultimately some level of RPA and intelligent document processing (IDP) tooling. The really ambitious ones get into AI as well. Many different technology roads will take them to their desired outcome.

What distinguishes automators from business analysts is that the former group actually builds something. As Leslie Willcocks and Mary Lacity wrote in one of the earliest books on RPA, "An RPA 'analyst' is a process expert who proactively seeks automation opportunities and typically writes detailed RPA requirements, whereas a typical 'business analyst' serves as a liaison between user needs and IT requirements."[5] A citizen automator may need to liaise, but they are not just a liaison. They make a difference in an organization's performance, however small—and that is what we find most exciting about the citizen movement as a whole.

Where Does Citizen Automation Belong?

Citizen automators use software, so they must be doing the work of IT. Yet, they are embedded in the business and only trying to transact critical business processes more effectively, so they must be doing the work of the business—and around we go. Unfortunately, there is little consensus around where this activity and the individuals performing it belong within an organization. In the earliest days of RPA-focused automation, it was not uncommon for practice leaders to admit openly (and on stage) that "my IT department doesn't even know I'm doing this." Many early-stage pilots were, and likely still are, deployed under the "seek forgiveness, not approval" approach. If IT did know what was happening, they would most certainly shut it down. For that reason, many early citizen automation efforts could easily be classified as "shadow" or "gray IT." This is unfortunate and unnecessary.

The fact is, there is actually no simple answer to where citizen automation should report. Choosing the proper home for such an initiative comes down as much to the culture and organizational setup of the enterprise as it

---

[5] L. P. Willcocks & M. C. Lacity, *Service Automation: Robots and the Future of Work.* Steve Brookes Publishing, 2016.

does to the spirit of what is trying to be accomplished with citizen automation. In our research, we have come across almost as many permutations as we have had discussions. There are organizations like WESCO where all forms of citizen development are owned by IT. Mass General Brigham had it reporting to finance, until the leader left, and IT took it over. Johnson & Johnson has a number of entities running with automation, not least of which is their Global Business Services operation, which works in concert with IT. The power company Entergy has automation initiatives reside within their Business Data Group. The rule of thumb seems to be that there is no clear rule of thumb.

To make the most of empowered domain experts, the age-old tug-of-war between business and IT needs to find some common ground. Perhaps the best place to do this is in hybrid and fusion teams,[6] enabled by specialist centers of excellence from across the AI spectrum and from across organizational functional areas. We'll explore this more in Part 4, "Setting Sail," when we discuss how to set up your own citizen empowerment initiatives.

What Is the Upside of Citizen Automation?

There are clearly many benefits to putting technical capabilities in the hands of SMEs. By enabling employees outside of the IT department to design and build automated tasks and workflows using RPA and the broader intelligent automation toolset, organizations will experience significant improvements in efficiency, productivity, and cost-effectiveness. Whether citizens are automating simple tasks only they touch or organization-wide process flows, the following benefits are some likely outcomes of a well-supported citizen.

Idea/Execution Overlap

IT projects fail at alarmingly high rates. A McKinsey study found that only 44% of IT projects deliver on their intended benefits.[7] If you consider the additional hurdles of coming in on time and on budget, the success rate drops to a paltry 0.5%. Ask your favorite generative AI model to explain

[6]https://www.gartner.com/en/information-technology/glossary/fusion-team.
[7]https://www.mckinsey.com/industries/public-sector/our-insights/unlocking-the-potential-of-public-sector-it-projects.

this, and it will cite top reasons as being poorly defined objectives and a lack of user involvement. The most commonly used software development framework of late, the agile/lean approach, begins with user stories for a reason. It's important to know who you're building for, and why. Yet many IT projects fail because the charter does not clearly articulate the purpose or the end-user needs. The gap between what is needed and what gets built is too great. Therefore, the project is deemed less than successful.

When the citizen is the user, the gap between the idea and the execution of that idea into a software solution becomes quite small or nonexistent. While citizens may not be fully versed in agile methodologies, there is usually no need for them to be. They simply understand what they need and are able to maintain a focus on the end goal. To date, there is no documented research on the impact that citizen automation has had on increasing the success rate of IT projects. But common sense dictates that when a user builds their own solution, the likelihood of their needs being met goes up. It does bear noting that statistics like those cited from McKinsey are for large-scale IT projects. Citizen automation projects will almost always be smaller endeavors, often focused on the development of solutions for individuals or departments.

Prototyping the Future State

What citizens build may not be full-blown applications and IT-grade enterprise solutions, but they do build something. An integration is developed, a workflow is made more efficient, or a decision is automated or improved. The spirit of this was best captured by the CIO of Kaiser Permanente in a meeting Ian had in 2015. After Ian explained RPA and how it complements (and doesn't compete with) the existing enterprise technical architecture, the CIO summarized the scope of RPA work as allowing her teams to "prototype the future state." We don't know of a better description. These prototyped future states illustrate what happens when five HR systems seamlessly "talk" to one another, or when a series of customer onboarding steps in a bank can be automatically triggered and completed without the need for manual intervention. These prototypes can serve as minimum viable products (MVPs), doing just enough to showcase the potential of automation and signaling to IT, "If you ever do build the functionality in to our core systems, this is what we need."

If an organization's IT team is responsive and recognizes these prototypes as a blueprint for the near- and mid-term IT roadmap of projects, a citizen will soon find their solution integrated into the enterprise technology landscape. Some organizations, like PwC and Shell, have a well-defined process for evaluating that potential. More commonly, the prototype could remain in place, operating as originally designed, for many years in anticipation of moving a specific process into an enterprise system or up to the cloud. In any case, there is significant value in allowing end users, the experts in their domain, to prototype what better looks like.

Increased Speed

In nearly every interview we have held with citizen automators (and those firms that had adopted the approach), the slow speed of enterprise IT was cited as a major catalyst for adoption of citizen automation. IT is busy, and roadmaps are full. No matter who you ask, you'll hear ranges of 6 to 12 to 18 months—sometimes quite a bit longer—as the estimate of when IT can get around to addressing the needs and requests of business. This is the story we heard from Renee Liu, an operations development director at the massive electronics manufacturer Jabil. A self-professed "digital transformation cheerleader," Renee works in an operations center of excellence (CoE) supporting 70 factories across three continents, serving more than 450 customers with requirements that change daily. Traditional IT solutions were taking 6 to 12 months to design and develop. By harnessing citizen automation, Renee and her team aim to rapidly respond to customer needs in a far more flexible and agile manner.

IT is often focused on maintaining and upgrading enterprise ERP and CRM systems, leaving them little time to work on point solutions and discrete automation solutions. With their attention spent on big projects, there just isn't enough time, resources, or impetus to be able to direct the IT team to many of the (smaller) projects that we would classify as citizen automation initiatives.

Of course, such acceleration is valuable only if it can be shown to be adding value to an enterprise's transformation goals. In the case of Jabil, speed and value worked hand in hand.

Employee Experience and Loyalty

One of the primary upsides of citizen automation—and often other forms of citizen development—is the empowerment it offers employees at all levels of an organization. By granting individuals the ability to automate and influence the way tasks, sequences, and more comprehensive processes are performed, citizen automation fosters a culture of innovation and self-sufficiency. What's more, citizen programs upskill employees, giving them interesting work and valuable future-proof skills. In turn, the associated career advancement opportunities establish higher levels of company loyalty and greater employee morale. More interesting work also creates lower churn rates of key individuals. As noted by Ben Berkowitz of Mass General Brigham, those accepted into his citizen developer program (they took a logic test as an entrance exam) proved to be his most loyal, and longest tenured, team members.

In all cases, citizen empowerment translates into increased agility, as teams swiftly adapt to changing business requirements and market dynamics by creating and deploying automation solutions tailored to their specific needs. The ability to respond rapidly to evolving challenges positions organizations well for sustained growth and resilience in today's dynamic business landscape. But, just as importantly, it allows for the SMEs to act on their expertise, building the solutions and sequences they know to be of value to themselves and the customers their enterprise serves. This level of empowerment is exactly what employees are increasingly looking for in a competitive labor market. In short, citizen initiatives help keep good citizens.

Fostering Cross-Departmental Innovation

We've already stressed the point that the "IT versus business" divide has been the culprit for many underwhelming software initiatives and outright barriers to progress on the digital front. It would then stand to reason that fewer silos, and greater levels of cross-functional and cross-departmental collaboration, would achieve higher degrees of innovation. By breaking down communication barriers and encouraging cross-functional participation in automation initiatives, organizations can harness diverse perspectives and expertise to drive creative problem-solving and continuous improvement. Citizen automators can help bring about this improvement if given the opportunity. Suffice it to say, those in the trenches who are speaking to customers, interacting with internal support functions, collaborating with external channel partners, and working with all other citizens in between have a unique read on what is needed to support a business ecosystem. The unique insights from each citizen's respective roles, contributing to the development of innovative solutions that address complex challenges, is the crux of why citizen-oriented innovation will prove to be so successful at scale.

What Can Go Wrong?

While the list of benefits is long, that's not to say there aren't potential risks and issues with a citizen automation approach. The biggest ones cited in our discussions were often based around data exposure, impact on core systems, and the general mayhem caused by too many untracked automations across an enterprise. We don't deny that unleashing non-IT professionals to do IT is a potentially risky proposition. Running a successful citizen program requires that an enterprise anticipate these risks and mitigate against them. We cover the mitigations in Part 4 on "Setting Sail" with all hands. For now, let's explore the risks.

Overhyped and Under-Delivered

Perhaps the biggest issue that many anticipate with citizen automation is that it simply doesn't work at scale or create any real value for the organization. This is a common belief among IT professionals, who often roll their eyes when you ask them about citizen automation. But our interviews with companies and the opinions of numerous advisors, consultants, and practitioners suggest that this is a trend that's here to stay.

Paving Cow Paths

A close cousin to the risk of under-delivering is the concept of incrementalism. The case can be made that citizen automation is likely to deliver small, nonstrategic, and incremental evolutions to any given process or sequence being addressed. We refer to this as "paving cow paths"—taking an old dirt path and simply covering it with asphalt and calling that innovation. In this context, this can mean simply taking a manual task and digitizing it just the way it is, without asking whether there is a different (and better) way to go about completing the process. In fact, this was the common practice in the earliest days of RPA, when explorations were often tool-first, rather than process-first. More mature initiatives have moved away from the tool-focused approach.

Over the last 10 years, there has been an energized and polarizing discussion around the wisdom of automating an inefficient process versus the approach of fixing the process first. This was perhaps most famously captured in a quote widely attributed to Bill Gates:

> "The first rule of any technology used in business is that automation applied to an efficient operation will magnify the efficiency. The second rule of any technology used in business is that automation applied to an inefficient operation will magnify the inefficiency."

Although we agree with Gates that in most cases processes should be improved before being automated,[8] even small changes add value. And they showcase where bigger changes might make sense in the longer run. Ultimately, automating the inefficient process that exists today will still likely result in a faster, cheaper process. By doing so, you learn more about the process than you would otherwise be able to if it was still being manually transacted.

Technical Debt

As well-intentioned as citizen automators may be, their relative lack of training or experience in software development best practices means they may inadvertently introduce inefficiencies, security vulnerabilities, or compatibility issues into the IT infrastructure. This accumulation of "technical debt" can hinder future enhancements, lead to increased maintenance costs and, ultimately, slow down innovation within the organization. In some cases, it can do even more harm by exposing data or interfering with the smooth operation of existing enterprise systems. In other scenarios, citizen automators can create solutions with little awareness of the existing IT roadmap. This can result in automations that conflict with soon-to-be

---

[8]Thomas H. Davenport and David Brain, "Before Automating Your Company's Processes, Find Ways to Improve them," *Harvard Business Review*, June 13, 2018, https://hbr .org/2018/06/before-automating-your-companys-processes-find-ways-to-improve-them.

launched capabilities or that are duplicative with other solutions already available within the organization's catalog. Such technical debt encapsulates the challenges and compromises that arise when nontechnical employees create applications or automate processes without a deep understanding of coding standards, scalability, and long-term maintenance. These issues are best abated through formal governance and oversight, which we discuss in Part 4.

The Future of Citizen Automation

The future of citizen automation is a story closely tied to the evolution of the tech stack available to empower the activity. The shift from RPA to a broader intelligent automation toolkit opened the aperture of workflow, allowing for more complex work to be automated. In a similar fashion, advancements in generative AI will transform the art of the possible for citizen automators. At the time of publication, the burgeoning number of large language models have created an explosion of use cases that all show-case an ability to write or create words, images, and videos. If carefully curated, so as to avoid the risk of hallucinations, this content can help in the development of customer service responses, internal documentation, and marketing material such as blogs and social posts. But, such tools are not yet able to do transactional work, at least not in any serious fashion.

This will all change with the advancement of generative models known as *large action models* (or *large agentive models*, LAMs). Their very purpose is to do work. They understand a person's intentions and then take actions to control the applications you use today, the very applications that citizen automators have been configuring software to animate. What's more, they'll do it using natural language, instead of code, low-code, or no-code pro-gramming alternatives.

"Actions will eat code,"[9] say Phil Fersht and Francis Carden, two early influencers and entrepreneurs in the RPA wave of work automation. In the not so distant future, citizen automators will be able to verbally describe how they would like to execute a given process, and a large action model will simply perform the work. When that time comes, the only barrier to all hands being on tech will be the lack of initiative by an individual, or the lack of access to the tools due to enterprise concern over enabling citizens with such capabilities. Both scenarios are likely to end poorly.

---

[9]https://www.horsesforsources.com/why-actions-will-eat-code_050724.

6

Citizen Data Science

Citizen data science as practiced in organizations really consists of two categories of activity. One might be more accurately called *citizen data analysis* because there isn't much science to it. Instead, it involves straightforward data analysis, generally with only descriptive statistics, visual analytics, or perhaps a bit of ordinary regression analysis. Few people seem to object to this idea, as it doesn't require a high degree of quantitative expertise, and creating a dashboard full of bar charts is unlikely to lead to really bad decisions.

The other category might be called real or true *citizen data science*, because it involves complex data analysis and the use of sophisticated predictive models. This activity has both proponents and conscientious objectors. It requires statistical expertise, and its outputs can be embedded into decision processes that, if made badly, can lead to a lot of trouble.

Both types usually involve some degree of data wrangling, although that within true citizen data science is typically more technically challenging. Some people worry about that wrangling because it sometimes leads to the creation of new data and "multiple versions of the truth." We'll describe the positive and negative attributions of both citizen data analysis and citizen data science in this chapter, beginning with citizen data analysis.

Citizen Data Analysis

For well over a decade the relatively simple analysis of data has increasingly been performed by citizens or people outside of the professional data analysis community. This type of work, historically called *business intelligence* (BI), involves the generation of frequency distributions, bar, pie, and line charts, so-called measures of central tendency (a sophisticated way to refer to means and medians), and simple statistical measures of relationships between variables such as correlations and regressions. These activities can usually be performed by anyone with a B grade or better in a college statistics course (so pull out those transcripts and see if you qualify!).

The technology to create such statistics isn't terribly complex either; it typically requires the ability to point and click with a mouse. Many citizens do analysis work with spreadsheets, which by this time the majority of data-literate employees can use reasonably well. Spreadsheets do often contain errors, and they make it very easy to generate "multiple versions of the truth," but nonetheless they have proven popular for many decades. Visual analytics can easily be generated and displayed not only with spreadsheets but also with easy-to-use, point-and-click software like Tableau or Qlik. These types of vendors have prospered greatly during the citizen data analysis era. More recently, companies have begun to use Power BI from Microsoft to accomplish many of these same tasks.

The result of these tools and activities is not only that many citizens have mastered data analysis but also that many organizations have freed up data analysis professionals to do more complex and fulfilling tasks than constantly developing dashboards and reports. Professionals and their managers in many companies have tried to instill a "self-service" ethos for this type of analysis, and citizens are probably (there is little data to confirm this) the primary creators of dashboards, charts, and data-oriented reports in most organizations.

However, it is probably also fair to assume that citizen analysis is a long way from being pervasive. A substantial majority of employees in organizations still do not have access to BI tools and cannot or do not perform citizen data analysis. In a global survey of corporate employees by Accenture and Qlik in 2020, only a quarter of those surveyed believe they're fully prepared to use data effectively, only 37% of employees trust their decisions more when based on data, and 48% frequently make decisions based on gut feeling. Data and analytic activity even seems to have some negative consequences. In the same survey, 74% of employees reported feeling overwhelmed or unhappy when working with data, and 61% believed that data overload has contributed to workplace stress.[1]

Companies are trying to help citizens develop more citizen analysis skills, but it's clearly not their highest priority. BARC, a German-based provider of business intelligence research and consulting, undertakes an annual global survey of business intelligence professionals. In four surveys between 2021 and 2024, the capability of vendors to enable "self-service analytics and data discovery" was ranked sixth out of 20 attributes, suggesting that it is a moderate but enduring priority of companies.[2] The same organization also reported that usage of self-service BI was stagnant at just over half of companies over the middle of the 2010s decade.[3] Perhaps generative AI will end the stagnation.

From an organizational perspective, there are three primary keys to enabling and encouraging citizen data analysis. One, of course, is education— about how to frame questions and use the tools, data that's available, and perhaps some limited statistics. Many organizations have included this type of education in "data literacy" programs that have been widely offered over the past decade. If your organization hasn't made one available, a quick Google search of "online 'data literacy' courses" yielded more than a million results. You should have no problem finding free or paid instruction.

The second is data. Organizations need to make it easy for citizens to access and use the right data—the right customer file, the right performance indicators, the right supply chain inventory. This is typically done with some kind of data catalog or marketplace that shows the available data that employees can use in their analyses. Ideally it would contain not only internal data but also externally sourced data on topics such as the economy, the weather, or industry-specific data.

The only problematic issue once widespread data access has been established is avoiding the creation of new data that might confuse

---

[1] Accenture and Qlik, "The Human Impact of Data Literacy," Jan. 16, 2020, `https://www.accenture.com/us-en/insights/technology/human-impact-data-literacy`.
[2] BARC, "BARC Data, BI, and Analytics Trend Monitor 2024," *Infographic*, 2023, `https://barc-research.com/infographic-data-bi-analytics-trend-monitor-2024`.
[3] BARC, "Self-Service Business Intelligence: An Overview," 2017, `https://bi-survey.com/self-service-bi`.

the enterprise. If you as a citizen data analyst develop, for example, a new definition of "customer" that includes the types of customers you or your department find most useful (say, you include prospects as well as existing customers), your new customer data element may sneak out into the rest of the organization. Then, when the CEO or other executives asks "just how many customers do we have in this company," they will become very frustrated when told that there are multiple answers depending on the definition of customer that is used. The education that employees get should emphasize the importance of using the "master" data source for enterprise data (ideally from an easy-to-use data catalog) and not modifying it to create new data and storing it. Of course, there are some data that are individual or departmental in scope, and citizens can usually do what they want with it. In highly regulated environments, citizens need to know the restrictions on data usage and sharing and adhere to them closely.

The final factor in increasing citizen data analysis is to create a culture that encourages—perhaps even mandates at times—the use of data in decision-making. In a McKinsey survey in 2019, respondents felt that among 10 different ways to establish a data culture, the most effective was having employees consistently use data in their decisions. The data practices that most differentiated high-performing companies from laggards included having at least one C-suite data leader, making data broadly accessible to frontline employees, and having a culture that supports rapid testing and iteration based on data.[4] Companies do this in multiple ways—education helps, for example—but we feel the most effective technique is for senior managers to set a good example by using data and analysis in their own decisions.

Although cultural change generally requires human intervention, it appears that new technology—especially a new technology like generative AI that captures human imaginations—can play a role in catalyzing a data-oriented culture. As Tom was drafting the foreword to the annual NewVantage Partners/Wavestone survey of data leaders in late 2023, he noticed a striking change.[5] A series of questions on whether organizations had created

---

[4] McKinsey & Co., "Catch Them If You Can: How Leaders in Data and Analytics Have Pulled Ahead," September 19, 2019, https://www.mckinsey.com/capabilities/quantumblack/our-insights/catch-them-if-you-can-how-leaders-in-data-and-analytics-have-pulled-ahead.
[5] Citation to NVP survey report once it is out.

a data-driven organization or established a data and analytics culture had been included in the survey in previous years. For the last several years they had shown no improvement and had even worsened. Whether an organization had "established a data and analytics culture," for example, had declined from 28% in 2019 to 19% in 2022 and 21% in 2023. But in the 2024 survey, it zoomed to 43%! "Created a data-driven organization" doubled from 24% in 2023 to 48% in 2024! What changed in the year between the 2023 and 2024 surveys, the first of which came out just as ChatGPT was announced? Generative AI seems the likely cause. At least in the perception of large organization data leaders, generative AI seems to have sparked a change in culture. We'll see, of course, if it continues to do so.

One other point on citizen data analysis: it has a tendency to evolve slowly into citizen data science. What is easy to do with analysis tools has come to include the creation of machine learning models, for example. Citizen-oriented tools like Tableau ("business science") and Qlik ("AutoML") now have machine learning capabilities. This can be an easy way to migrate citizens into doing some data science work, but as we'll describe in the next section, it requires more statistical expertise and someone with professional credentials to check on the model if it is important to the success of the business.

True Citizen Data Science

Of the many areas of citizen technology activity, true citizen data science is in some respects the most challenging. Like the other citizen domains, however, it is getting easier. It's not that the technologies for true data science—at least the ones designed for citizen use—are so difficult to use. As we just mentioned with regard to citizen data analysts, automated machine learning tools and now generative AI models can do many of the tasks that formerly required a data scientist. They include dealing with missing data, transforming variables or features, trying a variety of different algorithms to see which one best fits the data, and even automatically generating program code or an API to score or perform inference using the model. In many cases, all the citizen would need to do is to specify the outcome variable to be predicted and the data set to use.

The primary barrier to citizen data science, however, is the "science" part and in particular the deep statistical expertise necessary to interpret data science models and ensure that they are accurate in their predictions and do what they are intended to do. The number and types of algorithms and the complexity of the models used in data science have increased in recent years and go well beyond elementary regression analysis. Citizens who haven't learned enough statistics to fully understand their models may run into a variety of problems.

For example, automated machine learning programs may violate some assumptions involved in the use of a particular algorithm, such as "overfitting"—when machine learning models fit the training data closely but not the new data used for inference. Model accuracy, if used in important business processes like fraud detection, credit approval, and pricing, can have a major impact on a company's revenues and profits. Statistical models may also predict product safety, and if they're wrong, they could endanger customers. If a model employs excessive levels of bias, it can run afoul of regulators and create unhappy customers—not to mention bad press.

On the other hand, there are many true data science use cases involving predictive models/machine learning that are neither very hard to develop nor critical to an organization's success. Predicting how a customer might respond to a marketing offer is both not that difficult (assuming the right data is available) and, in the grand scheme of things, not that important. If the model isn't perfect, it can still be useful, and its imperfections probably won't have a big impact on a company's financial results.

In addition, some work can be done by citizen data scientists that falls short of the full responsibility for model creation and implementation activities. A citizen might, for example, create a model that fits the data using automated machine learning software. A data scientist can take a quick look at it and confirm that everything checks out. This saves the reviewing data scientists some time compared to developing the model themselves and, as long as it's not their only job, still lets them do some modeling themselves.

Data science was originally performed only by data scientists, but now there are many other related jobs—including data engineers, machine learning engineers, translators, data product managers, and so forth. All of these jobs require specific skills, but they aren't the same skills that being a data scientist requires. It's quite possible that citizens will have some of those skills if not all of them. In addition, despite some efforts at certifying data scientists,[6] few organizations have put formal classification or certification processes in place. Therefore, the distinction between professional data scientists and citizen data scientists is a permeable and shifting one. Citizens may not be able to perform all needed activities on data science projects, but in all likelihood they can perform some of them. We'll describe some possible configurations of citizen-involved data science in the following sections.

What Is the Upside of True Citizen Data Science?

As with other types of citizen development, real citizen data science has positive and negative attributes. On the positive side, there is simply too much data for professional data scientists to analyze and make sense of it all. Just like IT organizations, professional data science groups can't get to all possible data science projects. If citizen data scientists can take some of the load, the organization can make more effective use of its data and make better decisions with it.

As with all forms of citizen development, citizen data scientists have an advantage in that they often have intimate knowledge of the business problem to be addressed; they live with it every day. They know the shortcomings of the current situation, they know the (internal or external) customer, and they know the capabilities of the employees who will use the system. They may well be familiar with the data they want to use. So in many cases they are better equipped to solve business problems with AI and analytics than data scientists are.

Citizen data scientists within the business have another advantage over data scientists, who are often primarily focused on just solving the analytical or AI problem and creating a powerful and cool algorithm to do so. Citizens, on the other hand, are also motivated not just to develop a model that fits the data but to deploy the model into production and ensure that it actually gets used in the business, solves the business problem in the short term, and continues to do so over time.

---

[6] Usama Fayyad & Hamit Hamutcu, "Toward foundations for data science and analytics: A knowledge framework for professional standards." *Harvard Data Science Review*, 2(2), 2020. https://doi.org/10.1162/99608f92.1a99e67a.

This distinction between professional and citizen data scientists was reflected in an interview Tom did several years ago with a large bank's director of portfolio management and credit strategy. The group's work involves a mix of marketing and risk concerns, and the director had recently decided to adopt an automated machine learning tool to speed up model development.

He said:

> We put the technology in the hands of business users—people who understand why people do stuff. Historically I have hired people out of undergrad and trained them in data science. But with automated machine learning you don't really need to know much about technology or programming—it gives somewhat quantitatively-oriented people superpowers. My bias is to democratization, although we have a careful governance and approval process for systems developed by nonprofessional data scientists. We let pretty much everyone explore, but we are careful in what we deploy.
>
> What I realized was that data science traditionally consisted of math, computer science, and an understanding of the business domain. Now more and more of the math and computer science are automated. But the people who understand the data and the customer behavior are still needed and are much more powerful.
>
> The rest of the bank is working very hard to hire data scientists, but they are not really paying off because they don't understand the business. So I am firmly in the citizen data scientist camp. I call them 'purple people' because they understand a lot of the business and enough of the technology and the statistics.

Remember that this director was in a bank, where models have to be accurate and are often reviewed by external regulators. If citizen data scientists can be effective there, they can work in many less or nonregulated settings.

What Kinds of People Become Citizen Data Scientists?

The attributes and backgrounds of people who become citizen data scientists are highly correlated with their success. We've already described some of them in previous chapters. Charles Coleman, who created enormous value at Home Depot in the product assortment space, was a mechanical engineer with an MBA. With that quantitatively focused background, when he discovered some citizen data science and automation tools, he discovered that he could do a lot of work in a short time.

Amanda Woodly at 84.51°, the data science subsidiary of the Kroger Co., had a nonmathematical background in college. But through her work in demand, sales, and operational planning at various retailers, she discovered that she had a talent for math and data-driven decision-making. She now is a relatively business-oriented analyst in a business unit of the Kroger Co. that is replete with professional data scientists, and she works closely with them.

In short, citizen data scientists may not be fully trained in computer science or statistics, but they aren't afraid of computers or numbers either. They are passionate not about creating models but about using those computers and numbers to solve business problems. They are willing to learn new tools that expand their data science horizons—the more automated, the better.

Of course, some training in statistics and data management would be useful for any citizen. Companies like Shell and Airbus have created extensive online educational programs for employees wanting to be certified as citizen data scientists. At Shell, for example, the Udacity-created program in data science involves a "nanodegree" requiring four to six months to complete for employees working 10 to 15 hours per week. The program includes topics such as how to create supervised machine learning algorithms, Python programming, and data modeling.[7] Companies that do not have such formal certification programs in place may want to test employees before turning them loose as citizen data scientists.

Dan Jeavons, who is vice president for computational science and digital innovation at Shell, told us that these training programs have benefitted two types of people. One is different types of businesspeople—maintenance engineers, traders, and people in their service centers—who want to upgrade analyses that they use to do their jobs better. They learn some computer science skills and enough statistics to create basic predictive models.

---

[7] Susan Caminiti, "Royal Dutch Shell Reskills Workers in Artificial Intelligence as Part of Huge Energy Transition," *CNBC Work*, April 3, 2020, https://www.cnbc.com/2020/04/03/royal-dutch-shell-reskills-workers-in-ai-part-of-energy-transition.html.

These capabilities for citizens have the primary benefit, Jeavons said, of generating much better use cases. True data science work, as we've argued, is difficult for people with only small amounts of training. But they can both come up with better ideas for AI applications than they could previously and can communicate much more easily with professional data scientists. To facilitate this communication, Shell created embedded data science teams that live next to business people—some of whom have received data science training. The enhanced knowledge of citizens and their entry-level experience with data science, and the proximity to the professionals, leads to much better collaboration. The two groups can partner in a transparent way to build trust in the models, which means they are more likely to be successfully deployed.

The other type of beneficiaries are scientists. These include geophysicists, chemists, and highly quantitative engineers who are very familiar with the traditional statistics that lie behind today's AI but lack the up-to-date knowledge of computing capabilities and deep learning/generative AI models. They have benefited enormously from the data science training that Shell provides, and their science and engineering capabilities are being transformed as a result. Jeavons commented that deep learning models, for example, have been extremely helpful in the estimation of partial differential equations, which are critical to chemical engineering. In addition, with deep learning, simulations can be performed that are massively faster than those in the past.

What Can Go Wrong?

Some people are justifiably concerned about the concept and role of citizen data scientists in organizations. As we've already mentioned, there can be problems that result when relatively untrained citizens create analytical or AI models.

This perspective is ably represented by Scott Hallworth, who is the chief data and analytics officer at HP Inc.. Perhaps even more relevant is the fact that he was the chief model risk officer at Capital One for many years. Advanced risk management in highly regulated institutions has been at the core of his career.

About citizen data science, he had this to say:

You've got to be careful of the black box. If you don't know what's in a model and it's used for decision-making or customer interaction, it may have statistical bias or inappropriate features. Also, does the citizen data scientist have the rigor to know when there is degradation, drift, or overfitting in the model? Just like a new car, an analytics or machine learning model degrades in value immediately—even large language models degrade. The citizen data scientist needs to know how to read the dashboard and know when the model is drifting, when to take it in for routine maintenance, and when to get a full inspection once a year.

There is value to citizen data science but there has to be the guardrails and oversight to know when, where, and how to review the models. The most important criterion is required model and statistical threshold monitoring. Somebody has to set the dashboard to blink red when there is a malfunction. In financial services, in credit modeling there is no one dimension you are looking at, and you need to be attuned to multiple dimensions. If you are making credit decisions or monitoring the credit portfolio there is always a new data source, always a new trend to monitor. And of course it's always important to protect customer data.

Hallworth has fewer concerns about citizen low-code/no-code usage and citizen automation than he does with citizen data science. But even in those cases, he believes citizen work still needs quality tests if the outputs are high frequency or high severity.

Another conscientious objector to citizen data science is Zoher Karu, who is now vice president of data and analytics at Blue Shield of California. He's held similar jobs at Citigroup, eBay, and Sears Holdings in the past. When Tom asked him on a recent group call of senior data leaders how he felt about citizen data science, he remarked, "We try to keep sharp knives out of the hands of children."

When we interviewed him to get more detail on that intriguing comment, he softened his view a bit but had some real concerns.

The answer definitely depends on the analytical maturity of the organization. If there are teams scattered throughout the business with no oversight, do they really know how to do analytics? Maybe they report to people who aren't analytical, so who is providing the oversight? They may be marketing people who develop propensity or loyalty models, but they may not know right from wrong in terms of the right inputs or the construction of the model. I just worry about knowing whether the data science is using best practices. And automated tools will just create bad models faster for people who don't understand the key concepts.

Karu did agree that it is possible to certify people to practice citizen data science and that newer tools are perhaps more correct than they used to be. He even admitted the possibility that someday analytical and AI tools would have built-in guidelines that would keep amateurs away from trouble. But those tools are still evolving, he said.

He does support citizen data analysis, but in that area as well as in citizen data science he is concerned about the creation of new data:

I am fine with business users using data, interacting with dashboards, filtering data, and that sort of thing. But I worry about multiple groups creating new data—did they calculate it correctly and efficiently, are they using consistent enterprise definitions, or is it just a version of the data that supports their perspective? Might it lead to multiple versions of the truth? Is it secure? This is particularly important in organizations like mine where we handle sensitive consumer health information. So I say citizen data usage, yes; citizen data creation, no.

Both Hallworth's and Karu's comments should receive attention by organizations considering citizen data science on a substantial scale. It's possible to do it without encountering the problems they describe, but it won't happen without careful creation and monitoring of an organization's governance, guidance, and guardrail approaches.

What Kinds of Problems Should Citizen Data Scientists Take On?

The types of problems that are appropriate for citizen data scientists, then, are those that involve relatively straightforward technology and quantitative methods, that are based on well-structured data, and that do not involve highly critical or externally regulated business problems. Supervised learning models, for example, can easily be created by automated machine learning or generative AI data analysis programs and are relatively easy to interpret and deploy. A supervised learning model to predict how customers might respond to a digital ad run on a particular site at a particular time—based on past data about digital ad responses—would be a good example. Although the statistical methods involved in such an analysis might be complex, any citizen with a good understanding of regression analysis and the relevant data should be able to interpret and act on such a model.

Citizen data scientists should not be allowed to create or refine analytics or AI models that have life-or-death or business survival implications or those that will be closely examined by external regulators. Examples of problems that should not be worked on by citizen data scientists would be:

- A credit model in a bank that would be examined closely by regulators and cause substantial monetary losses to the bank if it were inaccurate
- A model predicting equipment failures in a nuclear energy plant that might lead to a meltdown if it were poorly constructed
- A deep learning model predicting whether radiological images showed cancerous lesions in patients that is both a life-or-death issue to patients and very difficult to understand and interpret
- A model that draws on external data from the Internet in real time that might allow cybersecurity hacks or breaches

To ensure that citizens are working on the right types of data science analyses, there needs to be some sort of assessment and approval process in place. If the model's outputs are being used in important decisions, they should be reviewed before being deployed into production. 84.51° has a "science review process" in which subject-matter experts—generally professional data scientists—can review the models developed by citizens and sign off on the science if it is acceptable.

Citizen Data Science for Generative AI

There is practically no limit to what citizen data scientists can do, including the creation of fine-tuned generative AI or large language models (LLMs). Although vendors have produced several high-quality base models, many companies want to customize them by adding their own content to the models.[8] Then they can be used for a variety of purposes, including internal knowledge management and external customer service.

Until recently, however, professional data science expertise was necessary to customize these models with a company's own content. You needed to employ a vector database with "embeddings"—words turned into numbers—and algorithms to assess the similarity of words. A citizen data scientist might be able to master those tasks, but it wouldn't be easy.

Now, however, a startup out of MIT called Pienso is based on helping citizens develop these tailored LLMs. To quote from the company's website:

> Non-technical users can now construct, deploy, and manage AI models, imbued with their own understanding of the data and context, all without the need for coding. By utilizing these aligned Large Language Models, organizations can build the AI applications they need now, faster, and flexibly retrain them in the future.

The company's CEO, Birago Jones, commented the following in an interview:

> The difference between democratizing AI and empowering people with AI comes down to who understands the data best—you [a data scientist] or a doctor or a journalist or someone who works with customers every day? Those are the people who should be creating the models. That's how you get insights out of your data.[9]

Pienso's customer Sky, a large TV and telecom company based in the United Kingdom, used its tools to better understand customer issues from call center transcripts. The company's Customer Insights team understood customers and their needs, but they didn't have data science skills, and the central data science team was otherwise engaged. After fine-tuning an LLM on their own call data, they are able to analyze each customer interaction

---

[8] Thomas H. Davenport and Maryam Alavi, "How to Train Generative AI Using Your Company's Data," *Harvard Business Review*, July 6, 2023, https://hbr.org/2023/07/how-to-train-generative-ai-using-your-companys-data.

[9] Zach Winn, "Putting AI into the hands of people with problems to solve," *MIT News*, Feb. 26, 2024, https://news.mit.edu/2024/pienso-putting-user-friendly-ai-problem-solving-0226.

with regard to topic, emotion, and sentiment. This work is one reason why Sky has lower customer complaints than any of its UK competition.[10]

The fact that Pienso had a tool of this type even before ChatGPT was announced in November 2022 suggests that even the most sophisticated machine learning models can be created and modified by citizens shortly after they are introduced. There is no reason to expect that other similar startups will work along these lines and that large vendors such as Google, Amazon, and Microsoft will eventually make similar capabilities available.

Citizen Data Science and Data Flow Automation

A major component of both data analysis and data science is getting the data for training and scoring (also known as *inference*) the models after training. It is often quite a tedious and time-consuming process to "wrangle" the data into the right place at the right time. Some of the citizen analysts and data scientists we've already profiled, such as Charles Coleman at Home Depot, succeeded in part because they were able to automate data flows into their models. This is one of the primary capabilities of Alteryx, which Coleman used to pull data into his models. "Mr. Citizen" at the large consumer products company uses it for the same purposes.

Another excellent example of the intersection between citizen data scientist and citizen automator—and Alteryx proponent—is Daniel Young. He refers to himself as an "actuarial data whisperer," "complex model translator," and "data democracy champion," although his actual job title is "Senior Manager, Risk Data Analytics and Modeling." He works at Haventree Bank, a residential mortgage bank in Canada. It's a relatively small bank but is growing rapidly across the country.

Haventree doesn't have a data science or AI department, but it still needs to make credit and risk decisions based on data, analytics, and algorithms. Young can create and interpret the loss models that the bank uses—typically based on regression analysis, which he learned in college and his MBA—but those models need data from different locations within the bank as well as from outside it. The bank's mortgages increase in risk, for example, with the natural disasters (fires, floods, tornadoes) that have

---

[10]"Congratulations to our customer Sky," Pienso website blog post, Sept. 1, 2023, https://pienso.com/congratulations-to-our-customer-sky.

befallen Canada in recent years or with falls in oil prices in Alberta. The loss models are increasingly a combination of financial intelligence and geospatial intelligence.

Young has led the initiative to employ Alteryx to create automated data workflows for risk models—and to develop the models too, which Alteryx can also do. Young has employed the workflows and models for ongoing risk management and also for special requests for data by regulators that needed to be addressed quickly. He says that the data workflows his team has built have saved 4,500 hours a year, and the work plan for this year can save another 4,000 hours annually. The team's work with rapid data workflows has also mitigated significant financial risks by enabling timely compliance. Young is also confident that if the Haventree IT organization had done the data workflows themselves, not only would they have taken much longer, they would have cost the bank hundreds of thousands more. Young has led the creation of a small Alteryx user group at the bank, and its application has spread to the financial reporting and planning/analysis teams.

Daniel Young's example nicely illustrates the blended nature of citizen development. He's a citizen data analyst and scientist, a citizen automator, and a citizen low-code/no-code application developer all at once—and a citizen development champion as well.

How Can Citizen Data Scientists Work in Data Science Teams?

In most cases today, data scientists are not unicorns who work alone on all aspects of a data science problem. Instead, they work on teams that may include not only professional data scientists but also data engineers, machine learning engineers, business/technology translators, data product managers, and the like. Citizen data scientists may play any of these roles except for professional data scientists (in which case they would no longer be citizens), and they may even perform aspects of the official data scientist role at times.

At 84.51°, for example, there have been citizen data scientists on staff for several years. They go by various titles; Amanda Woodly, for example, is a solution design consultant. They typically work on teams with a variety of skills involved; some could be described as citizen data scientists, but some are technology or analytical professionals of various types. For example,

Carrie Jones, the VP of solution leadership at 84.51°, describes her team-oriented role on LinkedIn this way:

> . . .responsible for leading and developing a cross-functional team of data scientists, insight analysts, and consultants to roll-out a best-in-class customer-centric assortment and space optimization, machine learning forecast, in-store inventory management science, and out-of-stock metric development. Guides team in implementing highly effective solutions that directly impact Kroger's assortment range, shelf presence, and in-stock position across all the Kroger stores and e-commerce offerings. Recognized subject matter expert on customer insights and data, retail merchandising, and inventory management.

These are not unimportant problems that Jones is describing; they are heavily involved in Kroger's success as a company. Many of the problems that these teams address are also large in scale. For example, the primary forecasting algorithm used by Kroger creates a sales forecast for every item (SKU) in every store every night. That's a problem that requires not only an accurate algorithm but also a lot of computing power. It shouldn't be the province of (only) amateurs to create and deploy, which is why 84.51° uses these multifaceted teams.

One important attribute of organizations in facilitating citizen data scientists is to respect the existing skills they have while offering them new ones. Citizen data scientists at 84.51° are hired in part because of their ability to understand and communicate about data and analytics-related business problems, but they can also develop skills in the area of model creation. They can take courses in automated machine learning and are sometimes invited to participate in modeling competitions using those tools. Nina Lerner, a professional data scientist who has worked with citizen data scientists at 84.51°, said in an interview that

> I have helped trained insights scientists [the term used at the company for citizen data scientists at the time] to use automated machine learning and use our model development process. There is more hand holding involved than when I work with people with strong statistical backgrounds. But "subject matter engineering"—really understanding the

business problem—always adds the most value in any modeling exercise. Our insight analysts tend to do more explaining to Kroger stakeholders about what value our data and models are providing. They know what questions a client might want answered and they create stories to explain the model outcomes.

How Will the Citizen Data Scientist Role Evolve Over Time?

We can think about the evolution of (true) citizen data scientists over time at both the individual and organizational levels. From the individual perspective, citizen data scientists have a variety of career alternatives.

- They can learn more about data science methods and tools over time and eventually become professional data scientists. This would probably require some additional credentials—a master's degree in data science or statistics, for example—as well as the accumulation of data science skills gained from working on projects.
- They could move into the IT function and focus on the technical or engineering aspects of data science—most likely the integration of data science models into existing technology architectures or perhaps the evaluation of AI offerings of vendors.
- They could adopt less technical approaches to making data science successful, such as specializing in business/technology translation. Although this has been labeled by McKinsey authors a "must-have role" in data science,[11] a more successful role in our view is that of the data product manager, who can perform some translation activities but is also responsible for bringing a data science project to production deployment and ongoing use.[12]

---

[11] Nicolaus Henke, Jordan Levine, and Paul McInerny, "You Don't Have to Be a Data Scientist to Fill This Must-Have Analytics Role," *Harvard Business Review*, Feb. 5, 2018, https://hbr.org/2018/02/you-dont-have-to-be-a-data-scientist-to-fill-this-must-have-analytics-role.

[12] Thomas H. Davenport, Randy Bean, and Shail Jain, "Why Your Company Needs Data Product Managers," *Harvard Business Review*, October 13, 2022, https://hbr.org/2022/10/why-your-company-needs-data-product-managers.

They could also move into business-only roles, but applying their citizen data science skills to making data- and analytics-based decisions. It seems likely that if the citizen data scientist capability is popular within companies, then it will be advantageous to disaggregate the role to some degree and describe the key elements and skills of citizen data science as well as citizen data analyst. Then the different roles related to citizen data science—and there will probably be more than what we have just described—can be described in terms of the data scientist/analyst elements and skills that are necessary in that role. Some companies, such as TD Bank, have done that type of disaggregation for professional analyst and data science roles, and it would be straightforward to extend it to citizens.[13]

From an organizational perspective, we expect that citizen development in many organizations will become pervasive. Remember, for example, the training that BMW was supplying to its 80,000 white-collar workers. Presumably a substantial number of them will become citizen data scientists or at least citizen data analysts.

Some degree of citizen data science is already fairly pervasive in some organizations, such as 84.51°. Lyndsey Padden, who oversees technical talent strategy for data science at the company, told us that virtually everyone they hire has some degree of quantitative focus when they are hired, and many develop more of that over time. That's at a data science company, but Padden said that there are also many educational offerings within the much larger Kroger organization that involve building data and analytical literacy. She expects that both forms of citizen and hard-core data analyst or scientist roles will eventually be quite common at 84.51° and Kroger alike.

As generative AI and other technologies mature, we expect that it will be routine for people to request complex machine learning models with a simple prompt. We also expect that some of the guidelines, guardrails, and governance approaches that are today necessary with data science—typically supplied by human professional data scientists—will be incorporated into AI systems. They could then warn citizens that their model is overfitted, that the algorithm type is inappropriate for the data set, or that the trained model

---

[13]Thomas H. Davenport, "How Large Companies Can Grow Their Data and Analytics Talent," *MIT Sloan Management Review*, Nov. 18, 2020, https://sloanreview.mit .edu/article/how-large-companies-can-grow-their-data-and-analytics-talent.

is not powerful enough at predicting to be worthy of production deployment. We're not far from this being possible today, and we're in the very
early days of generative AI and its application to data science.

If this all comes to pass, the term *citizen data scientist* will no longer be
necessary. Every citizen will effectively possess the same ability to create and
interpret statistical models as today's best human data scientists. At that point
there will be no further purpose to make a distinction between professionals and amateurs. Indeed, at that point there may no longer be a need for
professional data scientists.

7 | The Skills and Personality of Citizens

This chapter is intended for people who want to be citizens, as well as those within organizations who are responsible for identifying or creating more of them. It's especially for you if you've read this far and you're asking whether you have what it takes to be a citizen developer, automator, or data scientist. The short answer is probably "yes," because you clearly have an interest in the subject and the motivation to pursue it. Let's first take a look at the likely future of work and what will be required to be a successful worker in that future.

Workers of the Future, in the Future of Work

The fear that AI is coming for our jobs is a common theme, even if workers have so-called future-proof digital skills. We are relatively optimistic that most humans will not lose their jobs but rather that they will increasingly work alongside AI instead of being replaced by it.[1] That belief is captured in

---

[1] Thomas H. Davenport and Steven Miller, *Working with AI* (MIT Press, 2022).

a phrase we've begun to hear quite often—some variation of "AI won't take your job, but someone working with AI will." We're not sure how often that will happen, but in citizen development and other job domains, we do believe that AI and related tools will make workers more productive and effective. We didn't find any examples in our research of substantial layoffs resulting from automation, AI, or any other tools we explored.

However, at a minimum there will be job change from AI. In the book *The Work of the Future*, which arose out of a broad research project on AI and the labor force by MIT faculty, the authors begin with the following observation:

> No compelling historical or contemporary evidence suggests that technological advances are driving us toward a jobless future. On the contrary, we anticipate that in the next two decades, industrialized countries will have more job openings than workers to fill them, and that robotics and automation will play an increasingly crucial role in closing these gaps. Nevertheless, the implications of robotics and automation for workers will not be benign. These technologies, in concert with economic incentives, policy choices, and institutional forces, will alter the set of jobs available and the skills they demand.

Most of the citizen developers we have interviewed are doing their best to adapt to AI and other forms of technological change. Stevie Sims, a productive citizen developer at Shell, told us, "I don't see my next job being a traditional role that exists today. The way things are exponentially changing around us, it's hard to conceptualize traditional roles." We agree with Stevie. The detailed nature of the work of the future is somewhat hard to pin down. However, we believe we may have better luck forecasting the personality traits, mindset, and skills that will set up citizens and other types of employees for success, no matter the details of new jobs.

While there is no one specific profile of automation-resistant citizens, there are many common traits and telltale signs that combine to suggest that an individual is right for the journey. In the following sections we describe three areas—personality traits, mindset, and skills—that combine to create the archetype of the citizen.

Personality Traits of a Citizen Developer

While searching for common citizen prototypes, we found characteristics in the medium in which we all seem to signal our interests and strengths these days—our LinkedIn profiles. The following is an anonymous profile of a senior business analyst. It's not important where this person lives, who they work for, or what their specific demographic traits may be. What is important is the personality and skills mentioned in the profile.

> "With over 6 years of experience in business analysis and engineering, I specialize in supply chain processes. I am passionate about analyzing business problems and building solutions that streamline operations, enhance efficiency, and save costs. I hold certifications in Data Science, Google Business Intelligence and MS Power Platform."

A few things stand out. The profile does not use the term *citizen developer*. That it doesn't appear may be due to a lack of familiarity with the term. The individual is a business analyst, working in the "business," not the IT department. The person is a domain expert in a particular area—in this case, supply chain processes. The citizen is an expert in platforms that facilitate the development of solutions using low- and no-code technology—in this case, those provided by Google and Microsoft.

Passion

What drew our eye was this individual's self-reported "passion" for analyzing problems and building solutions. This may seem like an over-the-top embellishment, geared toward future employers. But when we spoke to enough of these people, we realized that "passion" is exactly the right word for it. Citizens truly love defining and solving problems.

Their passion stands out as an indispensable trait for citizen developers. Not merely an enthusiasm or love of technology and new tools, it is a profound drive to bring their creativity to work every day and solve problems as a mission. These are people not afraid to be innovators and to transform challenges into opportunities.

These passions are of great value to organizations, but they can also make a citizen hard to manage. They want to do more than their job description warrants. Some may interpret this passion as disruptive or dis-tracting. Or a citizen's drive to solve problems and do more can be har-nessed as a way to achieve value. Interpreting whether a passion is misplaced is up to the leadership and management teams on the ground. But, while perhaps more of a "handful" than the regular rank-and-file, these passionate citizens are the ones who bring the spark with them.

Instilling motivation in someone to be a citizen developer appears to be less successful. Citizens aren't assigned this role; they volunteer for it. As related to us by Philip Lakin, cofounder and CEO of NoCodeOps, a com-munity and automation management platform, "Recruiting citizens doesn't work. You have to attract them."

Curiosity and Willingness to Learn

The next trait we observed most frequently—often combined with passion—was a tenacious curiosity and desire to learn. In a discussion with Amanda Woodley, a citizen developer at Kroger's 84.51° data analysis busi-ness unit, she described her motivation for the role as follows:

> "My career path led me [to citizen development] because I was curious and wanted to know what's driving decisions. I am a synergistic, holistic brain person. I have had to understand how systems, processes, people, and vendors all connect."

It's curiosity like this that drives one to question the status quo—the current workflow or business process, the current technology, the current strategy. This natural inquisitiveness, if enabled, leads to a deeper under-standing of complex systems and an ability to identify gaps or potential improvements that may not be evident at a surface level.

Of course, enterprise leaders and their decisions and actions contribute to making such a culture possible. But the best way to realize such behaviors is to hire people with those traits and enable them to practice them at work each day—a bottom-up phenomenon.

An insatiable desire to understand the "how" and "why" behind each process and activity in an organization and a relentless pursuit to apply that knowledge creatively in daily work are difficult to teach. As Max Cheprasov, until recently the chief transformation officer of Tinuiti, told us, "Not everyone is an explorer." If aspiring citizens can't explore, they're likely to go elsewhere to an organization that values their personality.

Perseverance and Grit

A common theme in many of our discussions with citizens was scrappy perseverance. They make do with little or no support and even fewer resources. No one described this trait better than Michael McCullough, a successful citizen developer and champion at Amtrak when he said, "My journey in low-code started when I was in the military. We were asked to do the impossible with nothing—duct tape and bubble gum."

In other words, citizen developers often succeed thanks to their own tenacity and hard work, rather than the provision of resources and time from on high. Often that work takes place outside of regular hours. As shared by Renee Liu, head of citizen development at Jabil, of those in her organization, "Our employees were doing voluntary overtime. They had the customer in mind, and they wanted to do a good job."

Stevie Sims of Shell, whom we profiled in Chapter 3, "The Citizen Journey," said, "I was working my regular job [as an operator in a refinery], but also building apps on the side." There are citizens like these in departments across every enterprise. They bring their special brand of grit to challenges on a daily basis, often with little support. Michael McCullough of Amtrak, when asked how he learned to perform citizen development activities, replied, "Literally lots of YouTube, lots of coffee, lots of notes, and a lot of cussing."

Michael's perseverance paid off.

> "I figured out how to use this thing. What I loved about it was I could connect to any data source that I needed to. And that was the first time where I felt, here's something even though it's probably in its infancy, that is workable, it's doable. This is that one missing thing that I've always looked for, that now I can make something for me. I can scale it into a full-on production or enterprise application."

His grit paid off and sparked a high level of citizen development activity at Amtrak.

Creativity and Innovation

The aforementioned traits are critical to shaping the nature of a citizen willing to make things happen. The missing ingredient is the vision to choose the right activities to work on. This derives from the ability to ideate, innovate, and create.

The last decade has celebrated the concept of design thinking and its methodical way to conduct end-user assessments, creative brainstorms, ideation sessions, and rapid prototyping. This technique is certainly useful for successful citizen development. The Project Management Institute highlights design thinking in its Citizen Development Canvas, under the category titled "Project Delivery, Ideation 2.0." In that section, citizens are encouraged to "use collaborative tools and approaches to quickly generate and prioritize ideas and set the foundations for citizen development projects." We don't think it's necessary that citizens develop game-changing solutions at the beginning of the process. Often the iterative and evolutionary ideas they propose and prototype can set an organization on the right path.

Someone once described this form of iteration to Ian as "prototyping the future state." Indeed, creative and innovative citizens do just that with each new application, workflow, and model they develop. They turn ideas into real solutions that showcase new ways to get work done in a job function or department. Often this prototype serves to better inform an IT organization when they are ready to build more robust solutions that formalize and adopt features and capabilities that citizens wanted and built for themselves.

It's still too early to draw broad conclusions as to whether citizens are more creative than the average businessperson, but Alex Tsvayner, director of finance automation and analytics at S&P Global, believes they might be.

> "Citizen developers are usually folks that are more innovative and technically inclined and make up a fraction of employees in business teams. When they are left alone to innovate (and are supported by management and IT), they can do wonders!"

Mindset

In many discussions with citizens we had touched on mindset, including the discussion with Kristen, the "digital underwriter," mentioned in Chapter 3. She had what we call a "digital mindset," a positive orientation toward technology experimentation. Paul Leonardi and Tsedal Neeley have described this orientation in detail in their book *The Digital Mindset* (Harvard Business Review Press, 2022).

A mindset is not quite a trait or a skill; it's a way of thinking. Thus, we describe three additional forms of mindset (other than "digital") that we came across—entrepreneurial, computational, and hybrid—that are helpful for a large and stable citizen initiative.

Entrepreneurial Mindset

Entrepreneurs are attributed with having a mindset that allows them to see the big picture, be solution-oriented, able to identify how to add value, and ready to pivot when things don't work out. This holistic view is, no doubt, rare—to say nothing of a willingness to take on the risks of starting something new.

To be an entrepreneur is to be the opposite of a perfectionist. It's a "good enough" approach that goes well with being a citizen developer. Entrepreneurs often embrace the idea of a "minimum viable product" or MVP—an offering that provides value for customers, but isn't complete or polished. That concept is quite consistent with the types of apps, workflows, and models that citizen developers build. They are good enough to get the job done without being anyone's idea of perfection or elegance.

To be an entrepreneur also means, almost by definition, that you don't fit into traditional corporate cultures. Nor does an entrepreneur necessarily want to fit in. Early citizen developers report feeling this way. One such person told us, "I remember one day I was talking to my boss and I said to myself, "Why is it that I just don't feel like I fit into one space?" To his boss' credit, she said, "Because that's not your calling. That's not your journey. Your journey is to see the big picture, the big broad spectrum. You can identify with leadership, but at the same time, you also can understand individual people and how to solve their problems."

Of course, most citizen developers do not set out to start their own businesses. Instead, they set their sights on making change happen within their functions and departments. These "intrapraneurs" are primarily focused on solving problems, creating value, and developing solutions for their colleagues, channel partners, and customers.

We had the privilege of studying both intrapraneurial and entrepreneurial Citizen developers. We profiled several entrepreneurs in Chapter 3 on "The Citizen's Journey," including Christian Peverelli (WeAreNoCode), Heidi Ojha (Aware Health), and Antigoni Kourou (Nekod). All possess an entrepreneurial mindset and help others who do as well. We've described many more intrapreneurial citizens throughout the book.

Computational Mindset

There are several forms of mindset that came up in discussions and in our research. Some were around the ways a person approached a challenge, instead seeing it as an opportunity. Other mentions of mindset were geared toward how one analyzed and took on a complex situation. One such example of this is highlighted in training provided by UiPath in their "RPA Citizen Developer Foundation Course."

One of the strongest advocates for citizen development, UiPath, has long championed the "one robot for every person" narrative—asserting that automation is easy enough for everyone to be able to train and collaborate with it, as a form of digital assistant in their work.

In their training, UiPath specifically calls out that being a citizen developer can be quite challenging, and to face these challenges one needs to bring the right mindset. In the unit titled "Thinking Like a Citizen Developer," they refer to the mindset needed as *computational thinking*. Their definition breaks this concept down into four key techniques: decomposition, breaking problems into smaller, more manageable parts; pattern recognition, finding similarities between and within problems; abstraction, filtering out irrelevant details; and algorithm design, developing a set of rules for solving the problem.

This is a more comprehensive mindset and one that we feel is capturing both approach and a series of skills necessary to decompose, recognize patterns, abstract, and design. Nevertheless, the concept is a strong one and certainly a useful component to any citizen development training program.

Hybrid Mindset

One final mindset to discuss is really a combination of mindsets. The primary concept of citizen development is that people who are experts in their own roles or functions can also play technology-oriented roles to which they are not officially assigned. For instance, an HR transaction agent in a shared service center can also be an application developer or data scientist. One part of this role requires that they know the skills and mindsets required to perform their official job description. The other part of the mindset is to think and act like the voluntary persona into which they are stepping.

We have heard from many of the citizens we interviewed that the success of citizen development requires that they "think like" the person who usually inhabits the role they are assuming. They may not be IT professionals, but they need to think like them—at least to some degree. This might include, for example, identifying and designating a backup citizen to be knowledgeable about and responsible for a citizen-developed application if the original creator is no longer accessible for some reason.

The key attitude profiles we hear most often are that people developing apps, integrations, or data models must think like a risk officer, a customer advocate, a manager, or an executive. While it's a high bar to ask that any one person thinks like others—especially for roles with which they have no experience—at least some of the desired thoughts and actions are not from, as they say, nuclear physicist or astronaut jobs. Common sense and an ability to imagine oneself in someone else's shoes is often all that's necessary.

Some organizations have institutionalized the idea of hybrid mindsets. They seem most common in science and healthcare organizations like Mayo Clinic and Johnson & Johnson, but we've also encountered them in engineering-oriented companies like Shell and Arcturis, and even in law firms. We expect that they'll become more common and that organizations and individuals will begin to cultivate hybrid mindsets.

Skills of the Future

We began with citizens' personality traits because it's hard to train for them—they're more "nature" than "nurture." We also discussed that there are ways in which citizen developers think and approach a situation—mindsets. Now, assuming you see yourself (or people in your organization) in the series of traits and mindsets listed in this chapter, it's time to explore the skills necessary to succeed as a citizen developer.

Before we dive into the specific skills of the citizenry, let's begin with a review of those skills described as the skills of the future—sometimes called "21st-century skills." These skills are often presented as those capabilities that are critical for workers of the future to maintain their relevance and their jobs. They are frequently divided into soft and hard skills. They are also rarely accompanied with clear direction as to how one might attain or inculcate such skills.

One impressive skill compilation of this type is the World Economic Forum's (WEF) report on future jobs. The nearly 300-page report examines the changing landscape of work and the imperative to identify and prepare for shifting needs in employment globally. It forecasts that 44% of core job skills will change in the next five years. For some reason this was a decrease from the 57% they forecast in the same WEF report from 2020. Whatever the percentage might actually be, there is little doubt that jobs are changing. And, as outlined in Tom's work on AI-related skills with Julia Kirby in *Only Humans Need Apply* (Harper Business, 2016), workers must step up to the challenge.

An important step in doing so is to develop the right skills, not just any skills. The WEF report's authors list 26 skill areas, which they have divided into eight categories ranked in order of importance. The most important are cognitive and self-efficacy skills. Those skills in the physical ability and ethics (interestingly) categories rank the lowest. Specific skills rated most important within the categories include analytical thinking first, followed by creative thinking, resilience, flexibility and agility, motivation and self-awareness, and curiosity and lifelong learning. We would agree that these are important skills.

We'd also agree with the placement of technological literacy at number 6. Programming skills, however, rank a distant 20. With the advent of low-code/no-code and AI natural language coding, programming and programmers are just not as important as a result.

Skills of Citizen Developers

Having reviewed the entire catalog of those skills deemed necessary and future-proof, which are most critical to success in the citizen developer, automator, and data scientist roles? There are many possible ones to enumerate.

However, while we believe the topic of skills for citizen developers is an important one, we warn citizens and their organizations against excessively long skill lists. For example, one highly detailed list of required skills for data scientists includes 19 analytical skills, 9 "open-mindedness skills," 15 communications skills, 10 mathematical skills, 11 programming skills, and, if that weren't enough, an additional 26 "more data science skills."[2] Mastering the total of 90 skills would seem to be beyond even the most qualified professional data scientist.

Our research suggests that there are more than simply hard and soft skills to consider when finding and training a crew of empowered citizens, but not 90 different skills. We break these skills into four categories: domain specific, literacies, technical, and human.

Domain-Specific Skills

The current-day visionaries and titans of AI all appear to agree—the future belongs to those with specific domain expertise. Nvidia CEO and leather jacket-wearing darling of Wall Street, Jensen Huang, said this clearly in a presentation to the World Government Summit in Dubai in February 2024:

> "The people that understand how to solve a domain problem in digital biology or in education of young people or in manufacturing or in farming, those people who understand domain expertise now can utilize technology that is readily available to you. You now have a computer that will do what you tell it to do. It is vital that we upskill everyone, and the upskilling process, I believe, will be delightful."

Our citizen profiles across industries found examples of physicians, bricklayers, field service personnel, customer-care agents, and dozens more types of experts in their particular fields. Each possesses domain-specific skills that take study and experience to master. If they have the more generic citizen traits we discussed (creativity and grit, for example), then they may also have many ideas for how to do their work better.

What this group has historically lacked is technical know-how, creating an age-old gap between those who know the issue and those who build the

---

[2]Alison Doyle, "Important Job Skills for Data Scientists." *The Balance Careers* (June 3, 2019), https://www.thebalancecareers.com/list-of-data-scientist-skills-2062381.

technical solution to address it. The disconnect between the worker (often referred to as being on the "business" side) and the builder ("IT") has always been a root cause for IT/business friction. Agile methodologies tried to solve this with user stories, effectively a description of how a user gets value from a specific software feature. These were intended to inform the developer of what and why they were building applications. User stories are an effort to close the knowledge gap, but with citizen development the gap no longer needs to exist.

Building software-based solutions is soon to become a *de facto* part of many roles and jobs as technology increasingly becomes more human-oriented. As OpenAI founder and CEO Sam Altman predicted, "People will program a lot, but I think it'll be in a very different shape. Some people will program entirely in natural language."[3]

The citizens we interviewed were domain experts in their fields and often in several fields. What's more, many bring with them useful experiences through their education (both formal and self-directed), including doctors with analytics degrees, supply chain experts with user experience training, and more. Every effective citizen is an expert in something. With the right technology tools and encouragement, these experts can soar.

Literacies

It's tempting to jump now into the types of technical skills needed to build something. But, building a foundation on which to set those skills is a better, and more sustainable, first step. Laying that foundation is exactly what we see enterprises doing across the globe. We think of this as establishing a level of literacy in the key domains that make up the work of the future. The themes are data, analytics, and digital.

Data Literacy   The concept of data literacy is mentioned by many pundits and company learning and development people, but it often lacks precision and rigor. Fortunately, the idea has been explored in some detail by Usama Fayyad and Hamit Hamutcu (of the Institute for Experiential AI at Northeastern University), who cofounded the Initiative for Analytics and

---

[3] Sam Altman, "OpenAI CEO on the Future of Programming," clip from the Lex Fridman podcast, YouTube, March 25, 2023, https://www.youtube.com/watch?v=L_Guz73e6fw.

Data Science Standards (IADSS), to research and publish on data skills and professions. Hamutcu is also a cofounder of a company called Elements, focused on data skills assessment. They've created a concept called the data citizen, not to be confused with citizen data scientist or citizen developer, that's described in an IADSS research paper.

> ". . .we introduce the term 'Data Citizen' to designate individuals with the data literacy skills as defined within our framework. We would like to clearly differentiate this from a similar term already used within the industry, 'citizen data scientist'... This term is used to describe professionals who use tools and techniques that allow them to perform advanced data science and analytics tasks without necessarily possessing advanced skills and knowledge in this domain. In our definition, a Data Citizen is an inclusive term that can be applied to any professional within an organization, with core data literacy skills to be effective and efficient in their own line of work, i.e., using data to make better decisions. It does not require that such a person will be using tools of data science or analytics."

They propose three levels of data citizens (data citizen, data citizen+, and data citizen^2), each with a different set of skills. We won't enumerate all of them, but data citizen skills include critical thinking, going from business problem to data problem, basic arithmetic, spreadsheets, interpreting data visualizations, and familiarity with data security, data privacy, and AI ethics. Following the progression of these increasingly more advanced skillsets, some might choose to go beyond data literacy and become data professionals, e.g., data analysts or data scientists. But we, like Hamutcu and Fayyad, believe that these skills can be acquired by amateurs as well as professionals and that citizen developers should attempt to gain as many as possible. We expect that leading-edge organizations will eventually adopt these or similar skill categorizations and assessments of them and that highly skilled "data citizens" will be empowered to do sophisticated data modeling activities.

Analytics Literacy   The idea that much contemporary work and jobs require quantitative skills isn't new. The entire science/technology/engineering/math (STEM) movement in education (from elementary schools to colleges) is based on that assumption. Such skills are particularly important to citizen data analysis and science but are broadly relevant to other types of citizen developers (and "data citizens") as well.

In addition to their work on data citizenship, Fayyad and Hamutcu have also devoted considerable attention to the issue of data science skills. We won't replicate their work here, but we believe it is the most thorough approach to the topic. A few companies—TD Bank, for example—have developed categorization and classification schemes for their employees' analytics and data science skills. At TD, it was no minor effort, involving 7 job families, 65 different roles, 16 competencies, and a classification of 2,000 people. Still, we believe that more organizations need to do this type of classification and that clarity of skill requirements to perform data analysis and science work would make it easier for citizen data scientists to train for and undertake it. A few companies, like Johnson & Johnson, have begun to use AI to assess employee skills to guide personal development of employees and organizational workforce planning.[4]

However, recent research by the Burning Glass Institute suggests that data science skills are relevant to a large number of jobs in the United States. In a report suggestively titled "Data Science is for Everyone,"[5] the research found that nearly a quarter of U.S. jobs required at least one data science skill, including less data-intensive roles and those that don't require college degrees. The researchers also advanced their own categorization of data science skills, grouped into "getting the data," "exploring and analyzing the data," and communicating results. We would argue that many of these skills are a better fit with "citizen data analyst" roles than data scientist roles, but some of those data science skills are included as well.

This research implies strongly that citizen data analysis and science roles are increasingly popular, that they are becoming mainstream jobs in sophisticated economies, and that organizations should enumerate and assess the types of data analysis and science skills in which they are interested. We're

---

[4] Nick van der Meulen, Olgerta Tona, and Dorothy Leidner, "Resolving workforce skills gaps with AI-powered insights." *MIT Center for Information Systems Research* (April 18, 2024), https://cisr.mit.edu/publication/2024_0401_DigitalTalent Transformation_VanderMeulenTonaLeidner.
[5] Burning Glass Institute, "Data Science Is for Everyone," Research report, March 20, 2024, https://www.burningglassinstitute.org/research/data-science-is-for-everyone.

not sure that it's helpful to refer to all data-related skills as "data science skills," but that may help to draw attention to them.

Digital Literacy Defining *digital literacy* requires us first to define what *digital* means, and that's no small feat. It could apply to virtually everything humans have done with computers since the 1950s or so. It's even harder to define what any particular enterprise means by it; sometimes it's marketing, sometimes it has to do with operations, sometimes it's all of the above. Most dictionaries don't define the term; Wikipedia defines it as "an individual's ability to find, evaluate, and communicate information using typing or digital media platforms" (we find the "typing" reference somewhat odd). In an enterprise, digital literacy encompasses an employee's ability to capitalize on an ever-expanding toolkit of software solutions including cloud-based tools, analytics, automation, and more. The definition may not be clear, but enterprises are clearly racing to upskill large swaths of their staff to be more digital, or at least to declare that they are doing so.

To supply these capabilities, some of the world's largest services firms are offering to upskill employees and develop a broad "DNA" of those skills and behaviors deemed to be critical for organizational survival. Many learning and development departments the world over have established digital curricula, are running digital days of learning, and are working hard to teach employees how to use everything from Microsoft Office 365 and the Power Platform to tools like RPA and, increasingly, GenAI co-bots and digital assistants.

Accenture, a services firm with more than 740,000 employees, is making major investments in digital literacy. In March 2024, Accenture made public a $1 billion investment in the launch of LearnVantage, an AI-powered learning platform designed to help clients upskill their workforces. In the same press release, they also announced the acquisition of Udacity. Founded in 2011, Udacity was one of the earliest massive open online course (MOOC) platforms, with courses in topics including programming, analytics, and AI.

Courses like Udacity's are also found on other platforms such as Coursera, Udemy, Edx, and LinkedIn Learning. Courses in basic digital awareness can create a "white belt" level of knowledge in a broad set of relevant topics. For some this will lead to further study and experience in digital topics.

Ian has created several such courses on the LinkedIn Learning platform, introducing such topics as RPA and intelligent automation, process mining and discovery, and conversational AI. In the last several years, he has seen a significant increase in enrollment from large organizations that include his courses in their digital literacy curricula. It is clear that billions of hours are being spent watching such introductory courses (he's told by LinkedIn Learning that 387,000 hours have been spent watching his alone; unfortunately, he's not paid by hours watched).

We'll explore the efficacy of such training courses in more detail in Chapter 15, "Guidance." However, focusing on literacy in data, analytics, and digital technologies is one visible way in which enterprises are signaling that they take this transformation seriously. We agree that such skills are important, so it's encouraging to see the emphasis. However, to actually build applications, automations, and data models, an introductory level of literacy is not enough.

Technical Skills

Thanks to low and no-code tools, and the inevitability of more human language–oriented prompting, the technical bar for citizens gets lower with each passing day. Nevertheless, there are a few technical skill categories that came up in our research that are worth considering in any selection criteria, or training curriculum. They are as follows, structured by the three primary types of citizen developers we've discussed throughout the book:

Citizen Application Developer

- **Low-code/no-code platforms:** Understanding how to use common platforms allows for the creation of applications and automation workflows with minimal coding.
- **Basic programming knowledge:** While not always necessary, knowing the basics of languages such as Python, JavaScript, or HTML/CSS can be beneficial for customization beyond the capabilities of no-code tools.
- **Database management:** Familiarity with database concepts and simple querying languages like SQL can help in managing data, integrating applications with existing databases, or setting up new databases.

- **API integration:** Knowledge of how application program interfaces (APIs) work enables the use of various software tools and systems to extend the functionality of created applications.

- **Process mapping and automation:** The ability to understand and map out business processes, and knowledge of how to automate them effectively using digital tools, is helpful even for nonautomation projects.

- **Testing and debugging:** Basic skills in testing applications for functionality and usability, and identifying and fixing errors within the development environment, is helpful for more advanced citizen developers.

Citizen Automator

- **Understanding of RPA tools:** Familiarity with RPA software like UiPath, Blue Prism, Automation Anywhere, or Power Automate is critical, including knowing how to navigate these platforms and use their features to create bots.

- **Process mapping:** Even more than for citizen application developers, an ability to clearly understand and map business processes that are candidates for automation is critical. This includes identifying inputs, outputs, and detailed steps involved in a process. Increasingly it also involves knowledge of process improvement methods like Lean and Six Sigma.

- **Logical thinking and problem-solving:** Skills in logical reasoning are essential to structure workflows effectively and solve problems that may arise during the automation process.

- **Basic programming knowledge:** While not strictly necessary, understanding the basics of programming languages such as Python or VBScript can help in scripting complex actions within RPA tools.

- **Integration skills:** Knowledge of how to integrate RPA bots with different databases, applications, and systems using APIs or direct integration methods helps with incorporating automations into the broader IT architecture.

- **Testing and debugging:** Ability to test automated workflows for accuracy and efficiency, and to debug any issues that arise during the execution of tasks, is helpful with automation projects as well.
- **Data manipulation:** Understanding basic data handling techniques, including data extraction, entry, and processing, is useful because many RPA projects involve manipulating data across various formats and sources.

Citizen Data Analyst/Scientist

- **Data manipulation tools:** Proficiency in using tools like Excel, Google Sheets, and especially data manipulation languages such as Python or R for handling and analyzing large data sets is important for preparing data before analysis.
- **Statistical analysis and modeling:** Understanding of basic statistics and the ability to apply these concepts using tools to derive insights or make predictions from data is useful for citizen data analysts and critical for citizen data scientists.
- **Data visualization:** Skills in using visualization tools like Tableau, Power BI, or even Python libraries to create understandable and actionable charts and graphs is a core activity of data analysts.
- **Machine learning methods:** Citizen data scientists should be aware of key issues in creating predictive machine learning models, including dealing with missing data, model training, feature engineering, setting aside data for testing, and scoring/inference. They should also be familiar with typical mistakes such as overfitting or inappropriate feature types.
- **Machine learning platforms:** Familiarity with automated machine learning platforms like Google's AutoML, DataRobot, or Microsoft Azure Machine Learning is useful in building predictive models and managing them over time.
- **Decision-making methods and approaches:** Data analysis and science are typically used for making decisions, so citizens in this area should be aware of such decision approaches as decision trees, optimization, and predictive modeling.

In addition, all citizen roles will greatly benefit from the following:

■ **Compliance and security:** Knowledge of regulatory and compliance standards relevant to the processes being automated, as well as basic security principles to protect sensitive data handled by bots, is critical for risk avoidance.

■ **Understanding of data governance and ethics:** Awareness of data privacy, ethical considerations, and regulations (like GDPR) is crucial when handling sensitive or personal data.

The previous list should serve as general guidelines for any organization or individual looking to develop citizen skills. Specific training is obviously the next step. For instance, skills in low or no-code technology is a starting point, but which specific tool? We won't make recommendations here because: a) the landscape is changing so fast that it's impossible to say what is the right choice by the time you're reading this; and b) the catalog of such tools is vast, and your specific function, industry, and role are known only to you. Your organization may have clear preferences for tools as well.

Human Relationship Skills

While technical skills are an absolute necessity, the key to any citizen's success will have just as much to do with the human relationship side—their "soft skills." Without such interpersonal skills, the citizen will struggle to define opportunities, communicate ideas, garner support, and engage with other end users for whom they might be building applications, data models, or automations.

Forecasts and market research confirm our beliefs. As noted earlier, the World Economic Forum placed a heavy emphasis on soft skills as some of the most relevant and important in the battery of 21st century skills. The importance of human skills is confirmed by research conducted by outsourcing and shared services analyst firm HFS Research. In asking what skills (or lack thereof) were standing in the way of enterprises adopting and leveraging modern capabilities, including generative AI, the missing capabilities were not the technical ones. Instead, of the 105 organizations polled, the skills in highest demand were instead problem solving, adaptability, and critical thinking. Developer skills were the least likely to be needed and lacking. There are many skills considered to be soft (or human) that citizens need to possess or develop. Even the most technological of projects ultimately end up being human endeavors. They succeed or fail based on the level of respect and emphasis given to the human elements of the program—inspiring trust by managers, understanding of what workers do today, upskilling of those doing the work, and so forth. Whereas the needed technical skills vary by the type of citizen, soft skills apply equally to all citizen types.

Even in those quantitatively oriented roles like data scientist, the ability to work well with people and inspire their trust is equally important. The highest performance falls to those comfortable with being "purple people"—equally comfortable in the technical and human domain.[6] As Jim Wilson, a data engineer at insurance company XL Catlin, put it,

> "The businesspeople, the actuaries, know what data they need and can define requirements, but typically don't have the skill set to design a data architecture that gives them the data they need. Technology people typically don't understand the business requirements, but they can design the data architectures. It's like the people in IT speak blue, the people in business speak red, but we need people who speak purple in order to create an appropriate solution."

Communication and Collaboration Skills   Strong communication skills are essential for citizen data scientists, developers, and automators. They all need to effectively convey recommendations and insights to numerous stakeholders, including those in IT, security, risk, and (of course) business management. Citizens must be able to explain the purpose of solutions and distill complex data and analysis in a clear, concise manner that nontechnical audiences can understand.

The Project Management Institute (PMI) found that poor communication is responsible for 30% of all failed professional IT projects. When citizen developers are involved, the importance of communications is heightened, and therefore, the ability to communicate well becomes all the more important.

---

[6]Thomas H. Davenport, "Purple People at the Heart of Cognitive Tech," *The Wall Street Journal CIO Journal*, January 7, 2016.

One key communication and collaboration skill is effective storytelling about both problems and potential solutions. Good storytellers tell stories with data, evidence, visuals, heroes, and occasionally even villains (not, we hope, senior management). Some of our most compelling interviews and profiles were not because the individual created the most impressive data model or application (who are we to judge), but instead because the person we spoke to spun a tale of intrigue, challenges faced, ideas dreamt up, solutions developed, and success achieved. No doubt, their stories have compelled their management to support them, to fund them, and to celebrate them as shining examples of grassroots innovation.

Many citizen initiatives rely on fusion teams (combinations of citizens and IT professionals), centers of excellence, communities of practice, support networks, or any number of other congregations of people from across a firm. For that reason, we can't stress enough the importance of being able to work effectively with other humans.

Political Skills   Just as in national and local politics, solitary citizens seldom achieve their goals. The most effective ones create broader campaigns, build coalitions, and make back-room deals. Unfortunately, many people who are highly intelligent and technically capable are not aware of or good at organizational politics. Citizen developers may feel that they can do what they want and improve their own productivity and performance without help from others. But they can accomplish much more if they manage politics well.

We're not talking about citizen developers as Boss Tweed or some other political schemer. But they need to realize when their solutions will threaten or be offensive to people with power (official or unofficial) in organizations. They need to share information wisely and selectively in order to make their case and secure the resources they require. The effective citizen can still be honest and aboveboard, but it's also important to realize that politics are the art of the possible, not the ideal.

The Final Tally

Ultimately, the jury is out on the percentage of people in any organization who have the personality and skills to be citizen developers or have an interest in becoming one. We posed this question to a citizen development leadership group, spearheaded by LCNC veteran Matt Hubbard, and attended by pioneers and champions of the movement from such firms as Amtrak, Shell, SiriusXM, and more. Their average estimate for large enterprises was 12%. It was slightly higher for smaller firms. Perhaps progressively easier technology will inspire the panel to raise their estimates.

8

The Citizen Champion: With and Without Air Cover

Perhaps not surprisingly for a citizen technology program that is largely voluntary, someone has to step up or be appointed as champion of the initiative. In our research we've found a number of champions and are able to describe their essential tasks and some differences between them. Perhaps the major difference is whether they have senior executive support.

To "cross the chasm" (to use the Geoffrey Moore term) of user and organizational adoption of citizen development, encouragement and resources for the concept from senior executives—ideally, all the way to the CEO—are necessary. You simply can't have large numbers of employees changing their jobs and workflows with technology without someone in the thick-carpet corner offices knowing about it and at least accepting what's happening. What we're really looking for is enthusiasm among senior executives about citizen technology usage, and we hope we've given plenty of reasons why they should be enthusiastic. In short, it's really hard to digitally transform an organization without it.

There are several different patterns we've noticed with regard to executive support. One is to start citizen development from the beginning with it.

That's obviously the most desirable situation as long as it doesn't lead to compelling people to work with technology in ways that they don't want to. Starting with executive support typically means more resources, faster development of guidance and governance approaches, and more rapid impact on organizational performance. So we'll discuss an example of that first.

Shell: High Air Cover

We've discussed the high degree of executive "air cover" at Shell. Jay Crotts, the chief information officer who came up with the idea of the "DIY" program there, was profiled in the preface. We've also mentioned Nils Kappeyne at Shell, who was the first official champion of the DIY movement at that giant oil (and eventually, we hope, renewable energy) company. Kappeyne was very effective at many of the key tasks that make citizen technology initiatives successful.

As a result, citizen development spread rapidly across the company, with boot camps and hackathons around the world. Kappeyne noted,

> There was a flywheel going on here. The businesses were excited about citizen development, the hackathons were very successful, that fed a hunger in our people, and we were able to translate abstractions about data into things people could do. It really boomed.

In a situation like that, the role of the champion is to move fast and stay ahead of the fast-moving train. Kappeyne was also instrumental in creating the "red, amber, green" governance approach that has proven successful at Shell and several other companies we've talked to. It also involved finding like-minded people to work in the "DIY Center of Excellence" that Shell established.

Noel Carroll and Mary Maher, in their case study on citizen development at Shell, argue that five things had to take place for the movement to be successful:

- Providing the components and platforms to enable citizen development
- Introducing a standardized operating model with safe boundaries
- Developing a citizen development culture and building people's capabilities

- Coaching and guiding employees to innovate and improve process efficiencies
- Establishing and nurturing citizen developer communities across Shell[1]

Those tasks are effectively the primary responsibilities of the citizen development champion in an organization with plenty of air cover.

Dentsu and Tinuiti: Air Cover, but Citizen Focus When Ready

Max Cheprasov has been a champion of citizen development for several years within the context of technology-enabled operational transformation. As the chief automation officer at the giant advertising and marketing agency Dentsu, his leadership was instrumental in establishing an Automation Center of Excellence (CoE) in 2017. This CoE united more than 450 automation champions, including more than 150 trained citizen developers, to collaboratively create several hundred automation solutions. These solutions, ranging from large-scale process overhauls to targeted improvements, demonstrated an overall average ROI of 800%. This initiative resulted in more than 500,000 hours of productivity gains within the first three years, marking a significant leap toward redefining workplace efficiency.

At Dentsu, Cheprasov and his team navigated a highly fragmented global enterprise, comprising myriad business functions, processes, systems, and platforms. This highly decentralized structure was typical for marketing and advertising agencies at the time, but clients were beginning to request more integrated and coordinated solutions. As a leader of the "One Dentsu" initiative, Cheprasov led the use of intelligent automation as a catalyst for change management, innovation, and streamlined operations.

But his primary focus and interests were in broad organizational transformation, so in 2022 he took a role at Tinuiti as chief transformation officer. Tinuiti was also a marketing and advertising agency, but it differentiated itself in the industry with an analytics and AI-based platform to help clients decide on the optimal level of marketing investment. At Tinuiti, Cheprasov initiated a comprehensive overhaul of the service delivery model involving meticulous categorization and documentation of standardized solutions, supported by

---

[1] Noel Carroll and Mary Maher, "How Shell Fueled Digital Transformation by Establishing DIY Software Development," *MIS Quarterly Executive*, June 2023.

uniform standard operating procedures. Cheprasov viewed it as the foundation for identifying further automation opportunities to streamline operations.

From a citizen standpoint, Cheprasov emphasized the importance of preparing Tinuiti employees for AI-powered solutions. With the emergence of generative AI in early 2023, he spearheaded the TRaiLBLAZERS initiative, equipping the entire organization with foundational AI and automation skills. His objective was to go beyond skill-building to a culture of innovation that would enable the organization to transition from manual processes to AI-powered operations.

This initiative involved a transformation in how employees approached their work. Through strategic deployments of generative AI tools such as Read.ai for summarizing conversations and creating insightful meeting notes and Zoom AI companion for enhancing virtual communications, Cheprasov accelerated the organization's journey toward digital transformation. Integrating generative AI capabilities into project management software Wrike revolutionized the team's project management processes, facilitating the effortless generation of project briefs, draft plans, and brainstorming sessions. Enhancements to Google Workspaces with Duet AI streamlined day-to-day operations by helping employees draft, organize, visualize, and accelerate workflows. In total Cheprasov's organization provided access to more than 50 generative AI tools. This arsenal of capabilities empowered employees to leverage AI for creative problem-solving, operational efficiency, and superior client outcomes.

Cheprasov's experiences at Dentsu and Tinuiti illustrate a crucial principle: irrespective of an organization's current state, AI-powered tools can significantly enhance business operations when applied thoughtfully and strategically. However, maximizing the benefits of AI in the long term and at scale requires a robust foundation including process excellence, an efficient and integrated systems architecture, high-quality data, and a company-wide mindset committed to incorporating AI and automation. This transformation equips everyone within the organization with digital assistants, streamlining processes and fostering a culture of continuous innovation and improvement.

Arcadis: Growing Air Cover Over Time

But extensive executive support from the beginning is actually pretty rare. We haven't found it in most companies. Instead, the citizen development champion starts with few resources and little visibility and slowly builds community and capability over time. A great example of that champion role is illustrated by Freek Matheij, who is now "global citizen development, low-code & AI platforms director" at Arcadis. The company is a large (36,000 people working across 30 countries) engineering, design, and construction firm that takes on about 40,000 projects a year.

Matheij said that he has been attempting to grow citizen development as part of the broader Arcadis digital transformation since 2018 with the objective to "dare to be digital." He said that the movement has been "successful in terms of awareness but not that successful yet in terms of impact." He's a civil and structural engineer by training and worked for Arcadis for several years as a project manager. He started using low-code/no-code (LC/NC) tools himself and thought that they would be well-suited for use by the many engineers at Arcadis on their projects. He began to evangelize about citizen development but found that the IT organization considered it "shadow IT" and were not supportive of it. Eventually, however, he was pulled into IT to run the citizen development initiative.

Thus far, Arcadis has officially trained and certified only 500 citizen developers, using Pluralsight as their main upskilling platform. Matheij, however, says that he believes the company can eventually get up to many more, and there are already 4,000 citizens using the Power Platform tools. He's already set up standards, guidelines, guardrails, and security approaches and is planning to use gamification approaches to motivate more learning and tool use. Many engineers are already comfortable with programming, and since Matheij also directs AI usage at Arcadis, he believes that they will soon be using generative AI to prompt for the program code they would like to develop.

While Matheij is not yet happy with the scale and impact of citizen development, he is seeing signs of increased attention and "air cover." The company overall is strongly emphasizing the acquisition and use of digital skills, and developing digital products for customers is a strategic focus. Citizen development is mentioned several times in strategy documents for the company. The company's annual report even mentions how many "Arcadians" have been trained in citizen development, and the initiative is described in the Executive Board report—perhaps the first section devoted to citizen development in any annual report.[2]

---

[2] Arcadis Annual Integrated Report 2022, published Feb. 16, 2023.

Quiet Growth in Citizen Development at Amtrak

Citizen development in some organizations is such a good idea—or the champion does such a good job—that it can prosper and grow without a lot of executive support. That's the case at U.S. quasi-public passenger rail company Amtrak. Since its inception in 1971, Amtrak has struggled to get sufficient funding to build and operate a high-quality train network, but it has had an easier time getting citizens to build systems.

Michael McCullough is the citizen development champion at Amtrak, and perhaps an unlikely one. He was a Navy intelligence officer for 15 years, was hurt in Afghanistan, and was in and out of hospitals for two years. In the military he learned, he said, to "use what you have and get the job done." He later worked in the health insurance industry and had a supportive boss, Sarina Arcari. She encouraged him to experiment and see the big picture, and she later brought him into Amtrak where she was head of enterprise program management.

At one point McCullough was asked to display all project expenditures from across the company in one dashboard. He tried several tools to pull together the diverse information sources and eventually discovered Microsoft Power BI. Arcari told him to take the time he needed to learn the system, and he was able to create a dashboard quickly. Members of Amtrak's Executive Board saw the dashboard, were impressed, and asked how and by whom it was created. McCullough himself loved the exercise; he thought to himself,

> This is that one missing thing that I've always looked for. I can make something for me. I can scale it into a full production enterprise application and get it into production.

The IT organization, however, was not impressed. They viewed it as "shadow IT" and insisted that it be shut down. Executive board members, however, insisted that it be turned back on. That was the beginning of citizen development at Amtrak, although the company has 24,000 employees, and the sole citizen tool was one Power BI license.

McCullough continued working on a small scale until COVID hit, and Amtrak needed a quick solution to track the impact of the pandemic on employees and facilities. IT said that it could come up with a prototype in six weeks. McCullough worked for 12 hours and brought in a prototype the next day. When the word got out about the citizen-developed application, it "started the revolution," according to McCullough.

Demand for citizen capabilities soared, and the IT function was inundated with requests. So they brought McCullough over to coordinate the activity from within IT. But IT placed a number of stipulations and restrictions on how citizen development could operate at Amtrak. McCullough—not one to follow rules he doesn't agree with—ignored the restrictions for the most part. "People won't innovate with a 'you have to come to us' mentality from IT," he said. So he began the work of a citizen development champion in earnest, identifying tools, training, and events that would advance the movement. He spent a lot of time building relationships and communities across Amtrak, working with IT, security, and business units. He built a great relationship, he says, with Microsoft and the Power Platform suite.

McCullough developed moderate governance approaches that could accommodate both innovation and responsible use (he calls it "bumper bowling"—if you get too close to the gutters, you get bumped back in). He has only a few hard-and-fast rules.

- Every application, workflow, dashboard, etc. needs two owners at all times (in case one leaves).
- All citizen developers and applications must comply with security restrictions (set in Power Platform with permissions).
- There has to be a way to contact the developers without leaving the application—a "contact me" or "leave feedback" button.
- All applications have to be updated at least quarterly.

Five years ago, there were three certified "makers" (McCullough's preferred term over "developers") at Amtrak. The day we interviewed him, the number had risen to 1152. There were four developed applications five years ago, and now there are 24,300. About 19,000 employees have used the products at one time or another. McCullough now holds monthly roundtable meetings for makers that address new products, an innovative citizen application, or particularly productive makers.

Amtrak doesn't have the kind of culture that makes highly visible announcements about things like citizen development. McCullough describes it as a "stay in your lane" approach. And the only way that McCullough has to recognize successful citizens is to recognize them at roundtable meetings or give them a particularly nice piece of Microsoft swag. But it's clear that Amtrak is getting considerable value from citizen development, and McCullough has the goal of saving every employee four hours per week. Citizen data analysis has evolved beyond dashboards to statistical and predictive models. Perhaps the ultimate sign of his success is that after five years of asking for someone to help him, he's getting another citizen development helper.

Lessons from Citizen Development Champions

After speaking with several citizen development champions, we've come up with a laundry list of things champions can do to make citizen development more successful. Each activity is described here:

- It's helpful if citizen developers come from the business side of their organizations (as opposed to IT), or at least have some experience in the organization's business domain. Having a background similar to other citizens makes them more relatable, and it may temper the IT-centric perspective that deterred many citizens over the years.

- Champions should seek executive support, but they shouldn't quit if it's not forthcoming. We haven't done a statistical analysis, but it appears that citizen development is far more likely to be successful if senior executives provide resources and moral support. That said, there are some examples of flying under the radar and still managing to grow citizen activity, so the lack of air cover shouldn't make any champion give up unless the situation is clearly hopeless.

- Not all citizen applications are created equal, so champions should create or borrow some type of categorization scheme for how to address different types of citizen applications. The "red, yellow/amber, green" one developed by Shell is a good one, and we've described other possibilities for enabling and governing citizen development in Chapters 13 through 16.

- Show value in economic terms if possible. Senior executives may like or dislike the concept of citizen involvement in technology, but they'll be much more likely to feel there is something in it for them if that something involves increased dollars, euros, yen, etc. Some companies, like Shell and Johnson & Johnson, have tried to measure the value of every citizen application.

- Citizen development champions are like cruise ship social directors. They pursue every means possible to get citizen developers talking to each other, exchanging ideas, and recruiting new citizens. These means may include face-to-face events, webinars, hackathons, newsletters, Slack channels, one-on-one buttonholing, and so forth.
- Citizens typically develop a lot of assets—code components, machine learning features, automation workflows, etc.—and it's important for champions to establish repositories for them such as a marketplace or hub. This isn't, unfortunately, just a matter of storing some content in a database or website; it needs to be documented to be useful.
- Good champions try to protect their organizations from harm while avoiding a heavy governance hand. They know that strict governance approaches will deter some citizens from getting involved or letting others know that they are developing stuff. They think of their roles as "enablement"—making it easy to do the right thing—rather than police officer.
- As we've argued, highly productive citizens may leave the company—or become among the dreaded "overemployed"—if their work and creativity isn't recognized by their organizations. Champions should try to create recognition and motivation mechanisms if possible and encourage successful citizens' departments to give them the promotions and compensation bumps they deserve.
- Champions should push for adoption of more sophisticated usage of technologies and methods. Well-established tools and approaches can create a lot of value, but they ultimately will lead to stagnation. At this point, for example, champions should be trying to get citizens to adopt generative AI instead of LC/NC tools, intelligent process automation instead of robotic process automation (RPA), and citizen data science instead of citizen data dashboards.
- If citizens are not in IT organizations, they need to get past the idea that IT is the enemy. They should build a partnership with IT and together work out approaches to ensuring great outcomes for citizens as well as the organization.
- Citizen champions mentioned to us their strong relationships with vendors of citizen-oriented software, and we think that is generally a good idea. Just remember that there are a lot of vendors out there, and working with only one (we're looking at you, Microsoft) may be limiting.

Of course, there are exceptions to all of these guidelines and reasons why they might not work well within a particular organization. But we've shown them to several of the citizen development champions we have researched and interviewed, and they generally agree with them.

The Long-Term Fate of Citizen Development Champions

There are likely to be a variety of different career paths for these champions over the long term. Some will undoubtedly return to the business domain side from whence they came (if they ever left it), and we hope and trust they will be rewarded for the increased productivity and performance they helped achieve for their organizations. Some will probably become champions for some new technology, such as augmented reality or quantum computing.

But if citizen development becomes the primary way in which organizations develop applications, workflows, and AI models, perhaps the citizen development champion will become the effective chief information officer or head of application development. Certainly an entire organization that's primarily reliant upon citizens for its IT would need to employ very different management approaches and skills than those we find in IT today. The community-focused skills of the champion might be an excellent fit for such a role.

In the meantime, we hope that citizen development champions stay with their roles for a while. A few of those we interviewed said that they thought the citizen movements in their organizations were self-sustaining at this point, but we expect some ongoing championing would still be useful if not absolutely necessary for most organizations venturing into this territory.

Getting to Work

9 | The Citizen Tech Landscape

Dr. Martin Luther King famously noted, "The arc of the moral universe is long, but it bends toward justice." In a far less profound and important—but still interesting—context, we'd argue that the arc of the information technology universe is long, but it bends toward citizens. Tom is getting up there in age, and he started his career in computing several decades ago by helping citizens do what we now call *data science*. Ian is substantially younger, but he's been working with citizen automation tools (or what became them) for more than two decades now. We've both seen considerable bending of the arc already.

In this chapter, we're not going to tell you about punched cards and living room—sized computers. But citizen enablement with technology has been happening for long enough so that there ought to be some lessons we can learn from it. We can also draw from trends taking place in other realms of information technology to explain and predict what's been happening with citizen-oriented tech. We'll also describe how the previously separate domains of citizen application development, citizen automation, and citizen data analysis and science are converging.

The earliest use of the word *computer* referred not to a machine but to a person who performed complex calculations—as at NASA in the triple Oscar-winning film *Hidden Figures*. It's possible that the shift to AI for

135

citizen development will be as momentous as the shift from human to machine-based computers. This is happening so rapidly that it is difficult to anticipate exactly what's going to happen. We'll try to take a forward-looking perspective in this chapter—particularly at its end—but that won't prevent it from becoming technically obsolete within a few years. Perhaps someone will pick up the book and read this chapter in 2030 and say, "How very quaint!"

Information Technology Is Important—Duh!

Human computers notwithstanding, we mostly focus on computing machines now. The evolution of information technology at work is a tale of innovation, disruption, some resistance to change, and trillions of dollars of investment. All of this has gotten us to the point where every company is a software company, every company is a digital company, every company needs to make data-driven decisions, etc. You've heard all this before, but the implication of this evolution over several decades is that it's now essential for every person—or at least most of them—within a business to be some form of software developer, able to do more than simply operate the applications they have been provided by benevolent IT departments. AI will accelerate this trend and make it both easier and more important for everyone to develop and use information technology capabilities. Enough said.

What Makes a Tool Citizen-Ready?

A brief discussion on what makes a software tool citizen-ready may be helpful. Citizen-oriented software is all of the following:

- Is easy to use, with little or no programming and/or a graphical user interface
- Offers a broad range of functionality
- Is consistent with the user's industry or functional knowledge in terminology and outcomes
- Makes it difficult for the user to get into trouble
- Quickly produces the desired solution
- Is able to take advantage of previous efforts by the user or by other citizens in the same organization, at least as a starting point
- Offers considerable online and offline support

- Is robust, functional, and compatible enough to be accepted and supported by the organization's IT department
- Ideally offers a path to scaling and hardening the solution for broader enterprise use
- Is not overly expensive to buy or access

These are a broad range of criteria, and it's not easy for software vendors to meet all of them. The attributes involving enterprise IT compatibility suggest that vendors of existing IT software have a distinct advantage in developing citizen capabilities over stand-alone citizen software vendors. This is perhaps one of the reasons why large enterprise software vendors—Microsoft, Salesforce, and to some degree Google and Oracle—are prospering with citizen-oriented tools. Technically focused companies such as Amazon Web Services (and Google to some degree) tend to be more focused on professional users (even though there are potentially many more citizens they could sell to) and don't generally produce the ease of use needed by citizens.

The Evolution of Programming Languages

Just how has IT evolved toward more citizen involvement? The history of software development and programming is toward greater degrees of abstraction and separation of software from computing hardware. The increased abstraction level of software can be seen not just with obtaining computing resources but in the programming code itself. It has gotten less computer-esque and more human-esque over time. Programming experts typically speak in terms of generations, although there is some debate about whether we are currently in the fifth, sixth, or even seventh generation.

Whatever number you assign to today's AI models for code generation, they are the state of the art and—at least when refined further—will represent a new capability in software abstraction. It's hard to see how to improve on what generative AI can do, at least once it gets rid of its hallucination problems. We are effectively at the point where we have fully abstracted computer programs from the specific hardware or lower-level languages that run underneath them. Even today a citizen can simply type what they want into a prompt window and get a computer application, a web page, a statistical analysis, or a graphic display of data. It doesn't get much more citizen-friendly

than that. Most no-code tools are less sophisticated but still are a long way
from having to program in a computer language.

Current Citizen Tools and Platform Landscape

The citizen technology landscape is a somewhat complex one. Not only are
there the three categories we've discussed of citizen application development,
citizen automation, and citizen data analysis/science, there are subcategories
within them. Furthermore, the whole group of technologies is changing
rapidly, particularly with the advent of generative AI. At a minimum, there
will probably be generative AI user interfaces to every tool in every category. As we've suggested, we'll do our best to describe the current technology
landscape, but you'll need to keep watching the space if you want to be
up-to-date.

Low-Code/No-Code Application Platforms for Citizen Development

Most general-purpose low-code application development platforms, as we
noted earlier in the book, are primarily intended to enhance the productivity of professional developers. However, before you dismiss this category
from your consideration list as a citizen, things have become a bit more
complicated.

First, many low-code platform vendors have developed easier-to-use,
point-and-click versions of their software that are intended for citizen usage.
They are often called "studio" versions. In addition, some vendors of low-
code solutions say they can be used by technically astute citizen developers
and suggest that there is code generation going on in the background of
both low-code and no-code systems. In other words, the distinction between
low-code and no-code often doesn't hold up under further examination. It
is only sometimes useful in selecting among different vendor offerings.

Regardless of those complexities, some of the leading general-purpose
low-code tools are Microsoft's Power Apps, Mendix (owned by Siemens,
which has broadly adopted both low-code professional and citizen development for its own purposes), Appian (which has a business process management and automation flavor), OutSystems, AirTable (which claims to be

both low-code and no-code, and is a database/spreadsheet hybrid), ServiceNow (which has a strong workflow flavor), and large, multipurpose software vendors like Salesforce and Oracle.

Note that some of these low-code tools have specific orientations such as workflow or database. In fact, there is a realm of special-purpose low-code tools for narrower technology objectives. They include tools for specific technology development of web pages (e.g., SquareSpace), project management (e.g., Quickbase), physical asset management, financial reporting, supply chain and logistics, etc.

Some of these same vendors are also mentioned in lists of the best no-code application platforms, adding to the confusion in this category of citizen tools. But some multipurpose tools such as Zapier, Bubble, Google AppSheet, Zoho Creator, AgilePoint, BettyBlocks, Creatio, and Kissflow advertise themselves only as no-code and specifically are aimed at citizen developers. There are narrow-purpose no-code tools for some of the same application types as low-code options.

Citizen Automation Technologies

A distinct feature of citizen automation is the broad tech stack available to the citizen. While citizen developers will often use a single low-code or no-code tool to develop an application with the intent of creating a defined capability, citizen automators must often build Rube Goldberg contraptions—deftly tying together the right tools to digitize each step of a workflow. Depending on the task at hand, automators select the tools necessary to "see," to "interpret," to "execute," or to "communicate"—each an important building block of an end-to-end process. Choosing the capabilities necessary to complete the workflows and processes at hand is part of the craft.

For example, in many work processes there is often a need to "see" documents (often PDFs, checks, or paper) to identify numbers and names. Decisions must then be made. Data must be retrieved, manipulated, and entered. The work must flow from one task to another. This was all more than any one tool could handle. The industry struggled with what to call this toolkit.

Eventually the overall automation toolkit became more commonly known as *intelligent automation*, regardless of how much intelligence it actually contained. People's LinkedIn job titles evolved from "RPA expert" to "intelligent automation expert"—clearly a step up. Robotic process automation (RPA) centers of excellence were rebranded as *intelligent automation centers of excellence*. Newsletters, consortia, and entire companies rebranded accordingly. Ian co-authored a book called *Intelligent Automation: Welcome to the World of Hyperautomation*. Hyperautomation was one of the many contending terms for the same concept. It was a term Gartner developed, and it seemed to mean "lots of automation." We don't think it adds much to the dialogue on automation tools.

The intelligent automation toolkit is thus an amalgam of capabilities, each with a role to play in automating business processes. Each role can be understood as emulating a human talent that we bring to work each day.

This array of capabilities described in Ian's *Intelligent Automation* book is defined as follows (Figure 9.1):

> Intelligent Automation combines methods and technologies to execute business processes automatically on behalf of knowledge workers. This automation is achieved by mimicking the capabilities that knowledge workers use in performing their work activities (e.g., language, vision, execution, and thinking & learning).

Each category has gone through a great deal of investment and evolution in the last decade, making the tools more capable and, in many cases, easier to use. As stated earlier, the crux of citizen automation is the combination of a number of these tools to digitize integrations, workflows, and rule-based decisioning that makes up a lion's share of the work being performed.

While capabilities in the thinking and learning and language categories tend to be more professional developer-oriented because of their technical complexity, the execution and vision tools are more accessible by citizens and make up a majority of the solutions addressed by citizen automation initiatives.

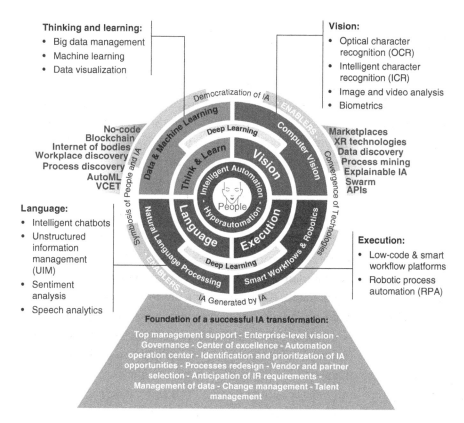

Thinking and learning:
• Big data management
• Machine learning
• Data visualization

Vision:
• Optical character recognition (OCR)
• Intelligent character recognition (ICR)
• Image and video analysis
• Biometrics

No-code
Blockchain
Internet of bodies
Workplace discovery
Process discovery
AutoML
VCET

Marketplaces
XR technologies
Data discovery
Process mining
Explainable IA
Swarm
APIs

Language:
• Intelligent chatbots
• Unstructured information management (UIM)
• Sentiment analysis
• Speech analytics

Execution:
• Low-code & smart workflow platforms
• Robotic process automation (RPA)

Foundation of a successful IA transformation:
Top management support - Enterprise-level vision - Governance - Center of excellence - Automation operation center - Identification and prioritization of IA opportunities - Processes redesign - Vendor and partner selection - Anticipation of IR requirements - Management of data - Change management - Talent management

Figure 9.1   The intelligent automation toolkit

Robotic Process Automation for Execution   Originally called "macros on steroids," RPA capabilities are the core to the citizen automation toolkit. Like macros, they allow a user to create scripts that execute clear transactional steps in a workflow. Unlike macros, RPA has the ability to interact with data across the full scope of an enterprise's systems portfolio. It can automate processes, for instance, that start with Microsoft Outlook, gather data via a Google Chrome browser, and enter said data into an enterprise resource planning (ERP) system (like SAP or Oracle). This gap filling and workflow execution is effectively gluing together systems.

Popular RPA tools include Blue Prism, UiPath, Automation Anywhere, Microsoft Power Automate, and a long list of other players. Some very recent start-ups promise to leverage the power of generative AI and large language models to disrupt more traditional industry leaders. They haven't yet succeeded but may eventually.

All of these execution tools were developed for the sake of making automation easier. The vendors themselves frequently emphasized ease of use, stressing the narrative that automating with this class of tools was "so easy a business analyst could do it." This citizen-focused marketing was emphasized further when several RPA vendors began to offer citizen-oriented versions of their software—again often with the "studio" term attached. In many cases, however, the chasm between business user skills and tool technical complexities were just too great. Attempts at "quick-starts' (for instance, getting a few members of an HR shared service team trained to configure automations) or "a robot for every person" all met similar fates. This was backed by numerous studies that showed, despite the hype and investment dollars generated, RPA was producing mixed results for organizations. In early studies by EY, 30–50% of projects were failing. A later study by Deloitte found that, of those that did succeed, a tiny fraction were able to scale. In the early days, RPA tools were just not easy enough to enable a true citizen automation revolution. They have become easier to use over time, however, and will no doubt become even more amenable to citizen automation when they add generative AI capabilities.

IDP: Helping RPA See   It is common for workflows to begin with an input. Often data in the form of PDFs, emails, attached spreadsheets, or other forms of information is what initiates a series of steps to identify, copy/paste, compute, and act on the information. Some such data comes into RPA already in machine-readable text or numbers, but other data is in more recalcitrant formats. The technology used to recognize alphanumeric characters on paper was long known as Optical Character Recognition (OCR). There are more modern versions, called Intelligent Character Recognition (ICR) that leverage natural language processing (NLP) to better extract and interpret the scanned information. All of these advanced capabilities are more commonly referred to as *intelligent document processing* (IDP).

These capabilities are the eyes of the digital workforce. IDP's benefits over OCR often include higher degrees of accuracy, a more flexible ability to find and interpret information found in nonstandard locations on a page, and the improved capability to recognize handwriting, poorly scanned characters, and less well-structured data. Tools commonly used in this category include ABBYY, AntWorks, WorkFusion, Taiger and more. However, as intelligent automation platforms flourished between 2015 and 2020, many of the traditional RPA firms also began to develop or acquire more robust IDP capabilities. Therefore, it is now common to see robust IDP features in UiPath, Microsoft Power Automate, Blue Prism, and other leading automation platforms.

Other Tools in the Automation Stack While RPA and IDP often make up most of the citizen automation tech stack, there are other complementary tools worth noting. First is process intelligence. With an origin in simple screen recorders, these tools have gained sophistication and are now able to assist in the mapping and measuring of how work is done. A series of tool categories including task mining, process mining, and process discovery fill out this set and promise to lead teams to optimal process flows while helping ferret out noncompliance and inefficiency. Other possible tools include chatbots for enhancing user experience and interaction with processes, and data mining, interpretation, and modeling (which we covered in more detail in Chapter 6, "Citizen Data Science").

One of the most recent combinations of automation technology and marketing is the "digital worker." The idea is that automation technology—RPA plus some other capabilities—can replace human workers entirely. This marketing approach is in part a response to the tremendous worker shortages that many organizations have experienced during and post-COVID. Several vendors have announced that they offer digital workers, but we don't think the term is yet accurate. These digital workers may be able to accomplish a few tasks rather than one—typically in a particular domain, such as anti-money laundering—but they can't do all the tasks that human financial fraud analysts can perform.

Citizen Data Science Technologies

In the early days of data science—though the term didn't exist yet—there were somewhat easy-to-use statistical analysis programs from companies like SAS, SPSS (now owned by IBM), Minitab, and Stata. If you wanted to run your data through an array of statistical models—first on mainframes, then on minicomputers, then on PCs, then in the cloud—these were the tools of choice.

For many professional data scientists today, however, the tools have changed. The open-source statistics system R became popular, and then many data scientists simply wrote Python programs to manage and then analyze their data. R is a marginally citizen-oriented toolkit, and Python is not generally for citizens at all. That helps us understand why many data science professionals think that citizen data science is an oxymoronic term.

Over the past several years, however, the world of data science technologies has changed dramatically. Some of these changes have affected professional data scientists, such as the rise of data science platforms from companies like Databricks and Domino Data Lab, which attempt to support the entire process of developing models from data acquisition and engineering to modeling to deployment and ongoing management. Cloud vendors such as AWS, Google Cloud, and Microsoft Azure also are increasingly offering such platforms. Some data scientists have also been willing to use automated machine learning (autoML) tools to enhance their productivity in model development, although many have not yet been convinced that machines can beat trained humans in these activities.

Specialized autoML systems, from vendors like DataRobot, H2O, and all of the cloud providers, have not really caught on with citizens either. In some cases this was because the tools were overly complex and really only understandable by professional data scientists. There were some examples of quantitatively oriented citizens (actuaries, financial analysts, market researchers) using these tools, but not enough to make it a terribly lucrative software category. And some companies (Dataiku, Aible, Squark) have focused on citizen autoML but have been only somewhat successful at best.

However, citizen data science tools are emerging from below—from business intelligence, data analysis, and visual analytics vendors. These are probably the tools—from vendors such as Tableau (owned by Salesforce), Qlik, Alteryx, and Microsoft Power BI—that are best suited to citizen data scientist users. As Thomas Dinsmore, a long-term analytics and data science expert, who has worked for several vendors in this space, told us in an interview:

> All of the BI vendors are adding machine learning capabilities. They will dominate the "citizen data science" category because they have deep pockets, strong customer franchises, and broad user appeal. Machine learning is most useful for business analytics when combined with other

tools. Stand-alone machine learning tools for business users aren't likely to survive.

In addition, we'd add that business intelligence companies are more used to having users (i.e., citizens) who are comfortable with easy-to-use, point-and-click software interfaces.

Dinsmore also suggested that data science capabilities would be integrated with function-specific tools with which citizen domain experts are likely to be comfortable. He mentioned some examples:

SAP [the large enterprise resource planning vendor] doesn't have a data science tool, but they do have sophisticated time series analysis capabilities embedded in their supply chain and logistics solution. Blue Horizon Infotech, a Dubai-based vendor, sells retail inventory management software. It has some sophisticated inventory planning and prediction capabilities, optimized for that specific process. We'll see more and more of those embedded data science tools.

New Developments for Citizens in Business Intelligence

In addition to the integration with data science capabilities, business intelligence is getting smarter in other ways. It is increasingly being combined with AI capabilities to enable automated discovery of patterns in data. It's sort of halfway between data visualization and analysis, and AI-based data science. This approach goes under a variety of names: "AI4BI," "smart data discovery," "automated data discovery" (though some use that term to mean simply finding the data you want or need), and "augmented analytics." Clearly, there is no widely accepted term, which means that it is still early days for this capability.

It works like this: instead of just displaying a bar chart displaying sales figures by region by quarter, it could point out that the Southern region has a tendency to underperform every year in the fourth quarter. We humans might be able to figure that out by staring at the bar chart for a while, but nobody has the time to stare at bar charts these days to try to figure out what's going on. Of course, one could also have figured out that relationship in the data with a correlation or regression analysis, but who has the time to do that either?

Salesforce.com was one of the first large vendors to adopt this approach, which was based on an acquisition of a company called BeyondCore. The feature has been named several things (including Einstein Analytics) over the past several years but is now called CRM Analytics and is part of Tableau. Other major vendors—Qlik, Microsoft Power BI, and Google's Looker—are closing in on this capability and have elements of it.

For example, at a U.S. industrial company (that doesn't want to be named) one manager there told us, "We are a data-driven company, but we don't have the time or skills to comb through the data." They are certainly not the only company that could be described this way.

This company had a corporate pricing team that saw the value of automated data discovery. The pricing team's analysts were citizens, not professional data scientists. One of their jobs was to assess the relationship between product pricing and business performance. At one point they were looking within a particular business unit to find the impact of pricing discounts on sales and revenues. The unit's discount program involved higher levels of discounts with greater numbers of units purchased in a tiered structure. The pricing team wasn't sure if the discounts were really helping the company; if they weren't getting more volume out of the price breaks, why offer them?

The team worked with the data on this topic internally for two months but found no clear patterns in the data. Then they decided to bring in a consultant with pricing expertise to look at the data. The consultants were given the data the team had been working with and were given six weeks to analyze it. They found no useful patterns in the data either.

The team felt defeated and was casting about for answers. One team member mentioned that she'd heard about data discovery capabilities from a vendor and suggested giving it a try on the same data set. No one was in a position to turn down the effort. The team arranged for a demo of the software.

Within two weeks, the software found an interesting pattern in the data—without any hypothesis or guidance from the team. It found that the actual pattern of customer discounts had little to do with the tiered discount structure based on purchase volume. In fact, most large customers were getting "special" discounts beyond what the tier discounts offered. The special discounts were being offered by the unit's salesforce on an ad hoc basis. If customers were receiving tiered discounts, it was probably because they weren't very price-conscious.

The team discussed this finding and concluded that it would be difficult or impossible to eliminate the special discounts from the sales force. So it recommended eliminating the tiered discount structure, which helped the unit avoid a substantial number of discounts. The software also revealed that some customers were "gaming" the discount structure with a loophole. Closing the loophole alone saved the company as much as the initial discount change, doubling the output of the project. Newly invigorated from this successful finding, the pricing team began to consult with other business units about how they could obtain similar types of results.

As in this example, the intersection of business intelligence and AI is clearly an appealing one. There are undoubtedly many companies that would like to employ citizen data analysts and receive the benefits of sophisticated data science. If we could only figure out what to call the category!

One other comment on business intelligence for citizen analysts: just as with data science software, there are many different industry- or function-specific BI offerings. They may be stand-alone or connected to a broader transactional system. Functions covered include HR, procurement, logistics, sales, marketing, customer service, and no doubt many more. Industries with custom-tailored BI software include retail, energy, financial services, healthcare, manufacturing, consumer goods, and so forth. These industry or function-specific software offerings make it easier for citizen analysts with domain knowledge to generate the right types of analyses and visualizations for their industry.

The Generative AI Era of Citizen Development

As we've suggested throughout this book, generative AI is going to have a dramatic effect on citizen development. There are three primary ways that it will transform the technology landscape, and today it's difficult to say which will be more influential.

The first and most obvious way will be through conversational user interfaces. Virtually every vendor of software today has announced or is soon to announce a generative AI interface. Now or in the very near future, someone interested in programming or accessing/analyzing data need only make a request to an AI system in regular language for a program containing a set of particular functions, an automation workflow with key steps and decisions, or a machine learning analysis involving particular variables or features. This sort of request would require virtually no computer language or tool knowledge and very little statistical knowledge.

The latter type of analysis has already become available. We've already created several machine learning models ourselves using OpenAI's Advanced Data Analysis feature, which generates Python code. Our prompt specifies only which data set to use and which variables are independent (predictors) and dependent (predicted). The resulting program deals with missing data (and tells you why it's taken a particular approach to it), does some feature engineering (variable transformations), tries several different algorithms to see which yields the best fit, and produces natural-language interpretations of the outcomes of the analysis. It's easier to use than any previous approach to automated machine learning, and should be accessible to virtually every citizen.

Generative AI is also leading to the collapse of the three citizen development categories we've defined. It can generate application code, generate automations, and generate data science analyses. One RPA vendor, UiPath, recently announced a set of large language models for accelerating the types of processes for which RPA has typically been employed, as well as tools for developing models with company-specific content. Microsoft is using generative AI CoPilots to assist with all of the different Power Platform tools across the spectrum of citizen development activity. Other vendors will integrate in this fashion as well with AI.

We're also beginning to see the creation of specialized "bots" that are intended to perform specific types of work. There are "digital workers" from RPA vendors and other start-ups that claim to perform an entire job (for example, anti-money laundering in a bank), although our investigations thus far suggest that they really perform just a few tasks and are certainly less flexible than human workers. There is a software development bot that claims to be able to write software programs from start to finish. Our guess is that for the next several years, these bots will be capable of making human citizens more productive and effective but won't replace them. But once we reach the era of artificial general intelligence (AGI), all bets are off.

Even now, we're on the cusp of dramatic change in how citizens do their work. Figure 9.2 from HFS Research suggests that we've exhausted the last wave of people-driven improvements and have entered into the "generative enterprise" in which AI, RPA, and other tools will spawn massive productivity gains. If that's true, some citizen developers are likely to no longer be necessary, and every citizen will need to change how they do their work.

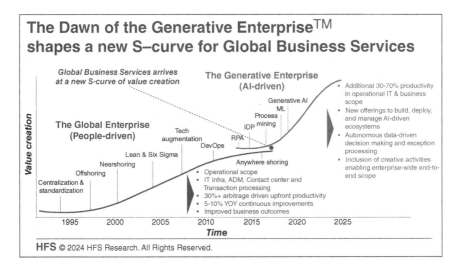

Figure 9.2   The generative enterprise

Source: HFS Research Ltd.

This type of change is happening today and will only become more common in the near future. For example, one vendor of workflow-oriented systems, Pega, has implemented Blueprint, a tool for using generative AI to design new workflows. Pega's systems are normally used at the enterprise level, and IT people are often involved in creating them. But designing with generative AI blueprints makes it easy for business and IT people to collaborate on a solution.

One of its customers, Deutsche Telekom—the largest telecommunications company in the world—is using Pega and Blueprint to rebuild its HR processes. It needed to rebuild and transform 800 HR processes, with different versions across the 25 companies in which it operates. Some, such as payroll, were mission-critical and were developed by IT professionals using traditional development tools. It has developed systems for 500 processes over the past six years.

However, 300 remain to be developed, and as Daniel Wenzel, head of the project, explained at Pega's 2024 user conference PegaWorld, "Good is good enough" for them. He also commented that "The biggest problem is having businesspeople to talk IT." With Blueprint, he said, businesspeople and IT can speak a common language, and business experts can describe processes in their own terms.

The company has a year and a half to develop systems for the remaining 300 processes, and it plans to use Blueprint for all of them. Wenzel expects that it will free up much time and many millions of euros compared to traditional development processes. The combination of generative AI and citizen involvement is transforming how digitization is done at Deutsche Telekom, and we believe it will do so at many other organizations.

10 | Benefits of Citizen Development

For many organizations, the development of technology by citizens is of tactical benefit. It allows applications, automations, models, web pages, and the like to be developed faster and with a better fit to the business need. When citizens focus on these smaller technology outputs, IT professionals can reshape the company—at least ideally.

Citizen-developed technologies may also involve less expense or more value for money, although most organizations don't measure the time and cost that citizens take in developing technologies or the value that they achieve. On the cost side of the equation, it may be that costs are simply being shifted from the IT organization—where they are somewhat more measurable—to other people in the company (note that this would not be unique; we've already shifted costs from the travel department and the secretarial pool to other employees). However, development with low-code/no-code tools tends to be relatively efficient, so the cost may be lower than with full-code solutions by professional developers.

On the value side, companies don't measure the right things from citizen development, in part because it is difficult and invasive to do so. In citizen automation initiatives, for example, some companies aggregate the number of minutes or hours saved by automations across the company, but it's quite rare to measure or account for what the employees do with all that saved time. Maybe they're selling more or innovating more, or maybe they are playing more Angry Birds or watching more of their kids' soccer games.

In terms of both cost and value from citizen development, we think that if an organization is going to adopt citizen activity on a large scale, it should at least do some experimentation across various contexts (LC/NC application development, automation, data analysis and data science) to see what the cost and value are. If both are in line with expectations, then it's reasonable to proceed on a large scale. As we'll describe next, that's where the strategic benefits lie.

Targeting and Scaling Improvement Benefits

The more strategic benefits of citizen activity, however, come with targeting, scale, experimentation and innovation, and better decision-making. Targeting of benefits from citizen development is critical for companies to achieve strategic value. Whether the objective is cost reduction, time savings, or strategic experimentation, these improvements will have much more business value if they are targeted to strategic areas of benefit. Unfortunately, however, not enough companies are doing it. Citizen development is often not closely linked with the value drivers of the business and the executives who are responsible for them.

One company that did link them is Stanley Black & Decker. Under CEO John Loree, the company was faced with major increases in tariffs and raw material costs. Loree had been CFO of the company before being named CEO in 2016, so he was comfortable with the levers that would make the company money. He identified several "value pools" that the company would focus on in restoring profitability to previous levels. They included such areas as digital procurement, pricing, inventory demand and supply, and cost categories for products. Loree believed that by applying tools like analytics and AI to these value pools that Stanley Black & Decker could achieve "margin resiliency" and set a goal of delivering a billion dollars in increased value over three years.

To help make that happen, Steve Brodrick was appointed chief transformation and analytics officer. Brodrick had previously been head of financial planning and analysis for the company, and he was familiar with both operations and analytics in that role. He knew that financial and performance information was scattered across the organization, and it needed to be integrated if it were to be made useful. Brodrick and his team also believed that the data and analytics would have to be employed broadly across the organization if the performance goals were to be achieved. They established a new strategy called "Democratizing Data"—an approach to empowering citizen developers to identify ways to improve the business in the value pool areas. They empowered 1,000 people around those pools and gave them tools to figure out where the use cases were.

A big part of the citizen empowerment was automation of data workflows. They used Alteryx to pull data together from a lot of different sources and gave citizen developers the ability to do automated analytics and, in some cases, data science AI models. The tools, Brodrick said, made data accessible and "decision ready," and then enabled automation, analytics, and—the most important step—taking action on the data and analyses. Stanley Black & Decker was able to uncover new sources of value quickly, identifying half a billion dollars in the first two years through steps such as cutting 30% out of indirect costs and optimizing pricing models.

Brodrick is now the chief transformation officer at Alteryx and talks to companies all around the globe about how they can make similar transformations possible. He agrees that not enough companies are viewing citizen development strategically and tying it to financial objectives and outcomes. To talk only about the time saved from citizen development, he argues, begs the question of what people do with the freed-up time. When he speaks to customers, he asks them, "With that freed-up time, where are you making different decisions and taking different actions? If you aren't asking those questions more, you can't drive profitability or growth."

As at Stanley Black & Decker, achieving strategic benefits from citizen development requires large-scale adoption. Scale-based benefits derive from broad adoption of citizen activities across a business, typically having the benefit of reducing costs or increasing speed. AT&T, for example, has developed more than 2,000 citizen automators and more than 3,000 citizen developers. The managers of these capabilities say that they have saved about 17 million minutes a year through automation, with a 20-fold return on investment. The combined citizen activity is estimated to have saved

AT&T more than $300 million a year. Although it may be challenging to directly trace those savings to AT&T's profitability, there is the opportunity to create strategic value if, as Brodrick noted, they ask the right questions about how the time savings are being used.

Johnson & Johnson (J&J) has achieved a similar scale and benefits. When it embarked upon an enterprise-wide "Intelligent Automation" initiative three years ago, the goal was to save the company half a billion dollars in costs. Having achieved that objective in 2023, J&J then achieved a billion dollars in savings in 2024 and set out to achieve two billion by 2025.

However, not every organization realizes the possible strategic benefits of citizen activity. For example, we worked with one pharmaceutical company that had both an articulated need for citizen activity and some of that activity underway. The company is only medium-sized within its industry, but its research productivity has been impressive of late. It plans to introduce several new drugs into the marketplace within only a few years.

One of its strategic goals is to maintain a high level of profitability by not adding a lot of head count as it adds products to its portfolio. We suggested that a broad citizen enablement program—with a particular emphasis on citizen automation, because it has a close tie to headcount needs—would be a good way to help achieve this goal. The company had already initiated an automation initiative, but it was rather small and low-key. Its leaders didn't seem to make the connection between broad citizen automation activities and the strategic goal it was pursuing. No doubt the citizen automation and other citizen activities at the company will continue to grow, but probably not at the pace it needs.

In addition to broad-scale cost reduction, increased speed of digitalization is potentially strategic, although difficult to operationalize and measure. Our assumption now is that most companies should be in a permanent state of digitalization and that they can use all the help from citizens that they can muster. But we've never heard of a company that claimed to be "90% digitalized," or even "roughly two-thirds of the way there." Even if a company digitalizes all its possible use cases, by the time it finished, some early implementations would be obsolete, and new technologies would have been added to the mix. So in general, we're not advocates of treating increased speed from citizen development as a strategic or tangible tactical benefit unless a company can determine with some rigor and clarity how much progress it is making toward digital transformation.

Where speed does seem to matter is when some type of natural disaster takes place, and the company needs a quicker response than IT can create. We'll describe later two examples of that at Shell, where a citizen developer quickly developed first a COVID application to track worker availability and then one dealing with the maintenance impacts of a severe hurricane. At another energy company, Chevron, a citizen developer created a tool for rapid damage reporting and resolution when flash floods hit many employees' homes in Africa. Also during COVID, the retailer H&M developed a citizen-created mobile app called FLEXI that kept track of where hybrid employees were working and whether there was sufficient space for employees to come into the office with limited capacity requirements.

Innovation and Experimentation Benefits

We believe that the greatest source of strategic benefits from citizen development will come from innovation and experimentation. Companies that depend in large part on their management, use, and analysis of information need every employee to digitally innovate. When they figure out a better process for doing business in a particular domain of the organization, they can quickly develop technology for supporting that approach. Others in the organization with a similar need can replicate or modify the original technology for their own purposes.

The most likely type of citizen activity in innovation and experimentation is citizen data science, and it is most likely to be found in industries where data and analysis are critical to the development of new products and services. One of those industries is in life sciences, where *informatics* is a field that rivals biology and chemistry in its current importance. In big pharmaceutical companies like Johnson & Johnson and Sanofi, in life sciences research centers like the Broad Institute, and in research-oriented medical centers like the Mayo Clinic, leaders are trying to cultivate as many citizen data scientists as possible.

These citizens are, of course, highly educated in their fields. One citizen data scientist who was hired by J&J, Charles Bridges, for example, has both a medical degree from Harvard Medical School and a PhD from MIT in chemical engineering.[1] But he had no training in data science. At J&J,

---

[1] "No Stone Unturned: How Charles Bridges Is Using Data Science to Combat a Rare, Incurable Disease," Johnson & Johnson Careers website, Feb. 28, 2020, https://www .careers.jnj.com/careers/no-stone-unturned-how-charles- bridges-is-using-data-science-to-combat-a-rare-incurable- disease.

he was focused on treatments for pulmonary arterial hypertension (high blood pressure in the lungs, an incurable disease today) and was using data science to analyze electronic health records to understand and predict the disease better. He has been named the first global chief technology officer of Actelion, a J&J business unit. He now works at a startup called CorVista Health that uses machine learning to analyze remote cardiac diagnostics, where he is EVP and chief scientific officer. For people with his medical and data science backgrounds, there is no shortage of employment opportunities.

Ryan DiRuzza is the talent acquisition leader in data sciences, digital health, and precision medicine at Johnson & Johnson. He hires people with a high level of data science skills, and J&J has about 600 of them—an impressive number. But many of them also have high levels of scientific education and expertise like Bridges. Some data scientist jobs are strictly that—hard-core data science and the ability to develop new algorithms or analyze novel forms of data. Most, however, are people with chemistry or biology PhDs who have moved into the data science space. They are effectively citizen data scientists but professional scientists.

In general, DiRuzza told us, the life sciences skills are harder to acquire than the data science ones.

> We typically look for people with chemistry or drug discovery backgrounds who have transitioned into machine learning in the last year or two. It's tough to take someone with a purely technical background in computer science and ML and ask them to help design molecules or proteins with generative AI. A base knowledge of chemistry or biology is more important than those pure data science technical skills. A 50/50 combination of scientist and data scientist might be the sweet spot, but they don't come along very often.

DiRuzza said that J&J sometimes hires people with science PhDs and trains them in the needed skills for data science. They wouldn't go into purely technical data science roles, he said, but rather into "stakeholder management" roles that are paired with business units and brands. They would typically translate between the pure scientists and the data scientists and perform tasks such as requirements gathering, relationship building, and internal consulting.

In another example of such skill combinations, Jim Collins, a prominent MIT bioengineering researcher, commented on a podcast that his research team would not have been able to develop a set of new antibiotics (sorely needed by the world, with none being created in decades) using machine learning-based experimentation techniques without "multilingual" scientists.[2] These are biology postdocs who learn about how machine learning works and machine learning grad students who learn enough about biology to help develop new drug molecules. They are highly trained professionals in one domain but citizens in another. Collins commented,

> As I look out in the next few decades in this exciting time of AI coming into biomedicine, I think the groups that will make a difference are those that have these multilingual young trainees and who are well set up to also inject human intelligence with machine intelligence.

Of course, in these companies doing advanced life sciences innovation work, if you have extensive scientific training, it makes it more likely that the needed data science expertise will be relatively easy to acquire.

The types of new capabilities developed by these hybrids also often involve better decision-making. Technology-savvy citizens can make decisions that are better informed by data than by intuition and are able to predict the future rather than report on the past. Since citizens are typically more aware of the types of decisions that need to be made and the business issues surrounding them, they may create better "decision science" applications than professional data analysts or scientists would. If, for example, you're trying to help your banking employer make better credit decisions, the best credit models may come from people who understand the bank's customers and the overall credit environment well and who can employ automated machine learning technology to train the needed predictive model.

We've seen similar combinations of skills in other fields like engineering and geology, and even law. And of course many hybrids are cropping up (pun intended) in business. As many fields and decisions become more data-intensive and new technologies make data analysis and modeling easier, it

---

[2] Eric Topol Ground Truths podcast, "Jim Collins: Discovery of the First New Structural Class of Antibiotics in Decades, Using A.I." Feb. 13, 2024, transcript at `https://erictopol.substack.com/p/jim-collins-discovery-of-the-first`.

eems likely that educational institutions will incorporate data science-oriented training for their students. MIT, for example, has a PhD program in computational systems biology that attempts to create "a new breed of quantitative biologists" from the start.[3] Many other research-oriented universities have similar programs. For those who weren't prepared to be citizens in graduate school, professional associations are also beginning to offer AI training programs; the American College of Radiology, for example, has created a Data Science Institute to train radiologists in the use and interpretation of AI image models.

In addition to citizen data science, it also seems likely that organizations will employ low-code/no-code system development and citizen automation tools to make innovative advances in many areas. In manufacturing, for example, the advent of tools like process mining (and a new technology called *visual process mining*) is making possible substantially more effective factories. Service-oriented businesses can improve their administrative processes dramatically using similar tools. Data- and technology-oriented engineers in plants are improving maintenance processes with predictive maintenance models and drone-based image recognition. Even military organizations are becoming much more technology-intensive and data-driven, and as AI takes further hold in "mechanized combat," there will need to be many soldiers who understand both warfighting and AI/automation tools.

Citizen automation with robotic process automation tools is generally viewed as creating small workflows for individual and departmental tasks. On the surface it doesn't appear to be a highly strategic activity, although it is a very useful one that can deliver benefits cheaply and rapidly. However, we can also think of RPA applications in a business innovation context. They are often used to connect, integrate, and transform information that comes from diverse systems across an enterprise. A new integrated system might be more desirable but would be expensive and time-consuming to implement. In that case, a citizen-developed automation could be viewed as creating a short-term solution that functions like an expensive integrated system. If it turns out to be a useful solution over time, then perhaps a new integrated system could someday take its place. This form of innovation could be quite useful for legacy information-intensive businesses with

---

[3] MIT Computational Systems Biology website, accessed Feb. 20, 2023, `https://csbphd.mit.edu/welcome-mit-computational-and-systems-biology-phd-program-csb`.

limited resources to rebuild their IT architectures—and of course that is the majority of legacy companies. We have more to say about this benefit in Chapter 5, "Citizen Automation."

In short, innovative organizations will continue to implement more technology into their operations, and all hands will need to be mobilized to create and use it effectively. No doubt those hands will produce technology solutions more rapidly than their backlogged IT departments could, and probably do it more cheaply. But the most strategic benefit is that the organizations can offer products and services to the marketplace that are dependent both on traditional skills and on those involving information technology and extensive data. Citizens will make that combination possible.

11 | The Organizational Response to Citizen Technology

We've focused thus far in this book on the idea and benefits of citizen technologies and the journeys that individual citizens have made toward the broad use of them. Now it's time to discuss the organizational response. That's a little difficult because it is in flux, and how organizations react to citizens taking over some of the traditional professional technology tasks varies not only across companies but also across time. We've interviewed or worked with multiple citizens who told us that at one point there was strong opposition to citizen development, but it has recently eased or even vanished. It does appear that the long-term trend is heading toward greater democratization and that absent some highly visible catastrophes, it's likely to continue.

The Two Stereotypical Positions

There are (or at least were. . .we're in the midst of change) two traditional positions relative to citizen development and technology usage—one positive and one negative. As you might expect, the positive attitudes were largely on the part of citizens themselves, and in many cases their managers as well. They advocated for citizen activities because they wanted to get things done—to support current and future business initiatives with technology—and because they were dissatisfied with the pace and perceived effectiveness of technology support from professional organizations like their IT groups. Laments like "I went to IT with a request to support my marketing campaign (or supply chain initiative or finance project or HR onboarding automation) and was told that it would take them more than a year to get to it" are all too common in many organizations. Such dissatisfaction is further fueled by vendors of citizen-oriented technologies, which are only too happy to allow citizens to download free trial versions of their software and learn what they can accomplish with it. And by all accounts, this usually works out pretty well. Citizens and their bosses are often delighted with what wonders citizen technology can bestow upon pressing business problems.

The loyal opposition to citizen development, of course, has usually come from IT professionals and their leaders. They typically object to the movement for a variety of reasons, some valid and some not.

- The systems developed by citizens incur risk, be it technical (not functioning correctly, or harming IT infrastructure), security, privacy, regulatory, financial, etc.
- Over time, the use of many citizen-developed systems may lead to a patchwork of systems that together incur a high level of technical debt.
- Citizen-developed systems need ongoing maintenance, the citizens who developed them may no longer be around, and IT professionals will be stuck with fixing them.
- Citizens may put IT professionals out of work.
- Many citizen-developed systems will create multiple versions of the truth within organizations.
- Citizen-developed systems that create predictive models or insights may lead to poor decisions.
- "Citizen-developed applications may not scale well and may not integrate well with existing systems," according to that master of bullet point generation, ChatGPT.

IT groups may refer to citizen development-oriented groups as *shadow IT* or *rogue IT*. But these citizen systems are only in the shadows because IT forces them to be. Despite the disparagement from IT organizations and professionals, we haven't found that their issues have yet led to insurmountable problems for the organizations we've interviewed. Some don't make much sense, such as the fear that citizen development will put IT people out of work. If that were true, why would there be such a backlog in most organizations? And most of the others can be addressed by good management of citizens and the related technologies. But we'd be lying if we denied the validity of these objections in total. As we'll discuss, some very sophisticated citizen-focused companies are worried about them.

Beyond the IT Resistance Stereotype

It's important to point out, however, that some IT organizations have not resisted citizen technology activity but rather actively encouraged it. Shell is an excellent example. In the late 2010s then–Group Chief Information Officer Jay Crotts believed that digitalizing the energy giant would be impossible without engaging many technologically informed and talented employees in the effort. He saw that many employees were getting easier-to-use tools in their hands and doing lots of clever things with them. As we alluded to in the preface, Crotts developed a data-centric "DIY" program to enable citizens to develop low-code/no-code applications and data science models.

Crotts wasn't worried about the "shadow IT" issue; he realized that employee-developed technology would exist in any case, and he wanted to bring such activity into the light. The mission of the DIY initiative was to "empower every employee to digitize work processes to improve productivity, increase agility, and create more value for customers."[1]

Kappeyne said that in the beginning the DIY focus was personal productivity applications using data that employees already had access to through Azure. Shell bought an enterprise license for the Microsoft Power Platform, and that became the primary development tool. They ran boot camps and hackathons for interested employees, and the DIY concept

---

[1] Noel Carroll and Mary Maher, "How Shell Fueled Digital Transformation by Establishing DIY Software Development," *MIS Quarterly Executive*, January 2023.

"really boomed," Kappeyne noted. Kappeyne had promised that the value of the effort would be 10 times the cost, and within six months they had measured $40 million in additional value—more than the 10 times the promise. For Kappeyne, a two-month assignment turned into a two-year love affair with the democratization of data and technology.

The team developed a framework for what kinds of citizen applications made sense. Applications that used low-code/no-code tools and approved data sources for individual applications were considered the "green zone," and employees were expected to build, deploy, and maintain the applications themselves. Amber zone applications could be prototyped by non-IT employees but needed to be reviewed before being deployed and could be used for only a year in any case. Red zone proposals involved access to sensitive data or involved external Internet connections and were generally rejected by the DIY reviewers in IT. There was also some degree of citizen automation, but Kappeyne generally insisted that it should be preceded by process improvement activities and that automation should be the final step in the process.

At the same time that Kappeyne was creating the DIY program, Dan Jeavons, Shell's head of advanced analytics and data science (also within the IT organization), was engaging the broader employee community in AI through a program called Shell.ai.[2] Shell had about 350 professional data scientists, but Jeavons was convinced that the company could achieve much more benefit from AI if he could train and mobilize many of the company's engineers and managers. Part of the program was to make available automated machine learning tools to these users, and enable them to train their own models. They also employed approved cloud-based data sets. Shell also made use of a common data format for time-series data—common from exploration and refining machinery—called Pi Tags.

Eventually the Shell.ai community came to encompass more than 5,000 members, many of whom were trained and certified in machine learning and data engineering approaches from the online education company Udacity. More than 1,000 people have earned "nanodegrees" in these fields. Jeavons said that with such training, many of its processes in areas like

---

[2] Shell's AI initiatives, including those involving citizen data science, are described in greater detail in Thomas H. Davenport and Nitin Mittal, *All In on AI: How Smart Companies Win Big with Artificial Intelligence,*" Harvard Business School Press, 2023.

maintenance have been transformed with tools like predictive maintenance models—originally designed by data scientists, but trained, monitored, and maintained by engineers. And as Crotts told us, many of the Shell engineers coming out of school today already know Python programming, so it's not much of a leap for them to experiment with data science.

An Emerging Third Party

But Shell is a relatively unusual example of IT leadership in citizen technology (although it is becoming more common), and there is still frequently a cultural conflict between IT leaders and business-side advocates of citizen activity. One of the factors we've found in the research for this book that seems to help address these often-opposing positions is intermediary organizations between IT and business groups. The role of these intermediaries is to create effective digital tools for employees or customers, but they are outside of IT. In such organizations it's usually IT's job to install and maintain the technology infrastructure and to manage transactional systems. These intermediary organizations don't address those issues, but rather the effective consumption and use of data and technology to address specific business issues. In trying to accomplish their objectives, they naturally turn to citizens.

The information and "expert solutions" company Wolters Kluwer, for example, needed to build a capability to create AI-based products. It previously had separate data science and operations teams, but the separation prevented them from speaking the same language, feeling each other's pain, and understanding each other's problems and issues. So, the company's Financial and Corporate Compliance division created an organization—called Customer Information Management/Operational Excellence (CIOx)—to better understand customer needs and build new products and solutions. Members of the group are expected to spend time with customers, identify their needs, and create solutions that fit customers' workflows and address their problems. The group developed a product development process with the steps of "ideate, test, incubate, scale." A team of product developers employs the process. CIOx wanted to be seen not as a research group but as having a solution mindset. The metrics for their success—and resulting reward mechanisms—should be the same as the businesses with which they were working. In short, they viewed themselves as "blue-collar

AI workers" focused on achieving outcomes rather than simply developing great models.

As data scientists and business subject-matter experts sat next to each other for several years, their skills started to blend. The business domain experts took on development roles. For example, Shelli Robinson was a frontline employee doing fulfillment operations with state government offices. She learned a variety of technical skills. Now she has created a platform to automate filing corporate reports to states. She also got tired of answering questions about how long it was taking to file documents, so she learned Power App and Power BI to create analytics about the process. Robinson taught herself these tools, but now there is an "Addicted to Learning" group sponsored by CIOx to teach people like her new tools. That group was created by Don McGimpsey, a "community organizer" for CIOx who reaches out to people, asks them what their problems are, and teaches them how to solve them.

Wolters Kluwer has created a variety of successful data products with a combination of professionals and citizens. For example, it created a "Legal-VIEW Bill Analyzer" that supports large companies' chief legal officers in reviewing law firm invoices for compliance with outside counsel billing guidelines. It uses two forms of AI—machine learning and a rule engine—to compare these companies' legal services agreements with what law firms actually bill them for and frequently finds errors in the bills. LegalVIEW BillAnalyzer can save companies up to 10% on their outside legal service costs and increases compliance with billing guidelines by up to 20%. The system also saves in-house counsel considerable time on investigating instances of overbilling.

Sharon Horozaniecki, a lawyer at Wolters Kluwer, is the head of the group that built and refines the LegalVIEW BillAnalyzer. She said that the development of the system was a good example of collaboration between professional data scientists and citizen developers. The data scientists built the machine learning model that identifies billing anomalies. The rule engine, called Sniffer, identifies other problems with the law firm billing data, such as a senior lawyer billing for copying documents. Much of the creation of the rules for Sniffer, and all of the ongoing refinements, are made by citizens in Horozaniecki's group. She says that in developing the system, her team learned a lot about data science, and the data scientists they work with learned a lot about law.

We found a similar intermediary organization at ProAssurance, an insurance company that is really, according to one executive we interviewed, "a data and technology company" more than an insurance company. The intermediary group is called Enterprise Digital Experience, and it's part of the Business Operations Logistics and Transformation organization (BOLT). Citizen development was once opposed by ProAssurance's IT organization, but now the Enterprise Digital Experience group makes extensive use of ServiceNow's citizen development capabilities to develop automation workflows for a variety of business problems. As we'll describe, this intermediary organization not only develops citizen applications but also ensures that they are safe and well-governed. But it seems unlikely that the citizen movement would have taken off without this group and the roles it plays.

"Governance" of Citizen Technologies

When many employees within an organization adopt citizen development approaches, their employers are often concerned about "governance" issues. We put the term in quotes because we're not big fans of it. We concede that it's important to ensure that citizen-developed applications and use cases are effective and accurate, that they meet ethical and regulatory standards, and that they don't cause harm. However, very few people relish the idea of their work being "governed." We prefer the term *enablement*, which to us involves making it easy for citizens to do the right thing with the technology they adopt and develop.

One of the organizations in this world with the greatest governance/enablement challenges involving citizen development is Microsoft. As we've noted, the set of capabilities in the company's Power Platform suite have been a boon to citizens across multiple realms—low-code/no-code application development with Power Apps, automation with Power Automate, and citizen data science with Power BI. The vendor has also embraced generative AI in its partnership with OpenAI and has created "copilots" in each of these areas that make it even easier for citizens to use powerful technologies.

At Microsoft, much of the push for technology democratization is coming not from individual users or the IT organization but rather the company's CEO. Satya Nadella has co-authored articles about the power of citizen development, and one includes this comment:

> To more evenly spread economic opportunity and resilience, we must democratize "tech intensity," a combination of tech and people skills—including among citizen developers. This so-called intensity is made up of three dimensions: the adoption of technology, the capability of individuals to use it, and their trust in the organizations deploying it. Tools from cloud computing to AI should be in the hands of every knowledge worker, first-line worker, organization, and public-sector agency around the world.[3]

Consistent with Nadella's advocacy of citizen development, Microsoft is also encouraging its own employees to develop technology capabilities *en masse*. Damon Buono, who is responsible for enterprise data governance at Microsoft, told us that the company's culture has a strong "use our product first" orientation. The emphasis across the company is to demonstrate how the company's tools can solve its own business problems, which can then be demonstrated to customers. Buono said he couldn't turn off that culture even if he wanted to, and he acknowledges its advantages for the company. However, he said that the downside to such a strong citizen culture is that it is very difficult to control who creates apps, automations, or data science models.

Buono said that the exact number of citizen-developed systems within Microsoft is impossible to know, but it feels like millions of each type to him. The lines blur across professional versus amateur every day: employees who were software engineers go back to school to learn some data science. Data engineers realize that they can create models too. Marketers realize that they can use automated machine learning APIs to predict what the customer wants to do next, and it works. Citizen business intelligence analysts see that Power BI can do machine learning. Seeing all this ease of use, many Microsoft employees get additional degrees or certificates in data science.

One can imagine that this proliferation of citizen-developed applications would keep a data governance person awake at night. Buono

---

[3] Satya Nadella and Marco Iansiti, "Want a More Equitable Future? Empower Citizen Developers," *Wired*, Dec. 9, 2020, https://www.wired.com/story/want-a-more-equitable-future-empower-citizen-developers.

acknowledges the possibility of "metrics collision" at the company and of multiple citizen-developed systems yielding multiple versions of the truth. He says that it hasn't caused any severe problems yet and notes that no citizen is trying to create a competing dashboard to the official one sponsored by Microsoft's chief financial officer. Nor is anyone competing with the HR department with an alternative set of numbers for employee churn. But with 50 officially sanctioned departmental business intelligence groups—each of which with its own data lake and its own key metrics—some metrics and insights collision is sure to happen.

Buono and his data governance colleagues across the company have tried to address this challenge in multiple ways. Microsoft is embracing self-service analytics at scale while also working to manage inevitable insight collisions through formal data product "endorsement" processes. Because Microsoft has a federated approach to IT and data management, Buono must work with these data-specific domains to scale these processes and identify the right data leaders who can certify, or endorse, data for discoverability and use.

Microsoft no longer has a corporate IT organization or a chief information officer, chief digital officer, or chief data officer. All of these technology and data leadership roles have been pushed down to the product group level. Buono leads data governance for the product group that creates governance products like Microsoft Purview (which provides security for important business data). The "enablement" approach is supported by providing citizen application developers with "built-in telemetry to data pipelines." Data products that include analytics and AI that could modify data can be published for broad internal use if they are approved by the Purview group. Buono refers to the approach as "noninvasive data governance."

It seems likely that Microsoft will be the bellwether for many companies in the near future. As everyone becomes capable of technology development work—"we're all programmers now," as one of our article titles puts it—there will need to be noninvasive ways of enabling good data and application development behaviors. Microsoft is wrestling with this problem now and will no doubt provide products to other organizations to facilitate their efforts.

Citizen Technology in Highly Regulated Businesses

The organizations that would seem to be in greatest need of "governance" are highly regulated organizations. It's one thing for citizen data scientists to develop a marketing model that is a bit off on what product to offer what customer. It's another thing altogether to use a biased model to underwrite loans or insurance policies (which can violate state or national laws) or to create a model predicting the onset of sepsis in a hospital that has many false positive and negative predictions (which really did happen, although it came from a major hospital software vendor and was probably created by professional data scientists and software developers).

However, highly regulated businesses are using citizen development tools, although they have more guardrails in place than companies in less regulated industries. For example, at ProAssurance, the regulated insurance company we mentioned that sells healthcare and legal professional liability policies, "governance" is not a negative term. In fact, when we asked Max Malloy, the head of enterprise digital experience at the company, what made citizen development work there, he mentioned "governance, governance, governance, governance." Citizen development, he said, is focused on "systems of action" rather than "systems of record." It's "the outer ring that touches the outside world," rather than the claims database or the underwriting algorithms. Citizen developers are also the primary developers of reporting capabilities and dashboards, which Malloy describes as "low-hanging fruit for IT people."

The primary tool that ProAssurance uses for citizen development comes from ServiceNow, and that tool automatically notifies the IT organization when a new automation has been developed. IT gets the chance to review it and ensure that it works as planned before it goes into production. IT review and the ServiceNow architecture (including the vendor's App Engine Studio for citizen development) guard against security breaches, hacks, and unauthorized integrations with transactional systems.

Mayo Clinic is another organization that, as a top-ranked medical center in the United States with multiple campuses, is highly regulated. Any application, automation, or predictive statistical model developed by citizens has to work well and not reveal any personally identifiable patient information. In some cases, new software for clinical use even needs to be approved by the FDA. Nevertheless, Ajai Seghal, Mayo's chief data and analytics officer, insists that software and AI tools need to be put in the hands of the people with the domain knowledge needed to leverage them. At Mayo Clinic, that is primarily the 40,000 physicians who work for the organization.

Seghal has two answers to the issue of how a regulated organization can ensure that data and AI are safe in the hands of citizens. One is data stewardship, and the other he calls *AI enablement*. Note that he doesn't use the term *governance* much; stewardship and enablement are more positive approaches to achieving the same outcome.

Data stewardship is a concept that has been difficult to sell in many organizations, but Mayo Clinic appears to be doing a good job of it. Stewardship means that it's the job of user groups to get the data ready for analysis—integrating it, ensuring quality and currency, and putting it in the organization's data library. Sehgal said that if you approach implementing stewardship as a transformational change—and take the requisite care to educate (with an extensive data literacy program), outline the value, and so forth—the business (or clinical in their case) stakeholders get it. The alternative to stewardship, he believes, is not IT doing those tasks, but rather no one performing the stewardship tasks and a resulting set of data problems. Generative AI, Seghal observes, has made it much easier to sell stewardship. People want generative AI use cases and are willing to do what's necessary to get their data ready.

The other key idea that helps with governance is AI enablement. Sehgal describes his AI role as head of enablement, and he has 60 or so people who help him fulfill it. Enablement consists of both technology and services that make building AI applications easier and safer. His group has built two versions of an "AI factory" that is a platform for building applications. Mayo Clinic has a partnership with Google, and the company's Vertex AI suite is a primary component of the platform. The platform also includes a toolset for gathering the needed regulatory information if the use case has to be approved by the FDA or other regulatory bodies.

On the services side, the AI enablement function provides consulting services, education, and even a degree program for medical AI. There is even a lawyer in the group to consult on regulatory issues. A key part of enablement consulting is to encourage people with use case ideas to come to them and discuss it before developing it. They provide guidance on tools, data, regulatory issues, and other related use cases within Mayo Clinic that may have already been developed. With all this enablement help and the success of the stewardship program, Sehgal and other senior executives at Mayo Clinic are confident that citizen development is both effective and safe. He said that the only problem with it is that his 60-person group of enablers isn't large enough to meet the heavy demand for help with generative AI. Even though Mayo Clinic has been exploring the technology since Sehgal arrived in 2020, the technology is sufficiently new and experimental that citizens who want to develop generative AI tools still need a lot of help.

Putting It All Together: Balancing Risk and Reward

Dr. Patrick Lechner is the head of process mining, robotic process automation, and low-code/no-code development at the German automobile and motorcycle manufacturer BMW. Lechner's virtual background for video calls features two hashtags: #TurningProcessIntoSuccess (reflecting process mining) and #CitizenDevelopment. BMW has an increasing number of employees who do their work at a computer (rather than on an assembly line, for example), and Lechner would be happy if each of them became a citizen developer. In fact, he and his colleagues are currently offering an education program—called "Digital Boost"—to approximately 80,000 employees. One module of the program focuses on citizen development and process improvement with technology.

He does not expect that all 80,000 become citizens because he's been working with citizen development for six years now—primarily with automation technologies—and some people just have a different focus. Some say they're too busy to learn, or they need more training. But BMW does have roughly 300 citizen automators who have been building and maintaining bots for a while now, and the company hopes to have many more after the educational boost. Still, Lechner says that for the foreseeable future there will be an option to order automations and apps from a "delivery factory" run by professionals. He believes that it's important to make citizen development a voluntary activity.

When asked why BMW is encouraging citizen development, Lechner gives the typical answer: because many departments want to develop IT solutions, and there just aren't enough IT resources to develop them. BMW's first foray into citizen technologies was with robotic process automation, using software from UiPath. But now it is also encouraging low-code/no-code development of individual or departmental applications with Microsoft Power Apps, and it is considering adding Power Automate to the robotic process automation (RPA) toolset. In citizen data science, BMW is using several toolsets and has also assembled its own platform for data science development, since they want to encourage more citizen development in this area, too. Lechner admits that "citizen data science is a bit tricky because you have to make sure it is done correctly," but he says there are plenty of BMW employees with the necessary quantitative skills to do citizen data science work. He should know; he has a PhD himself in applied math.

BMW has put into place most or all of the standard capabilities needed for citizen development to thrive. In addition to software standards and educational offerings, they include the following:

- **Community:** The citizen automators have a community from which to learn, and there is even an annual face-to-face event where people can find out what others are doing. The communities for low-code/no-code development and citizen data science are growing fast with already more than 1,000 active low-code/no-code developers across the BMW Group.

- **Centers of Excellence:** There is already a Center of Excellence at headquarters for supporting citizen automation and for developing automation bots when departments want them. It acts as a central hub, and there are regional "spoke" groups on each continent where BMW has operations.

- **Controls:** BMW tries to ensure that citizen-developed applications do what they are intended to do and that they have no negative impact on important transactional systems. Citizen applications that are intended for use by more than one person are inspected by internal or external IT professionals. Lechner says that some IT professionals are happy to work with citizen applications, and some would prefer to only create their own.

- **Central repository:** BMW maintains a central repository of citizen-developed applications, so that something that's already been developed by a citizen doesn't have to be reinvented. It's not always easy to find them with a search tool, however, because different citizen developers have different habits in furnishing metadata.

- **Central platforms and IT governance:** Patrick Lechner works for BMW's central IT organization, and it's his role to make citizen development successful. He said that from the IT perspective it's important to have centrally managed citizen tools. Historically there were a lot of applications with no IT awareness or support, and many were built in a noncompliant way. Now they have a platform that ensures that citizen-developed applications are compliant, such as only allowing certain connectors to core systems from Power Apps. Lechner doesn't worry that things will get out of control with citizen development.

Things aren't perfect yet with regard to citizen technology at BMW. Lechner says he would like some easier-to-use tools and feels that anything requiring more than a day of training is too complex. He wants more people to become citizens and hopes that the Digital Boost training—along with "multipliers" or citizens who train other citizens—will increase the numbers substantially. Otherwise, however, things are progressing quite well. Lechner has no doubt that citizen development will be essential to the ultimate success of digitization and widespread automation and data analysis at BMW.

We've concluded the chapter with the BMW story because it provides an effective contrast to the "IT versus citizens" narrative we described earlier. Citizen development at BMW is sponsored by the IT organization there, and it is putting considerable resources into training citizens and ensuring that their work is successful. We hope that many other organizations will transcend this ancient IT/business divide and get behind the citizen movement.

PART 4 | Setting Sail

12 | Preparing to Set Sail

You have probably realized that this book's title is a play on the phrase "all hands on deck," which originated in the context of sailing ships. When a ship was in a crisis, the captain would call for "all hands on deck," meaning that every member of the crew was needed to help. We can think of no better analogy for this moment in enterprise transformation. Everyone is needed.

And everyone is uniquely capable of adding value. As described by former Amtrak executive Sarina Arcari, "The frontline people know what the problem is, and they know what the solution is. That's where the gold is buried." There is much value in the insight and ingenuity that resides in the front line.

So let's prepare to set sail. This chapter and the next five explore what is needed to ensure a journey on which "all hands" are able to contribute, using technologies suited to their abilities and skill sets.

These chapters are not a formal toolkit for designing and deploying citizen initiatives nor a formal curriculum that can be followed to become a citizen developer. We are not so bold as to suggest that we have determined the best way to proceed on this journey. The optimal toolkit, approach, and learning path depends on internal, external, and environmental factors unique to a corporation's culture, industry, staff, and "innovation DNA." It also depends on the leadership team, comfort with risk, willingness to encourage experimentation, and tolerance for levels of agency and autonomy across the rank and file that make up the lion's share of the organization.

Though not a toolkit, these six chapters are still a sequential guide. We move sequentially through nine "forks in the road" that you will face as you orchestrate citizen development in your organization. Each fork is a decision to be made, and we illustrate each with two case examples that will bound your decision-making. As you move through the extreme case studies in each fork, you will likely see yourself somewhere between the two companies that we highlight. The hope is that you can locate your own organization somewhere on the spectrum between the companies we present in each fork and self-select the strategies and tools that align with the needs of your organization.

Over the course of the nine forks, we will also move sequentially through the 4Gs of citizen development enablement. The success of enterprise citizenry hinges on a robust *genesis* and then a mature set of *governance* policies, *guidance* resources, and *guardrails*. Yes, we continue to hesitate with the term *governance*, preferring *enablement* for its focus on support, rather than constraints. But there is still a place for harder-edge governance in the overall approach.

Maturity Models

As with many forms of change, a citizen development maturity model can illustrate where on the path you currently reside. Our discussions with organizations of all sizes suggest that most are still early in their journeys. As one executive described their effort, "It is a living, breathing experiment." Most of the companies we spoke with were aware that there was much more work to be done.

It is therefore valuable for anyone trying to champion their own grassroots technology innovation programs to have a set of stages against which to assess the current reality and with which to set goals and plans for future-state organizational coherence, investment, and direction.

Citizen Development Maturity Model

Our citizen development maturity model aims to describe the early-stage formative chaos of grassroots enthusiasm and tracks to a more mature set of practices and structures to ensure a scalable and safe approach to long-term citizen success.

Figure 12.1 shows—in the time-honored form of a six-stage maturity model counting Stage 0—the key stages in the evolution of citizen development. Note that there is no stage without any citizen development at all, since we have yet to find an organization that didn't have some of it.

Stage 0: Random Acts of Citizenry   If you don't know what stage of citizen development your company is in, you are likely in stage 0. Individuals and teams are independently tinkering, experimenting, and piloting, often with different tools. There are wide-ranging criteria, standards, training, goals, and results. There is much enthusiasm, but little direction.

This stage is often characterized by undercover behavior and "shadow IT." Here we see the agitators, disruptors, and creators we discussed in Chapter 7, "The Skills and Personality of Citizens," bringing their ingenuity to work whether their employers want them to or not. Citizens see problems and they solve them without authorization. This isn't an attempt to be disruptive, nor to create technical chaos, but rather the only way citizens are able to get things done.

Stage 1: Awareness   The activities in stage 0 eventually get noticed. Whether it's an IT administrator, a department head, or the chief executive officer (CEO), someone discovers that individuals are developing automations, apps, and models without permission or support. When that happens, an enterprise officially enters stage 1: awareness.

While alarms are ringing and managers are frantically trying to figure out how to deal with this situation, we will see the emergence of citizen champions; these leaders can take an enterprise perspective while celebrating the ingenuity of undercover innovators. If they're savvy, they will also articulate the value that's been created.

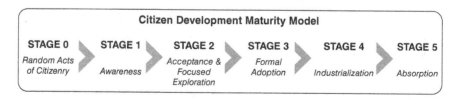

Figure 12.1   A citizen development maturity model

The awareness stage is also where the debate begins over whether to deactivate all citizen-developed solutions and impose a ban on the tools used to create them. This urge will be followed by the realization that most of the tools in question are part of the IT-approved technology suite sitting on everyone's desktops, perhaps causing a moment of embarrassment for IT or the CIO or even the CEO. As reality sets in that citizenry is not going away, the enterprise begins to transition to stage 2, either willingly or reluctantly.

Stage 2: Acceptance and Focused Exploration   At stage 2, meaningful structure begins to take shape. Much of Part 4 of this book is dedicated to exploring this structure. At this point, champions have likely won the support of at least some members of the executive suite. At this stage the direction of citizen sponsorship can flip from a bottom-up initiative to a top-down sponsored program. Mandates are declared in an effort to set goals, clarify strategy, and align resources to targeted outcomes and impacts.

Stage 2 is also the point when closer attention is paid to the tool portfolio, specifically the low-code and no-code solutions behind this innovation. Certain trusted tools will be championed while newer, more experimental tools will be put to the test in discrete pilots and proofs of concept.

The result of stage 2 is a recognition that nontechnical specialists have the potential to contribute to digital transformation initiatives across the enterprise. Citizens increasingly feel safe to come out of the shadows.

Stage 3: Formal Adoption   Thanks to the acceptance achieved in stage 2, citizen development enters a phase in which it is formalized, funded, and enabled. In the third stage, enterprises often assign a formal owner, organizational structures are designed (such as a center of excellence model or federated governance model), and formal reporting lines with clearly stated goals are declared.

In stage 3, formal governance, guidance, and guardrails will ensure that projects put into production meet defined standards without compromising systems or data. Structured training will show citizens what these standards actually are. This formalization will also put out a call for more citizens, which is when recruitment, training, skills assessments, certifications, and other qualification structures will be put in place. We have opinions about what methods work best to grow the ranks, which we discuss in Chapter 15, "Guidance."

As IT (sometimes begrudgingly) realizes that more hands on deck can be a good thing, their powers often combine with those of citizens. With such collaboration and both technical enablement from IT and robust organization support systems in place, citizens can begin to create more complex solutions. Citizen development is reaching its stride.

Stage 4: Industrialization Stage 4 is about scaling. Formal governance and guardrails are humming, citizens are signing up, impacts are reported out at executive meetings, and successes are being celebrated. Formal incentive programs appear to reward citizens at a level commensurate with their achievements. The organization begins to hire and train people in order to expand the ranks of citizens.

Pilots continue, but most projects have been moved to the leading platform in each of the citizen categories of automation, development, and data science (we cover this in Chapter 14, "Governance"). The goal is now to fully integrate citizen development into core enterprise processes and scale up initiatives across the board.

This could also be when enthusiasm wanes. If project impacts are not tracked carefully or if citizens are not rewarded sufficiently, there is a risk that things go back to "normal" and people return to focusing on their day jobs. In this case, the "I told you so" narrative will emerge from those who felt that "giving sharp knives to children" was never a recipe for long-term success. More likely, however, the tsunami of AI-powered tool introduction will help early adopters and tinkerers maintain their enthusiasm for building solutions.

Stage 5: Absorption The project management lifecycle typically ends with the project being absorbed into business-as-usual operations. Citizen development should follow this path as well. The very nature of "all hands" playing a role in AI-powered innovation requires all employees to have an opportunity to contribute. We are not just talking about everyone who works on a computer; ideally *everyone* in an organization will play a role in the citizen revolution, be it training, developing solutions, or collaborating with tools and information that augments them.

Citizen programs, if done right, will no longer merit stand-alone support functions and governance models. They will enter the stage in which "it's just how we work now." At this stage, every company is a software company, and every employee is a developer, data scientist, or automator. Citizen development will never go away, but as it becomes omnipresent, the need for formal programs supporting it will.

We don't anticipate many companies will reach stage 5, and we're not sure any have fully done so yet. But the organizations that do absorb citizenry into their day-to-day operations will become more nimble, competitive, and attractive to the best and the brightest talent.

As you are getting started with citizen development, we hope this maturity model helps you keep an eye on the destination. We will now discuss the crew needed for the landing party as you disembark.

Cast of Characters

These are the "hands" you will call on deck to ensure that you are tapping into a broad set of experiences, capabilities, and perspectives as you go. We divide this manifest into three main categories: leading roles, supporting roles, and stakeholders.

Figure 12.2 shows the leading and supporting roles in citizen development initiatives, as well as the key stakeholders whose buy-in and ongoing involvement are necessary for citizen development to thrive.

Leading Roles

Citizen development suffers from a branding issue. As we've indicated, the word *development* describes only a fraction of what citizens can do; it is important to highlight citizen automators, citizen data scientists, and citizen application developers separately.

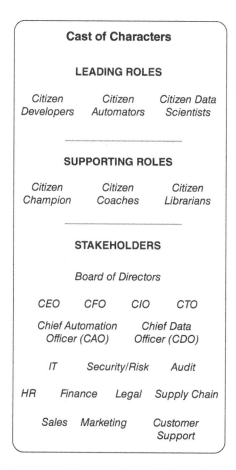

Cast of Characters

LEADING ROLES

| Citizen Developers | Citizen Automators | Citizen Data Scientists |

SUPPORTING ROLES

| Citizen Champion | Citizen Coaches | Citizen Librarians |

STAKEHOLDERS

Board of Directors

CEO   CFO   CIO   CTO

Chief Automation Officer (CAO)   Chief Data Officer (CDO)

IT   Security/Risk   Audit

HR   Finance   Legal   Supply Chain

Sales   Marketing   Customer Support

Figure 12.2   Primary and secondary citizen development roles

Citizen Developers   We've described citizen application developers in detail in Chapter 4, "Citizen Development Using Low-Code/No-Code Tools." As a brief reminder, they typically use low-code/no-code tools to develop individual or departmental applications.

Citizen Automators   Citizen automators, described in detail in Chapter 5, "Citizen Automation," are focused on digitizing manual workflows and automating rules-based decision-making. They typically use robotic process automation (RPA) software, sometimes combined with AI tools like document data extraction and process mining/discovery.

Citizen Data Scientists   Citizen data scientists and analysts are your data wranglers, analytical wizards, and dashboard dynamos. They are described in detail in Chapter 6 on "Citizen Data Science." They use tools like business intelligence, predictive analytics, and machine learning.

A Citizen by Any Other Name   The names we have given to each of the key players is less important than the roles they play. Alternative names we have heard and like include Super SME (Jabil), Embedded Developer (Mass General Brigham), Creator (Quixy), DIYer (Shell), Citizen Integrator (Kissflow), and finally, Maker (Amtrak).

Supporting Roles

This movement is made possible by a cast of characters. The few listed previously hold down the leading roles. But the protagonists depend on a slew of supporting cast members to make their roles possible. Here we list three that we believe are foundational to an enterprise-grade citizen program.

Citizen Champion   This is the advisor, the cheerleader, and occasionally the source of air-cover. The people in this role are quick to recognize the power of connecting grassroots inspiration to citizen-grade tools. Some champions merely enable citizens on their own teams, while others begin as citizens themselves before rising in the ranks to nurture and enable those that follow in their footsteps.

Citizen Coach   Early citizens are often self-taught. Thankfully for their successors, a more formal training, certification, and support program usually emerges over time. This is when the citizen coach appears. They teach the necessary skills, nurture the development of aspiring citizens, and assist in the ideation and review of new projects. We will discuss coaching in Chapter 15, "Guidance."

Citizen Librarian   Citizen programs run the risk of creating a large and uncatalogued pile of applications, integrations, and data models. These scattered assets have a few painful consequences: citizens may consistently reinvent wheels; organizations may go into severe technical debt. Having a librarian catalog the work products of citizens is a wise decision.

Some software platforms, such as UiPath, ServiceNow, and Power Platform, can be used to log and track that which has been built. This is fine if the enterprise has a monolithic citizen tech stack (only one tool), but this is an unlikely situation, especially in the long run.

Stakeholders

We need not tell you that the modern enterprise has many layers of management and far more divisions, departments, functions, and branches. Each and every one of these units is a stakeholder here. When all hands are on tech, those hands will be coming from every part of the business.

As citizen development gets off the ground, the executive ranks must understand what is happening, why it's happening, and what they need to do to support it happening. *Boards of directors* and *CEOs* should be aware of the role that citizen development plays in digital transformation and specify the types of citizen innovations that are most likely to enhance the organization's performance. The *CFO* and *finance* department should be focused on measuring and increasing the value of citizen activity and ensuring positive returns on it.

CIOs, IT, security, compliance, risk, and legal departments have often been in charge of saying "no," but they will need to learn how to say something different. Of course, having strong governance and guardrails in place is imperative, which should make these stakeholders breathe a little easier.

Operational departments such as *HR*, *sales*, *supply chain*, and *customer support* are where ideas will emerge; this is where the non-IT domain experts live. The leaders of such functions need to recognize that citizen activity is happening, guide it in the right strategic direction, and encourage more of it to take place. *HR*, of course, is also responsible for the recruiting, learning and development, and evaluation and reward processes that lead to citizen development.

Finally, *centers of excellence* must also be informed and engaged. Over the last two decades, there has been a proliferation of centers focusing on continuous improvement, learning and development, AI, ML, RPA, intelligent automation, data, and more. All of these centers are important stakeholders for citizen development and should integrate it into their offerings. An enterprise-grade citizen initiative hinges on the collaborative intersection of all the technology, data, process, and people discussed in this section.

The 4G Approach to Citizen-Readiness

We hope these examples, case studies, and individual profiles have convinced you that it is a worthwhile endeavor to empower domain experts. But how do you do this in your organization? The 4G approach that we will explore over Chapters 13–16 is designed to help streamline decision-making so that citizen development can meet its full potential. In the order that organizations will encounter them, these sequential parts are genesis, governance, guidance, and guardrails.

Figure 12.3 shows a high-level overview of each of the 4Gs, with the decision forks and key tools used in each one.

Each individual and initiative profiled so far faced the 4Gs and nine forks that we discuss in Chapters 13–16. But as you will see from the contrasting examples that we describe, companies with different needs make different choices about which path to take in each aspect of citizen enablement when they encounter these forks. We hope that by revisiting their choices and the contexts that led to them, you will gather the information needed to make the decisions at each of these forks that is right for you.

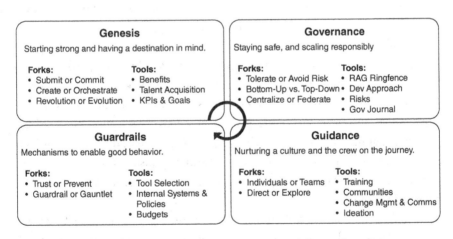

Figure 12.3   The 4Gs model for enabling citizen development

13 | Genesis

Like all evolutions, in the beginning there is darkness and chaos. In the beginning of any enterprise's journey to an established set of practices, policies, and rules, there is a chaos of various small projects and experimentations. These projects are mostly operating in the dark, often intentionally, keeping IT and leadership out of the projects for fear of them laying claim to the effort or simply putting an end to them.

The chaos phase is not necessarily bad, only uncoordinated. Citizen ingenuity sprouts up everywhere, and most companies will find it necessary to assess the citizen efforts that already exist and determine how best to enable them. The genesis section is about starting strong and having a destination in mind.

In this chapter, we will use three forks to help us to think through the decisions you will make (or have already made) during the genesis stage. After the discussion of the forks, we recommend a few best practices to fill the gaps between where your organization is now and where you want to go.

Genesis Fork 1: Submit or Just Commit

Our original name for this fork was "Prohibit, Submit, or Commit." We abandoned "Prohibit" for length and for practicality. You are welcome to try to prohibit citizen development, but you are highly unlikely to succeed. As tools become more pervasive and easier to use, there are just too many ways for citizens to circumvent your defenses and bring the latest technology to work. The "2024 Work Trend Index Annual Report," produced by Microsoft and LinkedIn, backs up this assertion: "Employees want AI at work—and they won't wait for companies to catch up."[1] Any efforts to prohibit citizen development are a waste of time, a drain to political capital, and a lost opportunity for transformation. If you're a persistent citizen bringing these tools to work, you have our permission to proceed. But please don't tell your management who authorized your rogue behavior.

Let's explore the first fork, submit or commit. Companies can resist at first, only to reluctantly submit to the idea of citizen development, or commit to making it a success early on.

Submit, Then Commit

The large consumer products company's citizen journey described at the beginning of this book has a happier ending but also offers a precautionary tale to companies considering submitting to or prohibiting citizens: the earlier you commit to citizen development, the better.

Five years ago, the company's IT team wasn't submitting to citizen development but was trying to prohibit it. Anyone outside of IT was discouraged from attempting data science, automation, or application development on their own. You may remember "Mr. Citizen" from the opening pages of this book. He was a supply chain manager when he first explored citizen development, and he describes the sentiment from IT towards this grassroots innovation at the time as "You can't do it; it doesn't work."

Even when citizens managed to complete and implement their projects, they were met with resistance from IT. Mr. Citizen and his team developed one automation that saved 48 hours of labor a week. Rather than supporting the citizen and his team or at least giving them a pat on the back, IT told him that he didn't need Alteryx because the citizen and his team could just write their SQL queries manually. But Mr. Citizen did need Alteryx, because he wasn't a programmer and couldn't write SQL queries manually. Despite this citizen's obvious success on previous automations, he struggled to get his IT organization to put Alteryx on the list of approved software tools.

---

[1] https://www.microsoft.com/en-us/worklab/work-trend-index/ai-at-work-is-here-now-comes-the-hard-part/#section3.

By not providing Mr. Citizen the tools he needed to realize his automation projects, IT was doing its best to prohibit them. But nobody could deny that his "shadow IT" saved more time and made better use of data throughout the organization.

The company finally realized that neither submitting to nor prohibiting citizenry would suffice. So they defined key principles, including referring to these projects as *citizen development* instead of *shadow IT*. They made clear what projects were in the best interest of the company and which were not. Eventually, engineers even created technical architecture to enable citizens' projects. As these projects saved time and money for domain experts and with new IT leadership, the company gradually underwent a mindset shift in favor of citizen development. Now it provides platforms, gives citizens tools, and creates communities that allow citizens to troubleshoot and learn together. To Mr. Citizen, however, it still seems a bit grudging.

If you're considering submitting to or trying to prohibit citizen development, we hope that the large consumer products company's journey convinces you otherwise. Grassroots data science, development, and automation will happen within your organization regardless of whether you condone or support it. But the sooner you do commit, the sooner these projects will bear fruit and the more delicious that fruit will be.

Commit

Perhaps no company has made as bold a commitment to citizen development as Microsoft. Richard Riley, head of marketing for the vendor's Power Platform, recounts that customers were often initially cautious about the idea, particularly if the CIO saw citizen development as a threat to the company's IT capabilities. Risk-averse cultures were also an issue. But Riley told us that knee-jerk reactions quickly shifted to "What is this?" and "How do we do this?" In fact, he said, "This flipped faster than anything I've seen in the tech industry."

Microsoft internally has embraced this revolution and its commitment to the concept has been a model of how to deploy the tech at scale. It didn't hurt, of course, that Microsoft became a leading provider of citizen-oriented software and that its CEO Satya Nadella became one of its strongest advocates.

Damon Buono, Microsoft's head of data governance, argues that the citizen movement has become so integrated into Microsoft's operations that now "there's no corporate IT organization in Microsoft." At Microsoft, everyone is expected to build products. With estimates of citizen-developed systems in the millions, seemingly everyone is meeting this expectation. These citizen-developed systems aren't merely internal. Microsoft consistently demonstrates how citizen tools can solve its own business problems and customers' problems alike. Buono said he couldn't turn off that culture even if he wanted to.

This infectious citizen culture is intentional at Microsoft, directly resulting from their commitment to citizen development. To enable the mass development of technology capability by all employees, Microsoft did away with centralized governance structures that may have hindered grassroots innovation. Microsoft no longer has a central corporate IT organization. There isn't a chief information officer, chief digital officer, or chief data officer either. All of these technology and data leadership roles have been pushed down to the product group level where they can enable rather than govern, and they do so primarily with (Microsoft) products rather than organizational structures.

Like all organizations, Microsoft had its initial reservations about citizen development. But now they're all in. The company recognized that prohibiting citizen development was impossible and turning a blind eye to it was irresponsible. So they chose to commit, and we strongly suggest you do the same. If it isn't already, the success of Microsoft's commitment to citizen development will become self-evident throughout this section of the book.

Assuming that domain experts will be creatively developing, automating, and analyzing whether you want them to or not, let's explore the options for what to do next. The first and most basic decision to make is whether to find your citizens or let them find you. Does your organization already have the individuals to scale citizen development? Or is it time to plant the seeds to grow this talent and initiative?

Fork 2: Create or Orchestrate

You can find your citizens or let them find you. Some companies aspire to have more citizens while others are overflowing with them. Taking inventory of the citizens in your company will help you decide if you need to create more citizen development or merely orchestrate the abundant citizens already at work.

Create Your Citizenry

As you may remember from Chapter 8 on "The Citizen Champion," citizen development at Amtrak began with a single citizen, Michael McCullough. Citizenry didn't spread organically as we have described in some companies; McCullough had to build Amtrak's citizen community from scratch.

We are not exaggerating when we say Amtrak started with one citizen. Following their first citizen data analysis project—a dashboard to display all project expenditures from across the company—Amtrak had exactly one Power BI license for its 24,000 employees.

McCullough continued his solo demonstration of the power of citizen data analysis. Amtrak needed a solution to track CDC data, outbreaks at their facilities, and healthy employee availability. IT said they could do it in six weeks; McCullough delivered a minimum viable product in 12 hours. When word got out about his miracle, McCullough noticed that people were increasingly hungry to be attached to successful projects.

McCullough took it on himself to inspire Amtrak's next generation of self-motivated digital problem-solvers. But as he plainly states, "I didn't feel like I needed to recruit them. I needed to inform them." McCollough believes that with the right tools, knowledge, and community, employees won't need convincing to adopt tools that solve problems and make their jobs easier.

But Amtrak employees didn't initially have the information they needed to succeed as citizens. McCullough changed that. He says that he felt, "We're not going to innovate, we're not going to grow, we're not going to move the needle if we are still stuck in a 'you guys come to us' mentality. . . I have to go to them. I have to provide the tools, the training, and the environment." That's exactly what McCullough did: he identified tools, training, and events that would inspire more citizen projects. He built communities across IT, security, and business units at Amtrak, and he formed a partnership with Microsoft to ensure seamless access to and troubleshooting with the Power Platform suite.

McCullough's efforts have led to a formidable supply of citizens: five years ago, there were three certified Amtrak "makers" (McCullough's word for developers) and four citizen-developed applications. There are now 1,152 makers and 24,300 maker applications. Approximately 19,000 Amtrak employees have made use of these apps. That's what we call viral growth!

It's rare for companies to have to work so intently to inspire a critical mass of citizens. More commonly, the seeds of a citizen army are already sown, and companies just need to channel their efforts toward their broader goals. In our next example, we will look at Johnson & Johnson, a company in which the average employee has a higher than average potential to execute citizen projects. All Johnson & Johnson had to do was point them in the right direction.

Orchestrate Your Citizenry

When Johnson and Johnson began their "Intelligent Automation" initiative in 2021, they had two goals: to free employees up to do more meaningful, purpose-driven work; and to save half a billion dollars in costs. Citizen automation has played a major role in accomplishing both of these goals. By the time J&J reached their cost-savings goal in 2023, they were heavily indexing on citizen data science as well.

But J&J didn't have to go out and find their citizens like Michael McCullough at Amtrak. J&J tends to hire talent with chemistry or drug discovery backgrounds, and these backgrounds lend themselves well to citizen data science and automation. The life sciences require "a logical mindset, technical competency, and an aptitude to learn,"[2] all qualities that leaders at J&J are explicitly looking for in citizen developers. These capabilities are also found in Johnson & Johnson's administrative functions. It should come as no surprise that an abundance of *professional* scientists and pharmaceutical business experts would yield widespread *citizen* data science as well.

Most employees at Johnson & Johnson are primed to succeed as citizen data scientists or automators; Johnson & Johnson just has to orchestrate them. And they have channeled their employees' high citizen potential with curated technical curricula, technology standards and criteria for assessing use cases. Employees have completed almost 30,000 courses using Johnson & Johnson's digital boot camp, which explains the fundamentals of AI, automation and data to aspiring citizens. More than 20,000 employees have

---

[2] https://sloanreview.mit.edu/article/harnessing-grassroots-automation.

completed a generative AI training course, which is required across the organization to deploy these tools for citizen projects.

Companies that make a habit out of hiring scientists, engineers, and expert administrators are most likely overflowing with potential citizens, but their efforts still have to be organized. According to Chris Gruber, senior director of Intelligent Automation & Digital Innovation, Global Services at Johnson & Johnson, this orchestration is well worth it: "Organizations can unlock new value by tapping into their team's expertise, offering the right training, and using technology. This way, they can achieve more than just small improvements and drive real, transformational change."

With your intrinsic or cultivated mass of citizens ready to deploy, it is time to start directing their efforts toward your organization goals.

Fork 3: Revolution or Evolution

Left to their own devices, citizens aspire to make themselves more productive and create value in their organizations. Often these efforts are dismissed by IT. But there are many ways in which citizen-scale innovations significantly move the needle. However, companies must make strategic decisions about how to channel and scale citizens' efforts.

Will you go deep and narrow, revolutionizing predetermined business processes with well-defined goals? Or will you go broad and shallow, allowing citizens to incrementally save costs and streamline ops in a more gradual process of organizational evolution?

Realistically, most companies will opt for a hybrid of revolution and evolution. Both are viable paths for citizens to benefit the bottom line. But the companies that consciously choose revolution, evolution, or an intentional blend of the two will best capture the value inherent in citizen development.

Revolution

Before Stanley Black & Decker (SB&D) enlisted citizens to improve its business, the company was in need of improved profit margins. Like many manufacturers, Stanley Black & Decker was facing crippling increases in tariffs and raw material costs throughout the early days of the pandemic. Margins shrank and profits dwindled.

But SB&D's CEO, John Loree, deployed citizens in a targeted approach to revolutionize their profit margins. As we mentioned in Chapter 10, "Benefits of Citizen Development," Loree identified specific "value pools" (digital procurement, pricing, inventory demand and supply, cost categories for products) that were ripe for improvement and set the goal of using AI and analytics to deliver a billion dollars in revenue over three years.

Key to this revolution was SB&D's "Data Democratization" program that empowered 1,000 employees with data and tools to find ways to improve the business across the distinct value pools. Their citizens leaned heavily on Alteryx, using automated data workflows, analytics, and data science AI models to slash time and costs from business processes. Product price optimization, as just one example, no longer required days or weeks; pricing happened with customers in real time. In the first year of the program, SB&D's citizens cut 30% of indirect costs and identified $500 million in profit.

SB&D executives needed dramatic improvement in margins and then provided the direction and support to meet their citizens' ambition. They dreamed big about the broad bottom-line potential of citizen development and then targeted the value pools toward which citizens would direct their efforts.

Companies that have predetermined goals for citizen development can prescribe specific tools and training that catalyze deeply rooted change. But as we will see in the next example, there is also value to be captured from allowing citizen development to evolve an organization more incrementally.

Evolution

"When you're the size of AT&T and you've had so many mergers and so many systems, there's just lots of manual processes." Those words from AT&T Vice President of Data Science Mark Austin explains the need for citizen automation at AT&T. AT&T never defined value pools for digital innovation. They didn't hatch grand plans for data democratization that initiated a citizen revolution. Instead, AT&T has fostered broad citizen evolution: incremental improvement of processes that, when aggregated, add up to an extraordinary savings in time and money.

In 2015, AT&T's service delivery team was so bogged down with manual, repetitive tasks that they began experimenting with robotic process automation (RPA). "These things would come in large batches, and they would have Excel files and people were literally typing these things individually into the systems because they weren't set up for batch," Austin explained to CIO.com.[3] "We heard about RPA at the time, and we started trying it and all of a sudden we were able to automate one process and then the next process and it kind of grew from there."

AT&T saved a minute here and a minute there; RPA was initially aimed at automating unpopular, monotonous tasks to simply improve employees' lives. But these incremental gains started to add up. After one year of experimentation, AT&T had created 350 automations. The savings garnered by these automations warranted the creation of an automation center of excellence to expand the program.

While AT&T's center of excellence houses 20 full-time employees that accelerate automation projects, the way they enable citizens is what really drives automation at scale. Through educating subject-matter experts to automate their own daily processes, AT&T has expanded to more than 3,000 automated bots, more than 90% of which have been built by citizens. And while the time and money saved from each automation may be incremental, the combined value across all the citizen-created automations—not to mention data science models—is immense. And now AT&T is increasingly involving citizens in the use of generative AI as well.

Austin's first piece of advice for companies considering RPA is to "start small." But AT&T's grassroots automation efforts demonstrate that thinking small can yield big gains when companies focus scaling such automations.

Starting Strong with the Fundamentals

Case studies go a long way, but we know you also need a set of fundamental principles and best practices to set up your citizen development program for success. We will highlight the fundamentals to identifying benefits, orchestrating talent, and setting goals.

Benefits

Our examples are rife with hours saved, efficiencies realized, and costs reduced. But there are also examples of employees liberated and engaged,

---

[3] https://www.cio.com/article/415235/atts-embraces-intelligent-automation-at-scale.html.

IT relieved and assisted, and customers empowered with actionable information and better service. In case you find yourself needing to champion citizen programs, Table 13.1 highlights these four stakeholders and key ways that grassroots ingenuity lends value.

Table 13.1   Stakeholders and Their Benefits

Stakeholders	Benefits
Organization	• Accelerates innovation and agility across the enterprise • Enhances process optimization and efficiency programs • Reduces costs and quality issues in sales, operations, and customer service • Addresses talent shortage of professional developers and data scientists • Fosters data-driven decision-making throughout the organization
Citizen	• Creates greater empowerment and ownership • Offers opportunities for modern skill development and career growth • Increases job satisfaction and employee experience • Enables better understanding of business processes • Provides opportunities for recognition and reward for creativity and value added to the business
IT Department	• Reduces shadow IT and mitigates associated risks and remediations • Reduces backlog of IT requests • Improves collaboration with business units and internal stakeholders • Increases speed of design, iteration, and implementation • Allows for more efficient use of existing IT resources and expertise

Stakeholders	Benefits
End customer/ user	• Increases speed and frequency of innovative solutions • Improves customer service and user experience design • Enables more personalized and efficient customer interactions • Allows access to more valuable and accurate data and insight

Talent

As discussed in "Fork 2: Create or Orchestrate," amassing a team of citizens is sometimes an act of creation and other times an act of orchestration. Clearly, there are many ways to attract and engage talent. The following list showcases some of the approaches worthy of your consideration:

- Creating awareness
  - Campaigns
  - Roadshows
  - Executive sponsorship statement

- Attracting and recruiting talent
  - Defined career roles and trajectories
  - Distinctions and rewards

- Assessing talent
  - Temperament and personality assessments
  - Logic and skill assessments

Key Performance Indicators

The citizen movement usually involves many micro-initiatives that add up to a broader revolution. Table 13.2 lists performance indicators that we have seen implemented most often. Instituting too many measures can be confusing and counterproductive; it is best to pick no more than you can reasonably track.

Table 13.2 Key Performance Indicators

KPI Category	KPIs
Adoption & Engagement	• Number of applications, automations, and models in development • Number of applications, automations, and models currently in use • Number of reusable components/pieces in circulation in module library • Average time to take a solution from idea to design to deployment • Number of cross functional projects spanning business functions • Tenure of citizens in the program • Number of applications or models developed per citizen • Dropout rate of citizens enrolled in the program
Innovation & Value	• Number of ideas and designs being developed • Number of ideas rejected or placed in backlog • Percent increase in customer satisfaction from new solutions
Operational Efficiency	• Number of processes automated or improved • Percent decrease in errors and processing times

KPI Category	KPIs
Skill Development	• Number of active citizen developers, automators, and data scientists • Number of applicants to join formal citizen training programs • Number of trained citizens • Number of certifications earned • Proficiency level of citizens achieved in chosen tools • Number of coaching and mentorship sessions conducted • Frequency of knowledge sharing and community events • Retention rate of skilled citizens
Governance & Compliance	• Number of requests to IT for support in development • Degree of compliance with data governance policies • Number of projects reviewed and approved • Percentage of projects meeting security standards • Percentage of projects passing quality assurance tests • Incidence of post-deployment issues or errors in citizen projects

14 | Governance

As Max Malloy, assistant vice president of enterprise digital experience at ProAssurance, said to us, the critical factor in any successful citizen development initiative is "governance, governance, governance, governance."

While we have expressed our concern with the controlling connotations of the word *governance*, we recognize the need for it. Measures to ensure the stability, safety, and scalability of citizen projects are essential. Governance structures make it easy for citizens to make good decisions.

According to the vendor Betty Blocks' guide for governing citizen development, "A solid governance model should serve as the backbone of any citizen development program."[1] But it is imperative to adapt the governance model that you adopt. There will be no one-size-fits-all. A high level of draconian control will likely drive citizens right back into the shadows. Designing the right level of governance is a balancing act between autonomy and control.

Each enterprise must choose the right levels of control and constraint to suit their needs. As Amtrak's Michael McCullough explains, "Your governance will fit where you are on your journey. Once citizen development becomes more established, your governance will adjust accordingly." Regardless of the maturity of your citizen development programs, you will

---

[1] https://query.prod.cms.rt.microsoft.com/cms/api/am/binary/RE4GSjX.

need to make decisions early on about your relationship to risk, where your governance comes from and where your governance lives.

For each of these decisions, the following forks highlight two companies that have right-sized their governance to their unique needs. The companies we compare often make contrasting choices about their governance structures, but governance decisions are unlikely to be as binary as they appear in the following examples. After our comparisons in the forks, we also recommend a few frameworks and best practices that have been used widely by companies with mature citizen development programs.

Fork 4: Tolerate Risk or Avoid Risk

Companies can tolerate varying levels of risk.

Risk Tolerance

Compared to some of the companies we have highlighted in the banking, medical, and transportation industries, Dentsu has a high tolerance for risk.

Dentsu is one of the largest advertising and public relations companies in the world, and its risk tolerance is partially a product of their industry. While the advertising and marketing services industry is governed by consumer protection regulations (such as data privacy and competition), the risks from a citizen project going awry at Dentsu pale in comparison to a misstep at Shell, Amtrak, or Johnson & Johnson.

But Dentsu isn't just in a low-risk industry; they have also primarily targeted low-risk automations, further encouraging their citizens to act boldly. At the start of their citizen automation initiative, Dentsu's former chief automation officer, Max Cheprasov, was on the hunt for high-frequency, high-density, highly structured tasks that took up a lot of time. Dentsu's citizen automators focused on automating tasks such as timesheet reporting, quality assurance checks, reminders, compiling vendor invoices, and merging disparate data sources. Cheprasov explains that picking this internal low-hanging fruit allowed Dentsu to simply "put something in the hands of employees, take out the bureaucracy, and accelerate innovation."

While tightly controlled citizen enablement might make sense for higher risk projects, Cheprasov reminded us that "top-down projects can take a long time. . .months." But low-risk internal projects in a relatively low-risk industry allow citizen-led automation to bloom quickly. Most of

Dentsu's aspiring automators had no prior technical background, but after just one week of training and a one-day coach-led workshop, they could start building automations for themselves and their teams. And these citizens are automating broadly across IT, finance, and digital media marketing.

Dentsu's bottom-up approach to automation yielded quick results. Working with UiPath's product StudioX, new citizens build a solution in one day. In fact, 50 citizen developers created 60 solutions in the first two days of their citizen automation initiative. At the time we spoke with Cheprasov, who has since moved on from Dentsu, citizens were responsible for 3,500 solutions averaging 800% return on investment (ROI). Given the low barriers to entry, both the number of automations and the number of citizens at Dentsu will likely continue growing for some time.

Risk Avoidance

Some organizations don't tolerate risk; they avoid it. But many of these risk-avoidant companies still produce robust citizen development programs through top-down governance. These companies can't afford to let their citizens run wild. You may remember the insurance data science leader who described how their organization strives "to keep sharp knives out of the hands of children." Citizen development can be a powerful tool for risk-averse organizations, especially if they establish top-down governance structures before citizen development proliferates.

Proassurance, which you may remember from Chapter 11 ("The Organizational Response to Citizen Technology"), is a specialty insurer focused on the healthcare sector, so they are naturally risk-averse. ProAssurance is also a data-driven organization. As their assistant VP of enterprise digital experience, Max Malloy, explains, "We are now a data and technology company just as much as we are an insurance company."

ProAssurance has to remain vigilant about the ways their data is put to use. But their risk aversion hasn't stopped Proassurance from committing to citizen development. Citizens first took on the digital experience aspects of automating the ticketing system for the IT help desk and soon graduated to real-time dashboards around anything associated with approvals, workflows, or claims processing. And now, Malloy claims it is easier to say what lower-complexity solutions they are *not* considering using citizen development for: "People's skillsets are becoming more fluid between business and IT…lines are really starting to get blurred."

Malloy also experienced the (now familiar) initial pushback from IT, but believes that this "heartburn" helped ProAssurance create the protective systems they needed for citizen development to actually work in a risk-averse environment. ProAssurance relies heavily on top-down, centralized governance and automated guardrails from its vendor ServiceNow to ensure that citizen development projects stay in bounds. The risk-averse structures that ProAssurance have put in place make it difficult for citizens to do the wrong thing: whenever anything has been built, their enterprise digital experience team is notified; then IT development leads are included in "approval threads" requiring that projects move through multiple checkpoints before going live; "process triggers" can shut down a project if citizens touch the wrong data or take action without required approvals.

Fork 5: Bottom Up vs. Top Down

A conversation about risk tolerance and risk aversion often maps directly onto decisions about governance structures. While not a hard-and-fast rule, risk-tolerant organizations are more likely to employ bottom-up governance; risk-averse organizations more commonly rely on top-down governance.

Top-Down Governance

The rigorously governed citizen development program at a nuclear utility company we researched is an example of risk aversion and top-town governance. This company produces and distributes electric power in the southern United States, and its commitment to nuclear energy has placed the company under strict regulatory scrutiny due to safety and environmental considerations.

But these restrictions haven't stopped the utility from enabling citizen developers. As the company's citizen development program manager, puts it, "In the age we're in, you have to upskill your people to do more with less. The way to do that is with automation." Initially, the company was attracted to citizen development because executives knew grassroots automation could help them gain an edge over competitors. But they also understood the potential downsides of citizen enablement. When nuclear energy is involved, the manager makes clear that "You don't want the Wild West."

The utility relied on top-down governance to balance the risk and reward of citizenry. The citizen development manager and his colleagues spent nine months building a three-tiered governance structure before their citizen development program even got off the ground. Their Tier 1 governance structures apply to personal productivity and have the loosest controls. Tier 2 kicks in if citizens' solutions impact multiple users or interface with production systems. Tier 3 requires system and organizational controls (SOCs), which are a series of standards, typically assessed by independent auditors, used to measure how safely citizens organize, secure, and transmit data.

The citizen development program has been live for about a year. Even with increasingly stringent top-down controls, citizen projects have made a big impact and expanded beyond their initial desire for automation. The manager speaks of "big power users that are building big things for the business" and notes that, "Robotic process automation is great, but it's only one use case." Citizens at this utility can "build an app, a business application flow, a chat bot, or an AI that brings in structured and unstructured data."

Without these clearly defined top-down governance structures, it's hard to imagine that the company's leadership or employees would have had the confidence to let citizen development fly.

Bottom-Up Governance

Not all companies have the need or ability to tightly regulate their citizens. Instead of stringent, top-down governance protocols, many companies take a bottom-up approach to regulating citizen activity. Bottom-up governance doesn't mean letting citizens run amok; it's just the minimal level of governance, often stemming from citizens themselves, that makes it easy for citizens to do the right thing

Microsoft uses the word *enablement* to refer to structures and processes that other companies would describe as governance. Citizen development is so core to working at Microsoft that Damon Buono, Microsoft's head of data governance (also referenced in Chapter 11 on the organizational response to citizen development) argues that it would be difficult to stifle and nearly impossible to turn off. Microsoft has, according to Buono, "millions of examples of citizen data science models…and millions and millions of dashboards." Attempting to tightly govern this level of citizenry would be challenging at best. Buono admits that they have limited control over who can and cannot build an app.

But they can control what access citizens have to important business data. Microsoft Purview is a product that allows a data governance team to approve or deny citizen access to sensitive data. Data products that could modify data can only be published for internal use if they are first approved by the Purview group, but the majority of governance structures are "non-invasive." Damon says, "If you introduce governance processes outside of the product-making process, they will be ignored. If a citizen is generating code, there are automated governance rules built in, but citizens are given the minimum possible restrictions to encourage the maximum amount of innovation." In other words, Microsoft's data governance structures are designed for enablement rather than control.

With millions of citizen-developed tools in circulation, both internally and with customers, Microsoft's minimalist governance approach doesn't seem to have inhibited grassroots innovation. If citizen control measures aren't absolutely necessary, they will not be implemented. The goal of Microsoft's governance structures are simply to "prevent citizens from shooting themselves in the foot."

Fork 6: Centralize or Federate

If you don't decide whether your governance will come from the top down or from the bottom up, it is unlikely to come consistently from any direction at all. Once you have made decisions about the directionality of your citizen development governance structures, the next step is deciding where these structures will live. Do they belong in a centralized, tightly guarded group where only the most qualified and conscientious are given access? Or are citizen projects freely deployed on federated teams and networks throughout the organization?

Your answer will likely fall somewhere in between these more extreme examples of centralization or federation. And if you're following these forks sequentially, you have already made some decisions about your relationship to risk and the direction (bottom up or top down) of your governance structures to help decide where to give citizens a rightful home within your company walls.

Centralized Governance

In the Preface to this book we gave a detailed account of how citizen development helped Shell accelerate in the race to digitize its business. Shell has become a canonical example of citizen enablement, which is why it is mentioned more than 60 times throughout our book. The level of centralized governance that Shell has created, especially for data, offers an example of how to protect information or systems that you can't afford for citizens to toy with.

When Shell's employees began to get citizen-oriented tools in their hands, Jay Crotts had serious concerns but saw an opportunity. Crotts is Shell's former group chief information officer and one of the earliest citizen champions (and the first mentioned in this book), but he couldn't help but imagine the worst-case scenarios if citizens showed poor judgment with personal data. When the European Union passed the General Data Protection Regulation in 2016, Crotts knew it was time to create a safe place to access and store data for citizen development.

To be clear, Crotts and his team didn't just create a centralized data repository out of fear. There were lots of smart and capable people taking initiative with data-driven projects at Shell, and they needed a place to access and store the data they would use. These needs and constraints spawned the "Do It Yourself Initiative," which included a centralized location to put data for DIY projects and a system that required citizens to request user authorization from designated owners of each data set. If you don't remember the DIY initiative, that probably means you skipped the preface of this book. We don't take it personally.

The team that started the DIY initiative believed that if they built a centralized, well-governed data repository, people would come to use it. And they were right. With more than 6,500 trained citizen developers, thousands of projects, and 10x returns on their investment, Shell has assumed a leading position in many aspects of citizen development.

Federated Governance

Shell found a way to use centralized data governance as an enabler to scale citizen development. But centralized governance can sometimes be a hindrance to scaling. The global tire manufacturing giant Michelin relied on distributed governance systems to educate and monitor citizens in each department. The combined examples of Shell and Michelin demonstrate how centralized governance (of data) and federated governance (of citizens) can work in tandem.

Michelin was initially attracted to citizen development because of the potential cost savings on offer with process automation. With such high demand for IT projects and the high cost and limited availability of IT talent, Michelin began to rely on domain experts to build their own tools. But now, the head of digital employee experience, Martin Nenov, sees citizen development as "empowerment—taking the tools, making their lives easier."

Robotic process automation (RPA) at Michelin first kicked off in 2018 with a small number of citizens motivated to learn UiPath. But citizens quickly escalated Michelin's automation capabilities. When Michelin switched to Microsoft Teams, everybody got their hands on RPA tools. And the IT organization was actually *responsible for* (not resistant to) putting RPA tools in the hands of domain experts.

RPA moved away from central IT and into distributed networks in a hurry. IT couldn't support all the citizen coaching requests coming in and was searching for a balanced governance structure. Nenov says they were "trying to control and democratize at the same time."

Michelin found this balance by forming a center of excellence. IT sends out teams to coach the federated departments where citizen development demand is strong. Each department had a unique RPA environment, so coaches support their unique needs. Each coach was assigned to specific plants, holding hackathons and targeted bootcamps in each department.

These federated citizen environments were not totally siloed. Each organizational unit has a citizen champion, and the champions are collectively woven together into a network. The distributed governance allows citizen development to grow organically while the network of champions allows leaders to still keep a close eye on what everybody is doing. Michelin gets the speed, innovation and empowerment that comes with federated governance, but with the network of champions they can ensure that projects aren't replicated and that citizens' lessons are passed on from one department to another.

This best-of-both-worlds approach at Michelin has yielded results. In just a few years, citizens have built more than 1,000 applications and more than 100,000 automations.

Enabling a Successful Voyage

A well-balanced governance approach is no small feat, but an organization's context provides a starting point. To properly weigh risk tolerance, direction of sponsorship, and control locations, look first to the way that your existing culture and leadership have balanced autonomy and control in the past. Whatever the culture, however, the goals of a governance framework should focus on reducing shadow IT, creating freedom for citizens to build securely, and relieving IT to focus on core systems.

The following are a set of best practices that can start your toolkit. It is by no means exhaustive, but they can be the foundational stones on which to build sturdy citizen development governance.

Risks

In the previous chapter, we explored the "Benefits of Citizen Development." We now examine the potential risks (see Table 14.1).

Table 14.1   Risks of Citizen Development

Risk Category	Risk Types
Data Risks	• Uncontrolled modification of important data elements • Noncompliance with industry data regulations or internal policies • Inconsistent data management practices leading to data quality issues
Integration Risks	• Challenges in integrating citizen-developed solutions with existing enterprise systems and applications • Compatibility issues and data silos • Duplication of efforts and redundant solutions

(continued)

Risk Category	Risk Types
Quality Risks	• Poorly designed or tested applications, automations, or models due to lack of technical or data expertise • Errors or bugs in citizen-developed solutions and data models • Lack of scalability or maintainability of citizen-developed solutions • Automation of bad or inefficient processes and workflows • Inclusion of corrupted or bad data into data models
Dependency Risks	• Over-reliance on citizen developers, leading to knowledge gaps and continuity issues • Lack of proper documentation and knowledge transfer • Difficulty in maintaining or enhancing citizen-developed solutions
Security Risks	• Potential security vulnerabilities due to untrained users creating applications without proper security measures • Unauthorized access to sensitive data or systems • Increased attack surface for cyber threats
Ethical Risks	• Potential bias or discrimination in citizen-developed models or algorithms • Poor decision-making from misinterpretation of data and insights • Ethical concerns around data privacy and consent
Resource Risks	• Overconsumption of computing resources or storage due to inefficient citizen-developed solutions • Increased IT support and maintenance costs • Licensing and compliance costs for citizen development platforms

Organizational Structure

Organizational approaches to citizen development are culture-specific. Some organizations choose to let solo citizens run wild, while others favor communal efforts and organize fusion teams or centers of excellence. The most common form that we came across in our research is a centralized body of specialists supporting federated branches and teams.

Many citizen efforts begin with individuals who gradually galvanize a few fellow pioneers to join them. Over time, departments form and or centers of excellence are established. Each approach makes sense for different levels of maturity. Table 14.2 showcases the most common structures and serves as a good introduction to our discussion of individuals and teams in Chapter 15, "Guidance."

Table 14.2 Common Organizational Structures for Citizen Development

Individual	Team	Fusion Teams	Center of Excellence
Solo creators, empowered to innovate often on simple and safe processes and data models.	Intradepartmental team, combining forces to work on larger, yet still somewhat basic processes and models.	Cross-functional temporarily assigned teams with IT and citizen members, sponsored to collaborate and develop more complex interdepartmental processes and models.	Coordinated interdepartmental dedicated teams focused on the most complex processes and models allowed, often supporting smaller teams as well.

Governance Models

Every citizen initiative needs a governance model. These structures ensure that teams can maximize return on investment (ROI), efficiency, and the quality of their work while safeguarding against risks and compliance issues.

Of the models we came across in our research, the most prominent came from the PMI Institute, the research firm Gartner, and a model used by Shell (showcased in a case study by Noel Carroll, University of Galway professor and founder of the Citizen Development Lab[2]). While they offer different levels of complexity, all are based on an XY chart with X mapping criticality (or risk) and Y mapping complexity. Those projects plotted closest to the axis are low criticality and low complexity and are therefore well suited for individuals or smaller teams, without additional support from IT. As you travel further up (more critical) and out (more complex), projects require more IT support and end up in a strata where only IT is allowed to proceed. These levels are often colored green (go), yellow (proceed with caution), and red (avoid). Some even have a black area, forbidden for any but the most experienced.

The more sophisticated frameworks bring in other parameters that give the governance model more nuance and fidelity. As illustrated in Figure 14.1, the y-axis may include size of team, level of compliance or regulation, scale of solution, and extent to which a solution spans outside of the enterprise to touch external systems and stakeholders. The x-axis may also measure data complexity characteristics (self-contained, shared, sensitive, etc.), user access rights, confidentiality, and adherence to enterprise standards and approved tools. A multivariate governance model like this can support quite sophisticated role-based authorizations.

A common theme in the most advanced citizen programs is the pursuit to "grow the green." These programs hope to enable citizens to take on more complex and critical projects. Steps to achieve growing the green (Shell calls it the DIY Zone) include enhanced risk and compliance training, well-designed guardrails, and an ongoing effort to earn the trust of IT and risk officers.

---

[2] Carroll, N., & Maher, M. (2023). "How Shell fueled a digital transformation by establishing DIY software development." *MIS Quarterly Executive*, 22(1), 1–16.

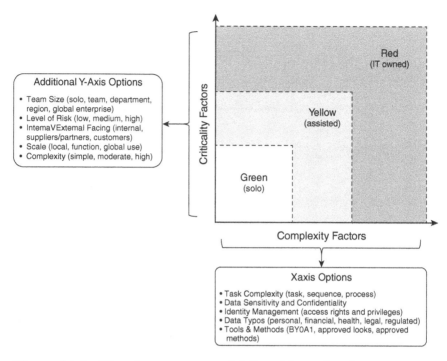

Additional Y-Axis Options

- Team Size (solo, team, department, region, global enterprise)
- Level of Risk (low, medium, high)
- Interna/VExternal Facing (internal, suppliers/partners, customers)
- Scale (local, function, global use)
- Complexity (simple, moderate, high)

Criticality Factors

Red
(IT owned)

Yellow
(assisted)

Green
(solo)

Complexity Factors

Xaxis Options

- Task Complexity (task, sequence, process)
- Data Sensitivity and Confidentiality
- Identity Management (access rights and privileges)
- Data Typos (personal, financial, health, legal, regulated)
- Tools & Methods (BY0A1, approved looks, approved methods)

Figure 14.1 The three-zone model for citizen development

15 | Guidance

Citizen development is done by people. Any successful digital strategy is at its core a successful human strategy. When digital initiatives fail, it is often due to a lack of emphasis on human considerations. It's rarely the technology that causes failure.

With governance structures in place, we now turn to elements that we classify under the umbrella of "guidance." Guidance includes the training and support an enterprise offers its citizens and the development of formal and informal communities.

These next forks explore the level of autonomy and exploration that citizens are afforded as they learn. While principles can be laid by organizations, your individuals will tell you what types of guidance actually resonate with them. We suggest you listen.

Fork 7: Solo or in Teams

Do you trust citizens to innovate on their own? Do you have the capacity for citizens to work in teams? The following examples illustrate both the individual and collective ends of the citizen collaboration spectrum, but this decision need not be a zero-sum game.

Go Alone

Arcadis is the second largest architecture firm in the world. They have more than 4,000 citizen developers, primarily focused on delivering services on projects to improve the quality of life in cities and communities. Each one of these citizen developers is an island. "If you build something, you're accountable for it," says Freek Matheij, Arcadis's global platform director.

At the moment, there are few fusion teams—collaborations of IT people and citizens—at Arcadis. In fact, in the genesis stage of citizen development, there were no teams at all. Eventually, successful citizen projects get plugged into an innovation pipeline. But until that point, Arcadis believes that when citizen development is an individual effort, it encourages individual responsibility.

Arcadis avoids collective citizenry because of their high level of organizational self-awareness. "We aren't ready for a lot of fusion development," says Matheij. "Not everybody wants to be a mentor, and we have to build a lot of trust to work up to collective responsibility." Arcadis knows that their IT teams are usually already taking on more than they can handle, so expecting them to coach thousands of citizens is unreasonable. Instead of adding the regulation of domain experts to IT's plate, the burden of responsibility falls squarely on the citizen who builds each project.

How does Arcadis keep their solitary citizen developers on track? It's their well-oiled blend of automated guardrails. You'll read more about how Arcadis's guardrails steer citizens toward good behavior in the next chapter.

Go Together

Arcadis is an extreme case of citizen individualism, but citizen development is often collaborative. While the next example offers an equally powerful perspective on the power of fusion teams, we don't expect you to start assigning your citizens and your data scientists seats next to each other. As is the case for all of these forks, your solution will likely fall somewhere in between these more extreme examples.

Wolters Kluwer is an information services company that we highlighted in Chapters 10 and 11 on the "Benefits of Citizen Development" and "The Organizational Response to Citizen Technology." How committed is Wolters Kluwer to fusion teams? They force domain experts and representatives of a customer-focused technology group (not IT) to sit together.

Five years ago Wolters Kluwer's data scientists and domain experts were on separate teams, but "if you don't make data scientists live in an ecosystem of operators, they don't speak the language, feel the pain, understand the problems." Those words come from Wolters Kluwer's global head of data and analytics, Abhishek Mittal. Mittal is part of the team that had the idea to have data scientists literally sit next to people on the operations team to observe each other's work.

When they kicked off this experiment, Wolters Kluwer didn't have a grand vision of citizen data scientists; the term didn't even exist yet. But their data scientists complained that in previous jobs they largely worked on theoretical problems that never went anywhere because user voice was never incorporated. And their subject-matter experts seemed to feel like the data scientists were opaque, mysterious, and generally removed from the normal operations of the business.

These forced fusion teams inadvertently created citizen developers and resulted in impactful projects. Through their mingling, domain experts and data scientists started to speak each other's language: skills started to blend; both sides became experts in each other's fields. Sandeep Sacheti, executive VP at Wolters Kluwer, noticed that domain experts started to see data scientists as "accessible people who want to solve problems and can be talked to."

And Wolters Kluwer's domain experts quickly acquired data science skills. While building Sniffer, the legal bill analyzer that we discussed in Chapter 11 on organizational response, their lawyers were able to independently execute much of the data science and even write the apps. The data scientists on the project are also now well versed in how to supercharge legal bill review.

Whether the goal is to turbocharge citizen development or simply to get siloed functions to speak each other's language, the fusion of business-oriented technology experts and technology-oriented domain experts can create teams much greater than the sum of their parts.

Fork 8: Direct or Explore

Think of the way you were taught in school. Did you have strict teachers, lectures, assignments, and rules? Or were you self-directed, pursuing knowledge and skills to advance your meaningful projects?

Most education systems rely heavily on explicit direct instruction, a content delivery method in which it is the teachers' job to pass down knowledge to students. But some education is less unidirectional, and less direct forms of instruction include "project-based learning." In project-based learning, learners work together and selectively seek out knowledge and skills that help them accomplish a collective goal.

As companies strive to fill skills and knowledge gaps in their citizens, there is a time and a place for both types of instruction. The genesis, governance, and guidance decisions you make in earlier forks will likely determine the blend of direct instruction and project-based exploration that makes sense for guiding your citizens.

Direct Instruction

PepsiCo took the leap into citizen automation because employees were facing bottlenecks. At first, everybody was chasing the same ~~IT~~ technology service delivery teams. When ~~IT~~ this approach couldn't meet demand, PepsiCo started hiring contractors and vendors. But there was still never enough ~~IT~~ support, to the point that leaders like Chris Knapik, PepsiCo's senior director of process transformation, and his team started wondering if subject- matter experts should run projects on their own. That's when PepsiCo started training citizen automators.

PepsiCo's first citizens were automators leaning heavily on UiPath, but they were not just cut loose to try their hands at RPA. PepsiCo built a rigorous curriculum that focused on raising awareness and skill acquisition. At its most basic level, the curriculum was meant to teach their workforce what citizen ~~automation~~ development is so that they could see the value it held to make their working lives easier. But the lessons were primarily devoted to skill acquisition, such as how to use the Microsoft Power Platform. Knapik and his colleagues believed that their citizens needed hard skills and awareness before they could run their own projects.

And their curriculum isn't just for entry-level citizenry. They have well-defined citizen competence levels at PepsiCo such as "citizen developer" and "advanced citizen developer." The way you climb to these higher stages is through serious engagement with the curriculum and with boot camps. If you want to take on bigger citizen projects at PepsiCo, you need to put in the coursework first.

Even though citizens can engage with the curriculum as individuals, collaborative learning still plays an important role for PepsiCo's citizens. When citizens get stuck, either with the curriculum or with a project, there are communities with active channels and governance groups waiting to be consulted. PepsiCo has teams in the form of a hub with citizen spokes coming off of it. One hub is often connected to others so that the spokes are intertwined in ways that best support a specific project or team. For those who believe that group learning is only compatible with project-based learning, PepsiCo's rigorous approach to direct instruction offers a counter-example.

Regardless of how much class time you have logged at PepsiCo, the learning never stops. Knapik points out that, "Even when you think you learned it all, tools like UiPath are robust and demanding." As citizens expand their individual skills and the total number of citizens expands as well, PepsiCo finds ways to keep the instruction coming. And their instruction has paid dividends. Though their citizens may have started as automators, their curriculum has allowed Pepsi's citizens to take on low-code/no-code and ~~data science~~process mining projects as well.

Project-Based Learning

Some companies, like Chevron, take a more exploratory approach to educating their citizens. To be clear, direct instruction and project-based learning are not mutually exclusive; most companies will rely on a proprietary blend of the two pedagogical methods. But Chevron offers a clear-cut illustration of project-based learning so that organizations can understand the finer points of citizen education.

Chevron has more than 2,500 citizen developers impacting nearly every arm of their business, from petrotechnical functions to corporate functions. Citizens work on projects in manufacturing, energy, human resources, and legal, to name just a few of the departments in which citizens are taking initiative.

But their learning process looks nothing like that of PepsiCo. Chevron's CIO, Bill Braun, argues in a CIO magazine article that "traditional instructor-led programs do not cut it in this space. . .We encourage our people to start with a solid use case—a clear opportunity that is not already addressed by our application portfolio. We then support them through a four-month program that blends some instruction and hands-on coaching."[1] Braun is describing a project-based learning process where citizens start with a use case and bootstrap the knowledge and skills they need to accomplish their project goals.

---

[1] Bob Violino, "Empowering Citizen Developers for Real Business Impact." CIO. Accessed May 15, 2024. `https://www.cio.com/article/646508/empowering-citizen-developers-for-real-business-impact.html`.

At Chevron, fast-paced, project-based citizenry is partially out of necessity: "Many times, these solutions are niche or needed for a fast response to a developing situation," Braun explains. When the homes of many of Chevron's Africa employees were damaged by flash flooding, a citizen data scientist quickly built a tool for damage reporting and solution tracking. Chevron often needs a solution fast, so they have to rely on their people closest to the problem to upskill themselves. They simply don't have time to start from a curriculum and build up from there.

Instead, Chevron's citizens build and learn simultaneously as the project requires: "Citizen developers are building applications while also learning new problem-solving techniques, ways to break down complexities, and how to teach others,"[2] Braun describes. While this project-based approach does result in completed projects, it also creates an infectious tendency for Chevron's employees to empower themselves and to empower others. As Braun puts it, "The real success is the impact they make as they graduate our programs, mentor others, and go on to build many solutions over time."[3]

Nurturing the Crew

To grow a critical mass of qualified citizens, organizations need to help them build their capabilities. Training, certification, community-building, and help with all stages of citizen development—including the earliest one of ideation and creativity—can all help in this regard.

Training

When it comes to imparting citizen-specific skills, there are a variety of viable tools and pedagogical frameworks on offer.

When it comes to online courses, LinkedIn Learning and Coursera were popular among the companies we surveyed. Vendors have their own academies and courses, as do some internal IT teams.

But training should be only a small part of your citizens' education. Enterprises need a balance of direct instruction and project-based learning. We have seen companies successfully employ a 70/20/10 ratio of experience, on-the-job training, and course-based training. While courses afford structured curricula, testing, and certifications, employees are often

---

[2] https://drive.google.com/file/d/1upM9tFcuef7P9pTwEB4KSgIXbnyNGcGV/view.
[3] Ibid.

"voluntold" to participate. And when the skills learned do not relate to an immediate project, they are usually forgotten. We will spare you a lecture on the "curve of forgetting" and encourage you to investigate it yourself.

Alternatively, "micro-credentials" are more specific and applied capabilities that require the accumulation of skills on the job. Micro-credentials are more relevant certifications that allow citizens to gain self-directed experience while also working toward a stamp of approval that will confer trust in them as they move through their citizen careers.

Levels of Citizen Certification

Earlier we discussed certification levels for citizens, akin to the karate belt hierarchy used in Six Sigma. We have also showcased Pepsi's and Mass General's skills certifications. Table 15.1 offers our own tiers of citizen growth, divided into the distinct citizen categories.

Table 15.1 Levels of Citizen Capability

	Developer	Automator	Data Scientist
Citizen I	• Basic understanding of app development concepts and frameworks • Proficient use of simple low-code/no-code tools for basic app creation • Certification demonstrating foundational skills • Completed one to three small-scale projects with supervision	• Basic understanding of automation concepts and frameworks • Proficient use of simple RPA and IDP tools for basic automation tasks • Certification demonstrating foundational skills • Completed one to three small-scale automation projects under supervision	• Basic understanding of data science concepts and frameworks • Proficient use of simple data analysis tools and techniques • Certification demonstrating foundational skills • Completed one to three small-scale data analysis projects under supervision

(continued)

	Developer	**Automator**	**Data Scientist**
Citizen II	• Proficiency in one or more low-code/ no-code tools for intermediate app creation • Certification demonstrating intermediate-level skills • Led at least one medium-scale project with minimal supervision • Understands and applies governance model principles and frameworks • Capable of integrating apps with existing systems and workflows	• Proficiency in one or more RPA and IDP tools for intermediate automation • Completed intermediate-level training • Led at least one medium-scale automation project with minimal supervision • Understands and applies governance model principles and frameworks for automation • Capable of integrating automated workflows while improving existing processes	• Proficiency in one or more data analysis tools for intermediate data science tasks • Completed intermediate-level training • Led at least one medium-scale data analysis project with minimal supervision • Understands and applies governance model princi-ples and frameworks for data manage-ment • Capable of extracting data insights with existing data lakes or systems

	Developer	Automator	Data Scientist
Citizen III	• Mastery of multiple low-code/no-code tools for advanced app development • Deep understanding of the strategic impact of app development on organizational goals • Certification demonstrating advanced skills • Led large-scale, multi-app/multi-department projects independently • Capable of managing risk, resources, and stakeholder expectations effectively • Expertise in optimizing app performance and user experience	• Mastery of multiple RPA and IDP tools for advanced automation • Deep understanding of the strategic impact of automation on organizational goals • Certification demonstrating advanced skills • Led large-scale, multiprocess/multidepartment automation projects independently • Capable of managing risk, resources, and stakeholder expectations effectively • Expertise in optimizing workflows and enhancing efficiency using automation and process improvement	• Mastery of multiple data analysis tools for advanced data science tasks • Deep understanding of the strategic impact of data science on organizational goals • Certification demonstrating advanced skills • Led large-scale, multidataset/multidepartment data analysis projects independently • Capable of managing risk, resources, and stakeholder expectations effectively • Expertise in optimizing data models and driving data-driven decision-making

Citizen Lite

Six Sigma also offers a lesser known white belt that imparts "the most basic level of understanding of the methodology."[4] It is not for practitioners but rather geared toward process experts who support the practitioners. We see room for a similar role in citizen programs. These lite citizens serve as scouts, locating target areas for citizen-built solutions.

Community Building

We've seen that networks and communities of citizens played an important role in the evolution of both individual citizens and the enterprise programs in which they operated. Table 15.2 showcases four of the most popular types of communities employed by the companies in our research. These communities are generally internal to particular organizations, but there are also multicompany online communities supported by vendors.

Table 15.2   Popular Types of Citizen Development Communities

Forms of Community and Support Networks

Communication	Collaboration	Support	Cross Polli-nation
• Roadshows	• Hackathons	• Coaching sessions	• Design blueprints
• Internal pod-casts	• Innovation competitions	• Open office-hours	• Best prac-tices
• Internal lives-treams	• Slack/Teams groupsGitHub/Discord	• Leadership forums	• Approved use cases
• All-hands calls			• Integrations and service catalogs
• Brown-bag lunches			

Ideation and Creativity

The way that citizens actually come up with ideas is a topic that has received little attention. One exception is in the PMI Citizen Development

---

[4]https://www.sixsigmaonline.org/six-sigma-white-belt-certification.

Certification course,[5] which has a unit specifically on ideation. Not only is it important to understand how to inspire and shape ideas, but it is also valuable for citizens to understand how to workshop prototypes with end users.

Aspiring citizens likely have a shallow familiarity with brainstorming methods, design thinking, storyboarding, and mindmapping, but rarely is it their specialty. It can be helpful to provide guides and templates to facilitate the identification of root causes, distill processes down to task-level granularity, turn problems into opportunities, and articulate user pain points and potential solutions.

---

[5]https://www.pmi.org/citizen-developer.

16 | Guardrails

Guardrails are like bumper bowling. They automatically provide specific rules, standards, and best practices designed to guide citizen behavior within a governance framework. They provide a safe space in which to operate, limiting behaviors and responses to ensure that activities stay within acceptable boundaries. Guardrails enable action within defined limits, offering freedom while ensuring compliance and mitigating risks.

According to John Bratincevic, a citizen development analyst at Forrester,

> "Going through approvals [to deploy an app] every time defeats the purpose of citizen development. What central IT should consider to enable citizen development at scale is providing more guardrails at the onset of development on a consistent platform, ideally reducing the many development and manual governance patterns that exist today."[1]

Guardrails aren't always but are often automated; they are built into the tools and systems that citizens use. They can limit access to sensitive data, or unverified applications. As our final fork discusses, companies must decide how much trust to allot to their citizen initiative.

---

[1] John Bratinsevic, "Low-Code Citizen Developer Programs," Forrester Research Report, August 3, 2021, accessed May 25, 2024 at https://www.flowforma.com/hubfs/Forrester%20Report%20Low-Code%20Citizen%20Developer%20Programs%20July%202021.pdf

Fork 9: Stewards or Shields

Do you trust citizens to avoid risk or put up shields to prevent it? Companies in tightly regulated industries require the most stringent guardrails, but the way they establish these protocols varies widely. Some companies rely on stewardship, through which the citizens closest to the data are trusted to decide how to protect and leverage it. Other companies use prevention mechanisms to ensure that their citizens have no choice but to make the "right" choice with sensitive information.

Depending on your industry, your governance structures, and the level of the guidance you have provided, you will likely need a combination of both the trust and prevention measures that Mayo Clinic and Arcadis employ.

Stewards

The healthcare sector has stringent information protection requirements regardless of whether citizens or IT are working with data. The Mayo Clinic is relying heavily on its domain experts to be stewards of the data they use for citizen projects. To quote ourselves from Chapter 11 on "The Organizational Response to Citizen Technology," "Stewardship means that it's the job of user groups to get the data ready for analysis—integrating it, ensuring quality and currency, and putting it in the organization's data library." Rather than putting in automated guardrails, Mayo Clinic is trusting its citizens to steward their data appropriately.

Mayo Clinic relies heavily on data stewardship partially so that citizenry can scale. You may remember Ajai Sehgal, Mayo's chief data and analytics officer, from our earlier comments. He believes that it is "not scalable to centralize the development of models...you need a lot of engagement with the people who created the data." Sehgal states it plainly: "Stewardship has to happen at the source." To have good data, you need good data governance and Sehgal argues that "business proponents are the best stewards of that data; they know it best and can best leverage it with AI."

Mayo puts domain experts in the best position to make good decisions with their data through robust education and guidance. Their "AI enablement program" starts with rigorous data literacy courses and offers consulting services, lawyers, and eventually a degree in medical AI. Citizens are encouraged to bring their ideas to the AI enablement team before they build it, and AI enablement highlights tools, data and regulatory issues to work through the process. Stewardship doesn't have to be less rigorous than putting up shields that prevent undesirable behavior; their thorough guidance systems allow Mayo Clinic to trust their citizens to do the right thing with data. There is some automation—one system alerts citizen developers if they are using regulated data—but the primary reliance is on the citizen stewards themselves.

If you don't have high-quality, well-governed data outputs in healthcare, you are in big trouble. As Sehgal argues, "Even using AI to summarize emails can get you in trouble." But Sehgal and his team have demonstrated that stewardship in citizen development will allow for transformational change. Sehgal says that when doubters see the guidance systems and potential value of stewardship laid out together, "They get it."

Mayo Clinic puts extraordinary trust in their citizens, especially for an organization in such a tightly-regulated industry. We do not expect all companies to afford their domain experts the same level of responsibility, so our next and final example offers a sharp contrast to the stewardship on display at Mayo Clinic.

Shields

Arcadis has a different approach to reducing risk in citizen development: protective barriers. We highlighted Arcadis earlier in Chapter 15, "Guidance," for the individual-focused approach that the company takes to citizen development. At Arcadis, there are no fusion teams; citizens are on their own. You may wonder: how does an architecture firm like Arcadis keep more than 4,000 citizens on track without the positive peer pressure typical of collaborative projects? The answer: automated guardrails.

Arcadis' IT organization developed guardrails because they need their citizens to be on their best behavior. When citizens do the right thing, they prefer to just leave them alone. Freek Matheij, Arcadis's global platform director says, "We want to empower people to stay in the green. We want to expand the green." Projects in the green zone have low business criticality (1 to 10 users) and low technological complexity. As projects reach more users, become more complex, or involve sensitive data or APIs, they gradually move from green to yellow to red and even to black.

The green/yellow/red sorting system isn't unique, but the automated guardrails tied to these colors are what stand out at Arcadis. At the beginning of their development efforts, citizens are expected to register their projects. As they do, they are asked a series of automated questions about their required funding, data sources and tools, the answers to which sort them into green, yellow, red, or black. When citizens work on low-impact, low-complexity projects that don't require funding or sensitive information, everybody at Arcadis wins: "If you stay in the green, you can do whatever you want. You can experiment. You can design. Nobody is going to bother you," says Matheij.

But if you touch the wrong platform or data sources, Matheij explains that "alarms go off. Now IT has the mandate to take control and delete elements of the project or delete a project entirely." When projects enter the red zone, IT can choose to take them on themselves. When a project gets sorted into black (likely because of a need for highly sensitive data), nobody is allowed to touch it. The yellow section is the trickiest at Arcadis (and at most other organizations using this classification, we found). In theory, "yellow" projects are ripe for citizen/IT collaborations, but as we discussed earlier in this section of the book, Arcadis hasn't built the capacity for many fusion teams yet. For now, most projects are getting sorted into red or green.

Arcadis makes their sorting and alarm criteria clear to citizens in the hope that this transparency will engender good behavior and independence. Their hope is that these guardrails don't inhibit citizen innovation but rather make it easier for citizens to operate unencumbered by IT governance structures.

Arcadis's guardrails set the boundaries. Within those limits, both citizens and IT can breathe easy knowing that missteps won't send a project, or the company as a whole into the gutter.

Facilitating Best Behaviors

We've argued that the best approach to avoiding citizen development risk is to make it easy for citizens to do the right thing. That is typically accomplished through a combination of human, automated, and financial guardrails.

Human Guardrails

One way to safeguard citizen solutions is to train your human citizens and managers to govern themselves and each other. Offering training on governance, security, compliance, and access management ensures that citizens know the lines, and how and why they should color inside of them. We provide some examples of policy guardrail domains in Table 16.1.

Table 16.1 Policy Guardrail Domains

Data Governance	Security	Compliance	Access Management
• Data classification and handling procedures	• Secure coding practices and code review processes	• Compliance frameworks (e.g., GDPR, HIPAA, PCI-DSS)	• Role-based access control (RBAC) policies
• Data retention and disposal policies	• Incident response and breach notification procedures	• Industry-specific compliance standards	• "Least privilege" information security principles and access review
• Data privacy and protection guidelines	• Security awareness and training programs	• Internal compliance policies and procedures	• Identity and access management (IAM) procedures

Automated Guardrails

The other way to encourage best behavior is to select tools that are designed with governance in mind. These built-in safety measures automate compliance, enforcement of access policies, safeguarding of data and systems, and activity tracking. Table 16.2 lists the automated guardrails to look for as you decide between tools.

Financial Guardrails

Good behavior can be enforced through financial controls including the allocation of budgets, financial tracking procedures, and reinvestment of realized savings. Table 16.3 lists some monetary guardrails at an enterprise's disposal.

Table 16.2   Automated Guardrails

Data Governance	Security	Compliance	Access Management
• Data masking and anonymization • Data encryption at rest and in transit • Data loss prevention (DLP) controls • Data access auditing and monitoring	• Vulnerability scanning and penetration testing • Application security testing and code analysis • Web application firewalls (WAFs) • Endpoint protection and antivirus measures	• Automated compliance monitoring and reporting • Continuous integration and deployment (CI/CD) pipelines with compliance checks • Automated policy enforcement and remediation	• Multifactor authentication (MFA) and single sign-on (SSO) • Privileged access management (PAM) solutions • User activity monitoring and auditing • Automated provisioning and deprovisioning

Table 16.3   Financial Guardrails

Monetary Guardrails	Description
Budget Allocation and Oversight	Establish a dedicated budget for citizen initiatives with clear approval processes and oversight mechanisms to ensure responsible policy compliance and to prevent overspending or noncompliant spending.
Cost Tracking and Monitoring	Implement tools and processes to track and monitor the costs associated with citizen development projects, including licensing fees spent on approved tools, infrastructure, and resources.

Monetary Guardrails	Description
Return on Investment (ROI) Measurement	Define and measure key performance indicators (KPIs) and metrics to quantify the business value and ROI of citizen initiatives, such as productivity gains, cost savings, and revenue generation, preventing shadow accounting.
Benefit Realization and Reinvestment	Establish a framework for capturing and quantifying the benefits realized from citizen development projects, and define policies for reinvesting a portion of the savings or benefits into compliant citizen initiatives.

This marks the end of the nine forks and the end of the 4Gs. We hope you feel empowered to make some decisions about your citizen development programs.

The earlier you make these decisions, the better. Launching a formal citizen development program is not going to get any less intimidating than it is today. As generative AI puts increasingly powerful and intuitive technology in the hands of your employees, orchestrating citizens will only become a more formidable task.

17 | The Future of Citizen Development

We've already seen a dramatic degree of change over the past decade or so in how information technologies are created in organizations, and this is likely to continue and even accelerate. One thing that will not change is the need for digital capabilities within organizations, and you would be hard-pressed to find a futurist who would say that the future of business will be less digital. If we care about digital skills and understanding across organizations, citizen development is the best way to go about it.

Many companies have already developed digital and data literacy programs. These are great, but they don't match actually developing and implementing IT applications. The best learning is always hands-on. In addition, of course, you can't compare the amount of IT and digital capability that will be developed by any IT organization to the volume and variety of applications that thousands of citizens (within a large organization) can create.

And those citizen-developed systems will have some highly desirable traits. They will fit the business need closely because citizens understand what those needs are. They will be innovative, because citizens will try to meet their IT and data needs in ways that IT veterans would never have thought of. As we've mentioned, citizen development will be a laboratory for innovations in processes, strategies, and business models that are supported by various forms of information technology.

In other words, citizen development isn't going away and will only become more pervasive.

Citizen Development: Too Pervasive to Have a Name?

However, that pervasiveness may mean that citizen development as a name and a concept disappears from the lexicon. It may be that in the future developing and implementing information technologies is simply part of everyone's job. And if everybody is doing it, why employ a separate name for it?

We had this discussion with Max Ioffe, who until recently was the global intelligent automation leader at WESCO Distribution. Max is a passionate advocate of citizen development and automation but wonders if the name is appropriate even now.

> "…is citizen development a relevant term today? Should it be changed to employee enablement to encompass both the personal productivity automations, traditional citizen development, citizen analytics, AI agents, etc."

We'd argue that the term still works today, but it may not work as well in the future if everyone is effectively a citizen. One wonders, however, whether everyone will be expected to have the skills to do IT work. If so, the lack of a voluntary component to citizenship may make the movement much less exciting and more a new form of drudgery.

We've already seen signs of this in our previous research. For example, Tom wrote a book in 2022 with Steve Miller called *Working with AI: Real Stories of Human/AI Collaboration*. It includes 29 case studies of people who work with AI on a daily basis and several chapters describing what we learned from them. One of the chapters was called "Everybody's a Techie" and this paragraph summarized what we found:

> Based on our recent observations, we believe there has been substantial progress towards addressing this business–IT gap within a wide range of

companies. And we think the reasons for this progress go far beyond the business analyst and other roles created to business-IT integration. Many of the people described in our collection of case examples are deeply involved with determining how to use data and technology to solve a particular business problem. They are based in business functions and units, rather than in the IT organization. They aren't formally trained in technology, and may not even have technology-oriented titles. If you were to hear them talk at work or watch them do their work, however, you'd have a difficult time distinguishing them from full-fledged IT people. The only difference is that they have a well-developed understanding of the business needs they are directly responsible for and of enabling technology, including the data and analytics in their specific job roles and business processes. In short, they are business-technology hybrids.

They might also have been described as citizen developers. Only a couple of the case studies in that book explicitly involved citizen development (or more specifically, citizen automation). The other case studies involved people with jobs that involved not only using an AI system but also helping to specify, develop, or maintain it. It seems likely, whatever one calls them, that such business/technology hybrids, citizens, or IT-enabled employees will continue to grow and prosper.

The Future of the IT Function and IT People

The future of citizen development, of course, is intertwined with the future of the information technology function within organizations. It seems unlikely that most IT groups will disappear altogether, but they are likely to undergo significant changes as citizens take on increasing percentages of application development, automation, and data analysis and science.

IT has already gone through considerable recent change in many companies because of the shift of computation and data storage to the cloud. IT market researchers predict that 80 or 85% of companies will close down their data centers by 2025 in favor of the cloud, and big companies like Capital One, FedEx, and Netflix have already done so. As this trend continues, it seems likely that managing technology infrastructure will increasingly be outsourced to external cloud providers. A big chunk of infrastructure-oriented IT professionals will be either working for external providers or not working at all.

In addition, much software—including that for citizen usage—will come from cloud providers, so software selection and maintenance will be less necessary as well. It does seem likely that IT, or at least people with IT professional skills, will continue to select, specify, configure, and maintain large-scale enterprise applications like enterprise resource planning (ERP) and customer relationship management (CRM). However, as these application packages move to the cloud, over time they require less work to install and maintain.

IT support services, like other forms of customer service, are likely to be performed with the help of AI, particularly generative AI. If we were chief information officers—and we thank our lucky stars that we are not, because it's often a tough and thankless job—we'd be planning for an IT organization that has substantially fewer employees. Most importantly from the standpoint of citizen development, the remaining staff will do different kinds of things.

Coaching and Assessing, Not Developing

The creation of IT applications will undoubtedly change as citizens take on more of the load for development of small applications. Large enterprise application (enterprise resource planning, customer relationship management, human resource management) development is already largely the province of external vendors, and this is unlikely to change.

Small applications are likely to be developed by citizens in the future—and perhaps even middle-size and middle-complexity ones. But as we have argued throughout this book, some of them will sometimes need help from professionals. We expect that the bulk of any remaining IT organization will consist of people whose job it is to make the work of citizens more effective and safe. That may involve motivating them to become citizens, teaching them how to do it well, organizing communities of them, coaching them, and reviewing their work to ensure that it meets standards and guidelines when necessary.

This is already the case for some IT people in some companies. The stereotype is that IT people would prefer to develop their own applications than to coach citizens in doing so, and no doubt this is accurate for some of them. But we've found several companies in which many IT people seem happy to do that type of work. For example, in ServiceNow (which has a citizen-oriented software offering), Chris Bedi, then the chief digital information officer (and now chief customer officer), commented the following in an interview on the role of IT professionals in citizen development:

> When someone wants to develop an app or workflow, they tell the central IT group what they want to do. Within 24 hours, we tell them if there is already an app to do this within the company, if the data are super-sensitive, or if it's too complex for them to do it on their own. If it meets those criteria, we offer them some training and they do it themselves. If it is too complex or there is a data issue, we help them. If their activity has died down after a while we will check in with them. Now in the beginning, my team did view it [citizen support] as extra work. They didn't find it threatening, they just wondered how to carve out the time for it. But then I assigned a program manager, and then another 1.5 FTEs to help. That's a total of 2.5 people to help citizens develop a thousand apps and save 40,000 labor hours. It's a pretty good deal for the company, and the people supporting the citizen developers like what they do. Citizen development is working well for us internally, and a lot of our customer CIOs also are encouraging it to accelerate digital transformation and free up scarce professional IT resources.

Ultimate Fusion

We've already mentioned the idea of "fusion teams," advanced by Gartner, that involves citizens working alongside professional IT people (or professional automators or data scientists, though they weren't in the original conception). We think this is a good idea and one that will probably be taken further over time.

However, we expect that the "ultimate fusion" would result in an inability to distinguish some citizen developers from professional ones—and we think that it's a positive development and that it will happen frequently. We've heard from many companies that already citizen developers have moved into IT, automation, or analytics/AI professional roles, and vice versa. And professional IT people are increasingly making use of low-code/no-code tools and AI-based coding and analysis software. Citizen developers and professional IT people already often resemble each other and overlap in terms of their ability not only to produce applications, automation workflows, and data analyses but also sometimes in their business domain knowledge and ability to translate between business and technical requirements.

If citizen developers and IT people become (more) indistinguishable, what does this mean for the future of the IT organization? It may disappear entirely as these ultimate fusion hybrids become pervasive across the business. More likely, we think that IT will become a center of IT excellence (CoE) that holds a relatively small number of technology experts. These people would identify promising new technologies, develop standards, create guidelines for interfaces between enterprise systems and those developed outside of IT, and plan for enterprise architectures. They could also be the arbiters of whether citizen-developed tools deserve promotion to enterprise-wide status and maintain the hub or marketplace in which those enterprise tools are stored and cataloged.

In addition, someone within the CoE will need to oversee talent management and community development for the fusion hybrids. It seems unlikely that organizations will develop and nurture many of these valuable individuals without a guiding hand. That hand can supply motivational incentives, meetings of the relevant individuals, reviews of how individual careers are progressing, educational opportunities, and so forth.

All of these supportive activities and organizational changes are worth the trouble if you believe, as we do, that these fusion hybrids will inherit the earth or will at least inherit the organizations to which they belong. What could be better than a large group of digitally savvy people who can identify, understand, and solve business problems with the aid of technology? We certainly believe that an organization that consists of many of these people will be more successful than those that maintain strict separation between IT and businesspeople. The time is now to begin creating such fusion hybrids.

Broader Tech and Data Leadership

It seems likely that even if the traditional IT organization goes away, there will still need to be some leadership within organizations for technology and data initiatives and activities. Over the past several years, the leadership roles in technology and data have proliferated—chief information officer, chief technology officer, chief digital officer, chief data (and or analytics/AI) officer, chief information security officer, etc. In a recent survey of technology executives, Tom learned that many of these leaders believe that there are too many such leaders and that the proliferation of them has created confusion within organizations about where to turn for what services.

Some organizations, including TIAA, Travelers Insurance, CarMax, and others, have created what Tom called *supertech leaders* who combine a number of these roles. They primarily report to the CEO and drive business change with technology. That's unlikely to be a need that goes away anytime soon.

And in most organizations, there is no organization that manages or facilitates citizen development. As we've argued, there are plenty of activities—genesis, governance, guardrails, and guidance, as we've referred to them—that benefit the rise and effectiveness of citizen development:

- Facilitating and championing citizen activities
- Ensuring that citizens are educated and have access to the right tools
- Embedding guardrails and governance into the infrastructure
- Maintaining data, application, and component marketplaces
- Checking on citizen-developed applications to ensure their efficacy and safety

We think it's likely that a "data and technology enablement" function—one possible name for it, anyway—could be created to oversee and perform any remaining IT functions and to lead technology-enabled business change. That function should also involve advancing the work that citizens do to help digitize company operations.

The Role of AI

AI, and generative AI in particular, is likely to play a major role in the future of citizen development. At the time we write this, it's mostly being used to write—or help humans write—emails and blog posts and to create fun images. Although it's already possible to use GenAI to write code, analyze data, and specify how an automation should work, those capabilities are far less well known and used. Perhaps it's because the popular uses of GenAI feel like fun, and these less popular ones feel like work.

It seems likely in the future that GenAI and conversational AI more broadly will be the front end to all citizen applications. That's possible today with many tools, but it takes at least a modicum of sophistication to create prompts that will get you the first cut at an app, a data analysis, or an automation workflow that you want. That's also true with code generation, and it's one reason why experienced coders tend to have better luck than inexperienced ones.

In the not-too-distant future, however—we're guessing within a year or two of when this book is published—it will be possible to have an iterative discussion with a GenAI interface about a machine learning analysis that might look like this:

GenAI—   What would you like to do?

Citizen—   I'd like to analyze a data set.

GenAI—   Do you already have the data set you'd like to analyze? If so, can you provide me with a link or upload a file?

Citizen—   Yes, I've just uploaded a .csv file.

GenAI—   Great, is there a particular variable in the file you would like to predict, or would you just like descriptive analytics on all of them?

Citizen—   I'd like to predict the variable in the column "Ad Response."

GenAI—   Do you mean the "Responded to Ad?" column?

Citizen—   Yes, that's it. Sorry, I forgot.

GenAI—   No problem. Do you want me to check all of the other variables to see how they can predict Ad Response or just some of them?

Citizen—   All of them except for the Customer Number variable.

GenAI—   OK, I'll get busy on that, and I'll let you know how I treated missing data, how I transformed some variables, the overall predictive effectiveness of the model, and which variables are most important in affecting the outcome. It should take only a few seconds, and I'll be happy to revise the model if you want.

In other words, generative AI will feel like the ultimate research assistant or programmer (because it is generating code to do this analysis). It will elicit what you want, work very quickly, and allow you to change your mind infinite times in specifying your app, automation, analysis, or model.

This can pretty much be done already with the Advanced Data Analysis component of ChatGPT, which generates Python code to do data analysis. All that's lacking is the iterative prompt capability, and some GenAI programs already allow some of that. There are also GenAI front ends to many data analysis and data query programs that generate SQL code. Within a few months every software vendor—LC/NC, automation, website development, etc.—will have similar offerings.

GenAI will also make it easier to find existing models, features, or software components that you can use to begin your citizen project. If there is no other benefit to not reinventing the wheel other than saving some compute energy, the citizen user might be told, "I've found a software component for taking credit card payments from the Consumer business unit's software marketplace. Should I use that as the starting point for your project?" Such marketplaces are often held back by human unwillingness or inability to describe the component in detail, but GenAI is great at categorizing and documenting software, so such repositories will probably become a lot more useful.

There are a variety of other AI capabilities that will make citizen development easier. There are already, for example, emerging tools to analyze images of process flows and determine what's taking so long in manufacturing the new part. There are automation tools that with very little coaching or prompting can become your new "accounts payable digital worker." There are even meta-automation tools that can tell you which automation programs are working well and which ones seem to be encountering glitches. There are software development agents that can already generate entire programs, though they are not yet perfected. It's clear, however, that more autonomy from AI will make citizen development easier and more common.

Perhaps the only thing that will be required of humans will be to know what we want from technology—and AI systems might even be able to help with that. If the GenAI system starts with "what do you want to do?" it could lead us through an analysis of our business situation and then tell us what we need to do—even using external data. For example, "It sounds like you might have an issue with slow accounts payable processes. Would you like me to compare your average payables age to other companies in your industry?" Overall, there isn't much that can't be done with this technology.

We've already mentioned that entrepreneurship is much easier than it used to be now that citizen tools can generate many of the systems that make a digitally-oriented business feasible. With AI and external component/ feature/workflow/data repositories, it will be possible for solo entrepreneurs to generate their businesses from scratch in a few minutes. All they will need is a good idea and perhaps a storefront, and no doubt AI will help them with those too.

We will spare you the possibilities—though of course we know them in detail—for what might be done with quantum computing, blockchain, augmented reality, and the Internet of Many, Many Things to make citizen development more productive and effective. But we're just getting started. Citizen development—or whatever it's going to be called in the future— will make businesses work better and faster and will make work more productive and fulfilling. Those who use and manage it well will be much more successful than those who do not. You won't want to miss this future, and it's already started.

A

Citizen-Ready Checklist

This checklist spans the entire 4G framework to cover all the key themes discussed in Part 4, "Setting Sail." Moving through the checklist will help organizations to start strong, scale safely, and achieve measurable impact.

We recognize that this checklist may induce information overload, so we have a few recommendations for how to work through it. First, you can think of this checklist as a recommended packing list; not all of the items may be necessary, but you should have a good reason if you decide not to pack something on the list. Second, many of these structures and processes already exist within your company and will require fine-tuning only for the context of citizen development. Don't reinvent the wheel. Finally, the citizen-ready checklist is a semi-sequential guide to implementing citizen development, but your organization may find the need for these actions in a different order. We encourage all companies to customize the checklist to suit their domain experts and the enterprise as a whole.

Preparing to Set Sail

Assess the Current State (Maturity Model)
- Identify citizen development projects already in motion.

- Catalog low-code/no-code tools currently in use for automation, app building, and analytics.
- Identify citizen champions associated with existing projects.
- Use findings from the previous items to map citizen maturity within the organization (stages 0–5.)

Genesis

Understand the Benefits
- Identify problems and inefficiencies to be addressed through citizen development.
- Identify benefits the organization expects from citizen development.
- Document case studies of existing projects to illustrate the potential benefits.
- Communicate the benefits of citizen development to stakeholders.

Choose a Strategy
- Choose primary goals for pursuing citizen development (based on ranked benefits).
- Determine ambitions of scale: revolution (big projects) versus evolution (many small projects).
- Determine how citizen development aligns with the overall business strategy.
- Outline specific outcomes expected from implementing citizen development.
- Choose to submit to current adoption activities, or commit to promoting and supporting citizen development across the organization.

Set KPIs
- Create a list of key performance indicators (KPIs) to potentially measure the program.
- Align KPIs with the overall business objectives and strategic goals.
- Choose KPIs that will be used to track progress over time.
- Determine how data is to be collected and analyzed to assess the effectiveness of citizen development projects; establish necessary mechanisms and procedures to do so.
- Design a process that supports the review and adjustment of KPIs as needed.

Secure Executive Sponsorship

- Assign a dedicated executive sponsor for the citizen development initiative.
- Define the role the executive sponsor will play in supporting citizen development.

Selection of Champion

- Identify all self-selected or designated champions for the citizen development initiative.
- Determine how the champions will communicate about citizen development across the organization.
- Implement support structures to assist the champion in driving citizen initiatives.

Find or Recruit Talent

- Define personality traits, mindset, and skills required for successful citizen developers within the organization.
- Identify employees who fit the criteria and have expressed interest.
- Work with HR to attract external talent with the necessary skills and mindset for citizen development.
- Develop clear roles, incentive structures, and career ladders for citizen developers.

Governance

Understand the Risks Involved

- Determine organizational tolerance of risk.
- Identify all potential risks associated with implementing citizen development in the organization.
- Decide how to safeguard against all major risk categories (data, integration, security, etc.).
- Determine what measures will be taken to ensure compliance with regulations and standards.
- Establish plans to handle issues with citizen development projects.

Create Organizational Structures

- Determine what organizational structures are aligned with corporate risk culture and support (solo, team, fusion, center of excellence [CoE]).

- If appropriate, establish fusion teams with clearly defined duration and overlap with other departments.
- If appropriate, establish a CoE to provide ongoing support, best practices, and governance.
- Define clear roles within the fusion teams or CoE and among all departmental touchpoints.
- Assign ownership to the individual(s) responsible for coordinating and managing citizen development activities across different departments.

Establish Necessary Governance

- Define the criteria for your governance model (for example, criticality and complexity).
- Decide on the direction of governance enforcement (top-down versus bottom-up).
- Adapt enterprise policies and guidelines to suit chosen governance model.
- Define reporting procedures and cadence to ensure transparency and accountability.
- Implement mechanisms to continuously monitor, review, and improve governance structures.
- Define clear data access and usage policies.

Guidance

Formalize Training

- Choose appropriate training ratio for the enterprise—balancing experience, on-the-job, and course-based training.
- Based on ratio chosen, develop (or subscribe to) resources to provide training material (online, vendor-specific, or in-house).
- Choose the scale at which to roll-out training: whole organization or select groups.
- Decide how training will be tailored to different roles and levels within the organization.
- Establish testing procedures to evaluate the effectiveness of training programs.
- Allocate resources (budget and trainers) to ensure continuous learning and development.

Define Certifications

- Define certification levels to validate the skills and competencies of citizen developers (i.e., Citizen I, II, III).
- Set criteria used to assess and award certification levels.
- Determine how the organization will promote and recognize certified citizen developers.
- Incorporate relevant partnerships and vendor-specific certifications into criteria as necessary (e.g., Microsoft, UiPath, Alteryx, etc.).
- Design governance training into each certification level including review of internal IT policies, security procedures, cybersecurity protocols, and best practices.
- Consider incentive structures and compensation associated with levels of certification and with levels of value created.

Create Awareness

- Determine communication strategies to raise awareness about citizen development across the organization (roadshows, internal podcast, all-hands events).
- Showcase the benefits and opportunities of citizen development for employees at all levels.
- Emphasize corporate sponsorship and support for the proposed initiative.
- Incorporate feedback loops and communication channels for employees to provide input (perhaps anonymously) to the design, promotion, and sponsorship of the program.
- Evangelize successes and lessons learned across the organization to generate excitement and encourage wider participation.

Encourage Collaboration

- Host events that encourage collaboration and good-natured competition among divisions and citizens (e.g., hackathons, innovation competitions).
- Encourage the creation of citizen-led internal communities to share lessons learned and best practices.
- Assign community leaders or champions to help foster a collaborative environment.
- Ensure collaboration between citizen developers, citizen automators, and citizen data scientists.

Set Up Support Mechanisms

- Designate champions or experienced citizens as mentors and coaches.
- Set regular office hours and forums to support citizens.
- Consider authorizing participation in industry forums outside of the company.

Provide Resources

- Develop internal resources (e.g., documentation, templates, solution module libraries, toolkits) to support citizen developers.
- Create a maintenance calendar to ensure all resources are kept up-to-date and relevant.
- Capture structured use cases for all known citizen-built solutions and models: highlight problem statement, tools used, solution developed, key performance indicators (KPIs) targeted, and benefits realized.
- Archive and evangelize successes, best practices, and lessons learned across the organization to generate excitement and encourage wider participation.

Enable Ideation

- Offer training and tools to support opportunity assessment and process redesign.
- Leverage community channels to disseminate ideas and invite voting/ranking of ideas for end-user validation and input.
- Consider using an ideation platform to host innovation activities, scoring, ranking, and monitoring of citizen activities; some vendor suites have these capabilities.

Guardrails

Data Governance

- Implement data classification and handling procedures for all citizen projects.
- Define data retention and disposal policies, with specific attention to industry-specific and IT-specific requirements.
- Establish data privacy and protection guidelines aligned to citizen certification levels.
- Enable data masking and anonymization.

■ Implement data encryption at rest and in transit.

■ Set up data loss prevention (DLP) controls.

Security

■ Enforce secure coding practices and code review processes, if necessary.

■ Develop incident response and breach notification procedures.

■ Provide ongoing security awareness and training programs.

■ Conduct regular vulnerability scanning and penetration testing of all models, apps, and automations created.

■ Apply application security testing and code analysis tools where necessary.

■ Deploy web application firewalls (WAFs) and endpoint protection measures.

Compliance

■ Follow industry-specific compliance standards.

■ Adhere to compliance frameworks such as GDPR, HIPAA, and PCI-DSS.

■ Adhere to existing internal compliance policies and procedures, adapting them as needed to best support citizen development initiatives.

■ Ensure chosen tools contain automated compliance monitoring and reporting functionality.

■ Ensure automated policy enforcement and remediation in authorized tools.

Access Management

■ Apply role-based access control (RBAC) policies, catered to the level of authorization granted to the specific citizen.

■ Implement "least privilege" principles and access review processes.

■ Establish citizen certification–based identity and access management (IAM) procedures.

■ Implement multifactor authentication (MFA) and single sign-on (SSO) solutions where not already present.

■ Deploy privileged access management (PAM) solutions.

■ Enable user activity monitoring and auditing.

Budget and Cost Oversight

- Establish a dedicated budget for citizen initiatives with clear approval processes and oversight mechanisms.
- Ensure responsible policy compliance to prevent overspending or noncompliant spending.
- Implement tools and processes to track and monitor costs associated with citizen development projects.
- Include licensing fees, infrastructure, and resources in the tracking.

Benefit Measurement and Tracking

- Revisit framework for quantifying benefits realized from citizen development projects.
- Revisit KPIs and metrics to quantify business value and return on investment (ROI), with a focus on quantifiable benefits including productivity gains, cost savings, and revenue generation.
- Define policies for reinvesting a portion of savings or benefits into compliant citizen initiatives.

B

Citizen Development Challenges Organizations Are Likely to Face

This table describes key organizational, cultural, behavioral, and infrastructural challenges to success with citizen development on a large scale. Knowing about them in advance may make it easier to address them when they arise.

Challenge Category	Challenges
Resistance to Change	• Executives uncomfortable with blurring lines between long-standing functional silos inside an enterprise • IT leadership unwilling to enable citizens with access and support • Citizens unwilling to take on added responsibilities to their "day jobs" • Management's unwillingness to allocate team time and resources to work perceived to be non-core
Data & System Readiness	• Data not structured, cleaned, or archived in a way that is easy for citizens to access • Systems either antiquated or locked down, making it difficult for citizens to interact with and automate within them
Political Jockeying	• IT (and other divisions) jockeying for ownership and authority over citizen programs • Business units fighting for control over citizen efforts to ensure focus on business unit-specific needs
Tool Selection & Alignment	• Lack of selection criteria, creating a large catalog of shadow IT tools to curate and reduce • Various tools with wide-ranging capabilities competing to be the dominant enterprise platform (i.e., Microsoft, UiPath, etc.)
Trust & Awareness	• IT skepticism that citizens can be trusted with enterprise systems and/or data • Lack of awareness across the enterprise about citizen programs and available guidance resources

C

Additional Resources

Our research benefited a great deal from the countless experts and pioneers who were kind enough to offer their time, stories, and lessons learned. During these conversations, we came across many resources that helped shape our perspectives and inform our writing. We've mentioned most of the relevant articles in our footnotes. Here are a few other resources we found to be particularly useful:

Certifications and Training
- Coursera AI courses by Andrew Ng and IBM
- Initiative for Analytics and Data Science Standards
- LinkedIn Learning Path: Become an RPA Developer
- LinkedIn Learning Path: Become a Data Scientist
- MIT Data Science and Machine Learning Program with IDSS
- PMI Citizen Developer Certification Courses
- Udemy Course: Data Science A-Z
- UiPath Citizen Certification
- UiPath Citizen Developer eBook

YouTube Educators
- Ian Barkin
- Pascal Bornet

- Tom Davenport
- FreeCodeCamp, Learn Data Science Tutorial
- Anders Jensen
- Andrew Ng
- Eric Siegel

Associations
- Data Science Association
- Institute for Robotic Process Automation/AI (IRPA AI)
- University of Galway, Citizen Development Lab

Communities
- Alteryx Community
- Citizen Developer Community
- Microsoft Power Platform Community
- NoCodeOps Community
- ServiceNow Community – Citizen Development Center
- UiPath Community
- WeAreNoCode Community

Books
- Pascal Bornet and Ian Barkin, *Intelligent Automation,* World Scientific, December 29, 2020.
- Thomas H. Davenport and Nitin Mittal, *All In on AI,* Harvard Business Review Press, January 24, 2023.
- Alex Gutman and Jordan Goldmeier, *Becoming a Data Head,* Wiley, May 11, 2021.
- Mary Lacity and Leslie Willcocks, *Robotic Process and Cognitive Automation: The Next Phase,* SB Publishing, February 12, 2018.
- Ethan Mollick, *Co-Intelligence: Living and Working with AI,* Portfolio, April 2, 2024.
- Project Management Institute, *Citizen Development: The Handbook for Creators and Change Makers,* Project Management Institute, January 30, 2021.
- Bill Schmarzo, *AI and Data Literacy,* Packt Publishing, August 9, 2023.
- Most low-code and no-code vendors have free e-books on citizen development

Acknowledgments

We knew something about the topic of this book before we started our research for it, but we learned vastly more from the many people we interviewed. We can't thank them all by name here, but we're thankful anyway. And there are some people and organizations that went beyond the call of politeness and really spent a lot of their precious time with us. They include:

Freek Matheij of Arcadis
Max Ioffe of WESCO
Benjamin Berkowitz of Vertex Pharmaceuticals
Christian Peverelli of WeAreNoCode
Michael McCullough of Amtrak
Matt Hubbard of AgilePoint
Jay Crotts, Nils Kappeyne, Paul Kobylanski, and Stevie Sims of Shell
Noel Carroll of the University of Galway
Amanda Woodly, Nina Lerner, and Lyndsey Padden of Kroger's 84.51°
    organization

In addition, Tom thanks his beloved spousal unit, Jodi, for her endless patience with this and 24 other books. She keeps asking, "Will 25 be enough?" He is also grateful to his son Chase for helping out with the book and drafting some great content in the final "Setting Sail" section on implementing citizen development programs.

Ian is grateful for the support of his wife, Shirley, and his daughters, Sophie and Emma, who are budding citizen developers in their own right. A special thanks goes to his mini golden-doodle, Tiger, for being a loyal companion during late nights of writing.

About the Authors

Thomas H. Davenport is Distinguished Professor at Babson College, the Bodily Bicentennial Professor of Analytics at the UVA Darden School of Business, fellow at the MIT Initiative on the Digital Economy, and senior advisor to Deloitte's AI practice. In addition to previous academic appointments at Harvard, Dartmouth, Oxford, Boston University, and the University of Texas, he's been a partner or senior consultant at McKinsey, EY, and Accenture. He's authored, co-authored, or edited 24 other books, including the bestsellers *Process Innovation*, *Working Knowledge*, *Competing on Analytics*, and *All In on AI*. He's also written more than 400 articles or columns for *Harvard Business Review*, *MIT Sloan Management Review*, *Forbes*, the *Wall Street Journal*, and the *Financial Times*. Davenport has been named one of the world's top 25 consultants by *Consulting* magazine, one of the top three business/technology analysts in the world by *Optimize* magazine, one of the 100 most influential people in the IT industry by Ziff-Davis magazines, and one of the world's top 50 business school professors by *Fortune* magazine. He's also been a LinkedIn Top Voice for both the education and tech sectors. He has advised or educated executives at many of the world's largest organizations on AI, analytics, digital transformation, and information technology management.

Ian Barkin is a serial entrepreneur with a background in automation, business process outsourcing, and consulting. He is cofounder of 2B Ventures, an investment and advisory firm with a portfolio of innovative companies focused on the future of work. Ian has held key strategic executive roles in some of the world's largest services firms and has been a pioneer in the robotic process automation (RPA) space as a cofounder of Symphony Ventures, a leading RPA consultancy. He is a LinkedIn Learning instructor with multiple courses on RPA, AI, and Digital Transformation, a co-author of the book *Intelligent Automation*, and co-author of articles in publications including *Harvard Business Review* and *MIT Sloan Management Review*. Ian is passionate about educating others through his courses, social media channels, and speaking engagements. He is a Bain advisor and serves on the advisory boards of Procesio, Skan.ai, and Ema.co. He has been recognized as one of the top 10 thought leaders in RPA by Thinkers 360, one of the 50 most powerful AI Influencers by Engatica, and a top 100 technology thought leader to follow by *The Awards Magazine*. Ian holds an MBA from the MIT Sloan School of Management and a BA from Middlebury College.

Chase Davenport is focused on the intersection of artificial intelligence and climate change. After many years as an AI researcher at Accenture, Chase founded the Ocean Beach Institute to bring intelligent technology to coastal climate issues.

Index

A

Accenture, 82–83, 115

Actelion, 156

AI (artificial intelligence). *See also* generative AI
  applications in citizen development, 3, 4, 6–7
  automation via AI, 6–7, 10, 17–19
  Chevron's project-based learning, 219
  conversational AI as front end to citizen
      applications, 241–242
  generative AI and its applications, 58–59
  impact on data culture, 84–85
  impact on entrepreneurship, 244
  impact on jobs, 101–102
  influence on employee expectations, 188
  integration into citizen development,
      190–192, 233
  integration with data analysis and
      automation, 243
  integration with workers, 101
  low-code/no-code tools, 52, 58–59, 116
  natural language coding, 112
  risk management through guardrails, 232
  role in citizen data science, 85, 99, 220
  role in data stewardship at Mayo Clinic, 228
  role in future of citizen development, 241–244
  role in IT democratization, 13, 18–19

AI enablement, 171

Alteryx, 14–15
  automation of data workflows, 153
  citizen data science tools, 144
  citizen development, 33, 38
  community resources for citizen developers, 256
  data workflows, 95
  integration with citizen certification
      programs, 249

Stanley Black & Decker's transformation, 153
  usage in risk management, 96

Altman, Sam, 112

Amazon Web Services (AWS), 137, 144

American College of Radiology, AI training
      programs, 158

Amtrak, 105–106, 128–130, 177, 191–192, 201

analytics literacy, 114–115

APIs (application programming
      interfaces), 66–67

Appian, 8, 16, 138

application development, 53–54, 57–61. *See also*
      low-code/no-code tools

application programming interfaces (APIs), 66–67

Arcadis, 127, 215–216, 229–230

Arcari, Sarina, 128, 177

AT&T, 17–18, 153

automation. *See also* automation programs; citizen
      automation; IPA (intelligent process
      automation); process improvement; RPA
      (robotic process automation); workflow
      automation
  back office, 69
  beginnings, 35–36
  business improvement, 21–22
  centers of excellence, 173
  centralized *vs.* federated governance, 206–208
  Chevron's project-based learning
      approach, 219
  citizen automation, 151–153, 172–174
  citizen contributions, 35–36, 38
  citizen development, 208, 218–219, 229–230,
      238–239, 238–239
  examples, 153–154, 193, 218–219, 238–239
  financial guardrails, 232–233

automation (*continued*)
front office, 69–70
future integration with AI, 241–244
history and development, 21–22, 71–72
impact on process efficiency, 220
incremental improvements, 195
integration with AI, 228
large-scale adoption and benefits, 153
in middle office, 70
pharmaceutical companies, 154
process improvement, 36–37, 194–195
risks and challenges, 78–80, 202–203
RPA (robotic process automation), 4, 6–7
ServiceNow, 7, 13
strategic value, 152–153
tools and technologies, 6–7, 10, 16–19, 63–66, 68–70, 173
transition to advanced tools, 36–38
automation programs, 6–7, 10

B
Babson College, 27
back office, 69
BARC (Business Application Research Center), 83
Bedi, Chris, 238–239
Berkowitz, Benjamin, 64, 72, 77
Betty Blocks guide for governing citizen development, 201
BeyondCore, 146
Blue Horizon Infotech, 145
Blue Prism, 141, 143
BMW, 99, 172–174
boards of directors, role in supporting citizen development, 185
Bratincevic, John, 227
Braun, Bill, 219–220
Bridges, Charles, 155–156
Brodrick, Steve, 153–154
Bubble, no-code platform, 139
Buono, Damon, 168–169, 190, 205–206
Burning Glass Institute, 114
business applications, 54–55, 61
business improvement, 21–23, 31
business intelligence, 35–36
business transformation, 7–8, 9–10, 12

C
Capital One, 90, 237
Carroll, Noel, 10, 124, 212
centralized governance, 204–207. *See also* federated governance; governance
CFO (Chief Financial Officer), 185

ChatGPT, role in IT resistance stereotype, 162
Cheprasov, Max, 104, 125–126, 202–203
Chevron, 155, 219–220
CIO (Chief Information Officer), 185, 190
CIOx (Customer Information Management/ Operational Excellence), 165–166
citizen application developer, 116–117
citizen automation. *See also* automation; RPA (robotic process automation)
benefits, 74–78
broad tech stack, 139–143
Chevron's project-based learning, 219
definition and scope, 63–64
education and training, 218–219
examples, 193–195, 202–203, 228–230
governance and risk management, 201–204
historical context, 70–72
IDP, 142–143
integration with financial controls, 232–233
integration with low-code/no-code tools, 219
intelligent automation, 140–143
large organizations, 195
process automation, 63–64
process efficiency, 193–195, 208
process intelligence, 143
risk management, 229–230
risks and challenges, 78–80
RPA tools, 141–143
tools used, 63–66, 68–73
types of work suited, 64–68
citizen automators. *See also* automation; citizen automation; citizen developer; RPA (robotic process automation)
alternative names, 184
characteristics, 64, 72–73
data manipulation, 118
examples from Shell, 72–73
necessary technical skills, 117
process mapping, 117
relation to AI tools, 183
role in digitizing manual workflows, 183
role in process improvement, 72–74
RPA tools, 117
testing and debugging, 118
tools used, 72–73
use of RPA software, 183
citizen certification, 221–223, 249
citizen coaches, 184
citizen data analysis, 82–85. *See also* data literacy; data science
citizen data analyst/scientist, 118. *See also* citizen developers
citizen data science. *See also* data science
advantages, 87

at BMW, 173
challenges, 86, 91, 144, 173
at Chevron, 219–220
education and certification, 221–223
education and training, 87, 89
evolution, 98, 143
integration with BI, 145–146
at Johnson & Johnson, 193
role in decision-making, 85, 87, 173
role in organizational transformation, 193
specialized autoML systems, 144
tools for, 143–145
citizen data scientists, 37, 40–41, 184. *See also*
    citizen data science
citizen developers. *See also* citizen development;
    fusion teams
alternative names, 184
creativity and innovation, 106
examples of successful
    implementations, 123–132
future integration with professional IT
    roles, 239–240
governance at Shell, 125
integration into enterprise processes, 181–182
low-code/no-code application
    development, 183
mindsets, 107–109
personality traits, 103–106
political skills, 121
potential evolution into "ultimate fusion"
    hybrids, 239–240
skills of the future, 110–121
tools and platforms, 127
transforming business processes, 236–240
citizen development
applications, 4, 7, 9–10
automation tools, 4, 6–7, 10, 17–19
benefits of, 10–11, 13–14
bottom-up *vs.* top-down governance, 204–206
centers of excellence at BMW, 173
centralized *vs.* federated governance, 206–208
certification and training levels, 221–223
challenges, 11, 13–14, 17–19, 187–189
champion roles, 123–132
citizen data scientists, 4–7, 10, 14, 18
citizen developers, 3–4, 7–10, 12–13, 18
collaboration with IT professionals, 56–58
collapse of development categories, 148
community engagement, 14–16
comparison with citizen automation, 63–64
conversational user interfaces, 147–148
decision-making in governance
    structures, 202–207
education models, 217–220

examples, 52–53, 56–57, 124–130, 163–165,
    170–171, 191–195, 211–213
executive support, 123–124
formal adoption, 180–181
fusion teams, 239–240
future trends and predictions, 235–244
generative AI impact, 147–149
governance, 124–125, 167–171
growth without executive support, 128–130
history and evolution, 51–53, 70–72
impact of guardrails, 231–233
impact on business, 87, 96, 237–240
importance of governance, 201, 215
importance of guardrails in
    governance, 227–230
individual *vs.* team-based approaches, 215–217
integration into business-as-usual
    operations, 181–182
intermediary organizations, 165–167
IT resistance, 162–163
low-code/no-code tools, 51–55, 57–62
management challenges, 60–61
online platforms and forums, 14–16
organizational response to, 161–174
positive and negative attitudes, 162
potential disappearance as a distinct
    concept, 236
preparation and planning for
    implementation, 177–178
risk management through guardrails,
    227–230
risk tolerance *vs.* risk avoidance, 202–204
role in data science, 88, 95
role of generative AI and automation, 241–244
role of IT and governance, 179–181, 215
roles and stakeholders, 182–185
stages of maturity, 179–181, 187–182
stewardship *vs.* shields approach, 228–229
strategic decisions in genesis stage, 187–193
support networks, 14–16
types of problems suitable for, 92–93
citizen development champion. *See also* citizen
    development
future career paths, 132
importance of executive support, 123–124
roles and responsibilities, 124–132
strategies for success, 130–132
citizen governance models. *See also* centralized
    governance; governance; guardrails
color-coded risk zones, 229–230
data stewardship approach, 228–229
DIY initiative, 207
federated approach, 208
financial controls, 231–233

citizen governance models (*continued*)
governance frameworks and best
practices, 212–213
three-tiered model at the nuclear utility
company, 204
citizen innovation, 165–167, 219–220
citizen journey, 33–35, 38–42
citizen librarians, 184
citizen stewardship, 228–230
citizen tech landscape, 136–139
citizen technology, 163–164, 167–169, 170–171
citizen tools, 35–39. *See also* automation;
software tools
citizen/professional collaboration, 56–58
cloud computing, 237
coaching, 238–239
coding, 51–52, 58–59, 62. *See also* generative AI;
low-code/no-code tools
Coleman, Charles, 38–40, 88, 95
Collins, Jim, 157
community building, 224–225
consulting, 37–39
CorVista Health, 156
COVID-19, 154–155
Creatio, no-code platform, 139
CRM (customer relationship management), 66, 238
CRM Analytics, 146
Crotts, Jay, 124, 163, 207
crowdsourcing, 24, 28–29
customer relationship management
(CRM), 66, 238
customer support, involvement in citizen
development, 185

D

data analysis, 29–30, 242–243. *See also* automation
data culture, 84
data governance, 190, 228–233. *See also* citizen
governance models; guardrails
data literacy, 84, 112–113. *See also* analytics
literacy; citizen data analysis
data science. *See also* citizen data science; citizen
data scientists; machine learning
automated machine learning, 37, 40, 85–86
challenges in adoption, 40–41
citizen data scientist roles, 40–41
citizen data scientists, 4–7, 10, 14, 18
citizen development initiatives, 184
citizen innovation, 155–157
combination with other fields, 157
data management tools, 4–6
evolution in organizations, 98
generative AI impact, 18–19
importance in life sciences, 155–157

integration with other citizen
technologies, 184
Johnson & Johnson, 155–157
machine learning, 6–7, 18–19
role of citizens, 85–86
tools used by citizen data scientists, 184
data stewardship, 228–229
Databricks, 144
data-driven decision-making, 83–84
Dataiku, 144
DataRobot, 144
Deloitte, study on RPA project success, 142
Dentsu International
Automation Center of Excellence, 125
citizen automation, 67
citizen development initiatives, 125–126
examples of citizen-driven projects,
202–203
integration of AI tools, 126
Berresse, Jessica, 67–68
Digital Boost program, 172–174
digital transformation
business and IT alignment, 7–9
challenges and failures, 9–10
citizen involvement, 9–10, 12
examples from various industries, 34–38
fueled by citizen development, 51–53, 59
importance of digital agility, 10, 13–14
role of citizens in driving
transformation, 35–36
role of LC/NC tools, 51–53, 59
digitalization, 154
Dinsmore, Thomas, 144–145
direct instruction, 218–219. *See also* training
DiRuzza, Ryan, 156–157
DIY initiative (Shell), 207

E

education, 218–223, 255–256. *See also* training
enablement, 16–19. *See also* citizen development;
governance; guardrails
enterprising resource planning (ERP), 66
entrepreneurship, 244
Excel, 35–38, 46–47

F

Fayyad, Usama, 112–114
federalism in IT, 12–14
federated governance, 207–208. *See also*
centralized governance; governance
FedEx, example of cloud migration, 237
finance, 185
financial guardrails, 232–233. *See also* governance

Ford Motor Company, 33
front office, 69–70
fusion teams, 56–58, 239–240

G
Gartner, 7, 13, 239–240
generative AI, 84, 93. *See also* AI (artificial
    intelligence); intelligent automation;
    machine learning; RPA (robotic process
    automation); IDP (intelligent document
    processing)
    applications in LC/NC development, 58–59
    capabilities, 241–243
    conversational interfaces, 147–148
    future potential for automation, 80
    impact on citizen development,
        18–19, 147–149
    impact on data science, 85, 99
    integration with business operations, 126
    integration with RPA and
        Power Platform, 148
    machine learning models, 6, 18–19
    potential for no-code environments, 59
    role in automation, 68–69
    role in code generation, 58–59
    tools at Tinuiti, 126
    tools for citizens, 93–94
    training at Johnson & Johnson, 193
    use in citizen development, 127
genesis, 187–193
geology, combination with data science, 157
Gershenfeld, Neil, 26
Google, 14
    AppSheet platform, 139
    business intelligence certification, 103
    cloud services for data science, 144
    Looker BI tool, 146
    role in citizen automation, 137
governance. *See also* centralized governance;
    citizen development; data governance;
    data stewardship; enablement; guardrails;
    guidance; IT (information technology)
    AI enablement at Mayo Clinic, 171
    balancing autonomy and control, 201
    balancing innovation and control, 193
    balancing stewardship and automated
        controls, 227–230
    bottom-up *vs.* top-down structures, 204–206
    centralized *vs.* federated approaches, 206–208
    challenges and tools for scaling, 181
    challenges in citizen technology, 167–171
    challenges in large organizations, 193
    citizen development, 178, 180–181, 193,
        201, 215, 227

    examples of governance models, 211–213
    financial controls as a governance
        tool, 231–233
    guardrails in citizen development, 227
    highly regulated environments,
        17–19, 170–171
    integration into enterprise processes, 181
    integration with education and
        guidance, 217–219
    Mayo Clinic *vs.* Arcadis approaches, 228–230
    Mayo Clinic's data stewardship, 171
    Microsoft's approach, 168–169
    models for citizen development, 12–14, 17–19
    ProAssurance's focus on governance, 170
    risk tolerance *vs.* risk avoidance, 202–204
    roles and responsibilities, 16–18
guardrails, 17–19, 186, 227–233. *See also* citizen
    stewardship; enablement; governance
guidance. *See also* education; governance
    citizen development, 215
    community building, 224–225
    instruction and training, 217–219

H
H2O.ai, 144
Hallworth, Scott, 90–91
Hamutcu, Hamit, 112–114
Haventree Bank, 96
HFS Research, study on human skills demand,
    119
History of IT, 3–4, 7–9. *See also* citizen
    development
Home Depot, 38–39, 88
Horozaniecki, Sharon, 166
HP Inc., 90
HR (Human Resources), role in recruitment and
    training for citizen development, 185
Huang, Jensen, 111

I
IADSS (Initiative for Analytics and Data Science
    Standards), 113
ideation, 224–225. *See also* community building
IDP (intelligent document processing), 142–143.
    See also RPA (robotic process
    automation)
innovation, 24–25, 31, 155–159. *See also* citizen
    innovation
integration, 66–67
intelligent automation, 140–143. *See also* citizen
    automation; RPA (robotic process
    automation)
Ioffe, Max, 236

IPA (intelligent process automation), 64–66. *See also* automation; RPA (robotic process automation)

IT (information technology), 179–181, 188–190, 237–240

IT professionals, 53, 56–58, 60–61. *See also* fusion teams

IT roles, 4–7, 10, 12–13, 18. *See also* citizen developers

J

Jabil, citizen automation examples, 76

Jacobson, Alan, 33

Jeavons, Dan, 89–90, 164

Johnson & Johnson, 73, 154–157, 193

Jones, Carrie, 97

K

Kappeyne, Nils, 124–125, 163–164

Kirby, Julia, 110

Kroger Co., 40–41, 89, 97, 104

L

large action models (LAMs), 80

Lean, 10, 22, 36, 117, 149

Lechner, Patrick, 172–174

LegalVIEW BillAnalyzer, 166

life sciences, 155–157

Lilly, Eli, 28

Liu, Renee, 72, 76, 105

Loree, John, 152, 194

low-code, 183

low-code platforms, 141

low-code/no-code tools, 138–139. *See also* application development; software tools
definition and applications, 51–55
examples from Siemens and Shell, 52–53, 56–57
examples of use in various industries, 34, 44–45
generative AI as a no-code solution, 58–59
integration into citizen development, 34, 44–45
management challenges, 60–61
role in citizen development, 51–55, 57–62

M

machine learning
automated tools, 6–7, 18–19, 37, 40, 85
challenges in citizen usage, 86, 91
challenges in understanding and implementation, 37, 40
citizen-developed models, 6–7, 18–19
integration with citizen development, 93–94

Maher, Mary, 124

maker movement, 26 27. *See also* citizen development

Malloy, Max, 170, 201, 203–204

Mass General Brigham, 17, 72–73, 77, 184

Massachusetts Institute of Technology (MIT), 158

Matheij, Freek, 127, 216, 229–230

maturity models, 178–181

Mayo Clinic, 18, 155, 228–230

McCullough, Michael, 105, 128–130, 191–192

McKinsey & Co., 84

medical research, 29–30

Mendix, 53, 56–58, 138

Michelin, 207–208

micro-credentials, 30

Microsoft, 11, 14–15, 18
Buono's approach to data governance, 205–206
Buono's role in data governance, 168–169
challenges with citizen-developed systems, 168–169
commitment to citizen development, 189–190
community resources for citizen developers, 256
decentralized governance and citizen enablement, 190, 205–206
generative AI, 148
IDP features, 143
impact of AI on citizen development, 241–244
integration with citizen certification programs, 249
internal adoption of citizen tools, 190
noninvasive data governance, 169
non-invasive governance practices, 205–206
Power Automate for RPA, 141
Power Platform tools, 54, 138–139, 144, 167
Satya Nadella's advocacy of citizen development, 167–168
survey on LC/NC adoption, 54

Microsoft Excel, 73

middle office, 70

minimum viable products (MVPs), 75

Minitab, 143

MIT (Massachusetts Institute of Technology), 158

Mittal, Abhishek, 217

mobile app development during COVID, 155

monarchy in IT, 12–13

N

Nadella, Satya, 11, 167–168

natural disasters, 155

Netflix, 237

no-code, 183

no-code platforms, 139, 141

O

Ojha, Heidi, 44–45
open innovation, 24–25, 28–29
OpenAI, Advanced Data Analysis feature, 148
open-source software, 25–26
Oracle, 137–138, 141
ornithology, 28–29
OutSystems, 138

P

PepsiCo, 218–219
pharmaceutical companies, 154
Pienso, 94–95
platforms
    low-code/no-code, 4, 6–7, 9–10,
        18–19, 139, 141
    mobile app development, 9–10
    ServiceNow, 7, 13
Power, Brad, 29
Power Apps, 163–164, 172–173
Power Automate, 172–173
Power BI
    AI integration in BI, 146
    at Amtrak, 128, 191
    analytics and machine learning capabilities, 167
    citizen data science tool at Microsoft, 167
    machine learning capabilities, 144
    role in citizen data science, 191
    role in citizen development, 128, 148
    role in Shell's digital transformation, 42
    transition from Excel to advanced data
        visualization, 42
Power Platform, 42, 54
ProAssurance, 170, 203–204
process improvement. *See also* automation
    connection with automation, 21–22
    examples from various industries,
        34–38, 74–76
    focus of BMW's Digital Boost program, 172
    role in citizen automation, 36–37,
        64–65, 72–74
    Six Sigma and Lean, 22
product development, 24–25
professional development, 56–58. *See also*
        fusion teams
PMI (Project Management Institute)
    Citizen Development Canvas, 106
    communication importance in projects, 120
project-based learning, 219–220. *See also* training
Project Management Institute (PMI). *See* PMI
        (Project Management Institute)
prototyping, 75
pulmonary arterial hypertension, 155–156

Q

Qlik, 82-83, 144, 146
Quickbase, 139

R

R (programming language), 144
radiology, 158
risk management. *See also* governance
    anarchy in IT, 12–13
    centralized and federated governance
        approaches, 206–208
    governance and oversight, 16–19
    impact on automation and data
        governance, 208–209
    motivation and incentives, 11, 13–14
    tolerance *vs.* avoidance in citizen
        projects, 202–204
Robinson, Shelli, 166
RPA (robotic process automation). *See also*
        automation; citizen automation; IPA
        (intelligent process automation)
    comparison with IPA, 64–66
    definition and scope, 64–66
    evolution towards intelligent automation, 140
    impact on process efficiency, 194–195
    importance in citizen automation, 117
    integration with AI and automation, 233
    integration with AI and cloud computing, 243
    integration with other citizen
        technologies, 172–173
    risk management in citizen
        automation, 202–203
    risks and challenges, 78–79
    role in Arcadis' automated guardrails, 229–230
    role in automation history, 22
    role in citizen automation, 141–142, 183
    role in citizen automation at BMW, 172–173
    role in future of citizen development, 241–244
    tools and technologies, 64–66, 68–73,
        141–142, 172–173, 183
    UiPath tools, 117
    use in Arcadis' automated guardrails, 229–230
    use in AT&T's citizen automation, 194–195
    use in citizen development at Michelin, 208

S

Salesforce
    CRM Analytics, 146
    role in citizen development, 137
    Tableau platform, 144
Sandeep Sacheti, 217
Sanofi, 155

SAP, 145
Schauber, Daniel, 46–47
Sears, Maya, 30
Seghal, Ajai, 170–171
ServiceNow, 138, 170, 238–239
shadow IT, 3, 6–8
Shell, 17. *See also* low-code/no-code tools
    case study, 125
    centralized governance, 207
    citizen automation, 72–73
    citizen development during natural
        disasters, 155
    citizen development initiatives,
        41–43, 102, 105
    Crotts, Jay, 124, 163, 207
    data science training programs, 89
    development of COVID application, 155
    digital transformation initiatives, 163–165
    DIY initiative and citizen tools, 207
    DIY movement using LC/NC tools, 52–53
    DIY program, 124–125, 163–164
    examples of citizen-developed
        applications, 52–53
    examples of process improvement, 72–73
    executive support for citizen
        development, 124
    governance approach, 125
    impact on AI applications, 90
    Jeavons, Dan, 89–90, 164
    Kappeyne, Nils, 124–125, 163–164
    Power Platform applications, 42
    response to hurricane impacts, 155
    role in digital transformation, 52–53
    Shell.ai program, 164–165
    Sims, Stevie, 41–43, 102, 105
Shell.ai, 164–165
shields, 229–230
Siemens, 53, 56–58
Sims, Stevie, 41–43, 102, 105
Six Sigma, 10, 22, 36, 117, 149, 224
Sky, 95
Sniffer, 166
software tools, 33, 35–38, 42, 46–47. *See also*
    low-code/no-code tools
SPSS, 143
stakeholders, 185
Stanley Black & Decker, 152–153, 193
Stata, 143
stewardship, 229–230
supertech leadership, 241

supply chain, 185
systems integration, 66–67

T
Tableau, 23, 38–39, 82, 85, 144, 146
Taiger, 143
Taylor, Frederick 21–22
Taylorism, 21
technical debt, 79–80. *See also* risk management
technology architecture, 22
TIAA, 240
Tinuiti, 105, 126
top-down governance, 204–205. *See also*
    centralized governance; governance
training. *See also* citizen development; direct
    instruction; education
    for citizen developers, 59–60
    generative AI training, 193
    importance in citizen development, 193
    importance in project-based learning, 219
    role in citizen certification and skill
        development, 193, 221–223
    Siemens' approach to LC/NC training, 57–58

U
Udacity, 115
UiPath, 108, 141, 143, 148, 203, 208, 249, 256
US government, citizen science programs, 29
user adoption, 123–124

V
value pools, 152–153
visualization tools, 23
von Hippel, Eric, 23–25

W
warfare, 158
WESCO Distribution, 73, 236
Willcocks, Leslie, 73
Wolters Kluwer, 18, 165–166, 216
Woodly, Amanda, 40–41, 89, 96
workflow automation, 21–22
WorkFusion, 143

Y
Young, Daniel, 95–96
yourencore, 28